Fierce Dancing

C. J. Stone was born in Birmingham in 1953. His father was an electrician, his mother a hairdresser. He was educated at Sheldon Heath Comprehensive School in Birmingham, and then at Cardiff University. In 1974 – under pressure from the prevailing ethos – he dropped out without finishing his degree. Thereafter he did a variety of jobs: barman, cellarman, machine-operator, dustman, road-sweeper, playgroup-leader, care-worker and archaeological digger. He finally finished his degree in 1984 at Bristol Polytechnic. He became a full-time political agitator, involved in the Miners' Strike, the Poll Tax protests and, latterly, against the Criminal Justice Act. Since September 1993 he has been responsible for the Housing Benefit Hill column in the *Guardian Weekend Magazine* and, more recently, a regular column in the *Big Issue*. *Fierce Dancing* is his first book.

Fierce Dancing

Adventures in the Underground

C. J. STONE

illustrations by Eldad Druks

faber and faber
LONDON · BOSTON

First published in 1996
by Faber and Faber Limited
3 Queen Square London WC1N 3AU

Photoset by Parker Typesetting Service, Leicester
Printed in England by Clays Ltd, St Ives plc

Song lyrics p. 198 © 1996 Warner/Tamerlare
Warner/Chappell Music Ltd, London W1Y 3FA
Reproduced by permission of International Music Publications Limited

A CIP record for this book
is available from the British Library
ISBN 0-571-17603-5

10 9 8 7 6 5 4 3 2 1

Contents

For Joe: for keeping me sane.

'We shall celebrate with
such fierce dancing the
Death of your Institutions.'

Maya – Windsor Free Nation News, 1974

Prologue: New Year

The last thing I remember was the whisky. I remember the soft, golden glow in the glass as I raised it to my lips like a warm promise. It twinkled at me merrily, reflecting the multicoloured Christmas lights stretched across the bar. And that's it. No more. I disappeared. I was absorbed into that amber light like a drop into the ocean. I was gone; vanished like a cheap magician's magic trick down a trap door into the basement depths; banished to the nether regions where the light barely shines and where consciousness is just a dim and distant flicker. I woke up on my own bed, fully dressed on New Year's Day, with a raging thirst, a sore nose, and the vaguest gossamer-like images of some sexual altercation with a woman I hardly knew.

There's a place I know called alcohol heaven. I've been there once or twice. It's not like God's heaven, because it doesn't last for ever. It's nothing like E heaven either, because it's not entirely dependent on the drug. You have to be in the right mood. You have to have the right people around you. You have to be in the right place at the right time. It's no good simply drinking.

But, when the conditions are right, alcohol heaven really exists. I'd been there last night, briefly.

Kodan and Marion had come round with a half-bottle of brandy Kodan had pinched from the superstore. We'd shared that and some khat that someone had given me – we chewed the khat stems down to a fibrous pulp, and then washed the tongue-cleaving bitterness away with drafts of liquid fire. It seemed like a good combination. After that, we'd gone out.

Khat is a North African herbal stimulant, by the way. You shouldn't really take it with alcohol.

But I was in a good mood. It was New Year's Eve. The brandy had warmed the heart, while the khat was stimulating the brain. We shared a pint in the Lazy Barman and I was in alcohol heaven. Strangely exuberant, as I'd said at the time.

After that I'd struck out on my own. I'm not really sure why I'd left Kodan and Marion. I think it may have had something to do with not wanting to be a gooseberry. After all, they were in love, whereas I was on my own. So the truth is, I was on a personal quest: high up in alcohol heaven and looking for love.

I went to the Logical Cadaver and drank a pint, then to the Crow's Nest. After that – and the whisky – I don't remember a thing.

I decided I needed to see Fen. It was a bright, clear New Year's Day morning as I walked the mile or two along the suburban streets of our town to where Fen lives, on a forgotten council estate in the middle of nowhere.

Fen is an old friend of mine. He's impossibly thin, built like a taut bow ready to spring. He once told me that he's this thin because he's preparing to leave the earth. That's the way Fen talks. He's in his mid-thirties, with long greying hair and a thin goatee beard. There's something of the devil in him, and something of the elf. He's a painter and decorator by trade (currently unemployed), and an astrologer by persuasion. Fen is my type of the self-educated working class. He was reading before he ever went to school. He taught himself. But the scope of his education is entirely outside the norms of the formal system. He was always a rebel. He hated school and left without any qualifications. After that he got into drugs. Glue at first (from which he boasts a collapsed lung) and then cannabis. The cannabis saved him. Later he started taking LSD. For two years in his mid-twenties he took it religiously (that's his word): four or five tabs every weekend, and a couple during the week to keep him going. He says that for those two years he never came down.

I woke Fen up. He was bleary-eyed and blinking in the morning light. He invited me in and put the kettle on.

Fen said, 'What happened to you last night? I bought you a whisky and then you disappeared.'

'That's about the long and short of it,' I answered. 'I disappeared.'

'I thought I saw you at the Assembly Rooms. Everyone else was there.'

'I don't know if I was there or not. I didn't notice anyone. I think I've broken my nose,' I added. 'It hurts like fuck. I think somebody must have hit me.'

I was still haunted by this faint image of a woman. She had straight black hair and was wearing a rat-tailed Afghan coat. I must have been round her house, though I couldn't remember at what point. I had the vaguest recollection of her pushing me away. What was she doing? What was I doing? Was it her who had punched me? It was all too embarrassing to contemplate. I felt certain that it involved an indiscreet proposition of some kind.

'Fucking alcohol,' I said.

3

And Fen said, 'Alcohol reverses the psychic polarities.'

That's what I love about him. He's the only man who can use an expression like 'psychic polarities' at nine o'clock in the morning and still sound sane. I laughed.

So we were in Fen's messy living room, surrounded by astrology books and dog-ends and ancient copies of the *Daily Sport*. We were drinking tea and smoking: me cigarettes, Fen spliffs. Fen doesn't believe in tidying up. There's no carpet on his floor and he uses the floor as an ashtray. I tried flicking my ash on the floor too, but I couldn't handle it. I had to have an ashtray. I was in an absurd dilemma, surrounded by ash and yet having to insist on a clean ashtray. It was like a piece of anti-art: a whole room full of ash and roaches and cigarette butts, and a clean, sparkling ashtray in the middle of it.

I wanted to tell Fen my theory of miracles. I wanted to tell him my version of the loaves and fishes story.

This is it. The crowd are out there in the mountains and hungry. Well, one lad had the foresight to bring his lunch with him, didn't he? Five loaves and two fishes. And he was willing to share it. Did everyone else forget? In that immense crowd, was there only one with the good sense to pack some food before setting out? Of course not. Some had food tucked away and some didn't. Some of them were rich and came well-stocked. Even those who were poor had their lunch with them, like the boy: a few crusts of bread and some meat or fish or salty goat's cheese. The miracle of the loaves and the fishes is a social miracle. Once the loaves and fishes were being shared, and everyone else brought out what they had hidden, there was more than enough to go round. This is the secret of the loaves and the fishes: that there's more than enough to go round.

This is the secret of free festivals, too. I'd been thinking of the loaves and fishes story as an image for this book.

Fen rejected my theory. Fen believes in miracles. Real miracles. He believes that the fundamental property of the universe itself is that it is miraculous. He says that the universe is constantly spewing out matter. He rejects the Big Bang theory. He says that pulsars create matter out of nothing. The whole thing is a cycle. Pulsars pour out matter, black holes draw in matter. They are two sides of the same process. And truly developed beings can harness this fundamental principle and create matter. They can create miracles. Thus Jesus was able, in fact, to turn the loaves and the fishes into a feast of plenty. He created it, as the universe creates itself, out of nothing.

Then he launched into his theory of existence. Human beings, he said, far from being no more than glorified animals, are divine beings. We were with God at the beginning. We are almost godlike in ourselves. We helped create the universe. We've been around for ever. We've trailed from star system to star system from the beginning of time. Our last home was Sirius. When we arrived on this planet we were huge gaseous beings made up of a double pyramid structure: two pyramids facing each other at the base, with a gap in between. So I'm sitting here on an ordinary winter's morning, with a God-awful hangover and an aching feeling in my insides as if something is ripping me apart, and Fen is talking about huge gaseous pyramidic beings from Sirius. And I can't help it. I just start laughing.

'Oh, come on ...' I said.

'Yes,' he said, in all seriousness, 'and when we were in Atlantis we created the animals. The whole animal kingdom is a massive genetic experiment started by us. We even created our own bodies, which we now inhabit like machines. Our bodies are part of this experiment. We've forgotten, that's all.'

'You don't expect me to believe all that, do you Fen? It doesn't make any sense.'

He looked at me, slightly hurt.

'Oh, all right then. I might as well believe it, mightn't I?'

And we both laughed.

Talking to Fen is the perfect cure for a hangover.

He has a different view of the world than most of us. Acid-inspired, you could say. Acid-addled, you might add, if you were in a cynical frame of mind. Well, it doesn't matter to me one way or the other. Fen makes me laugh and that's good enough for me.

Fen is extremely talented, by the way. He does astrological readings and hand-paints intricate birth charts, complete with all the arcane symbols of the trade. It doesn't matter whether you believe in the philosophical basis of astrology (I'm none too sure myself), the fact is he has an uncanny insight into the structures of the personality and a great depth of vision. He is often alarmingly accurate. In another world – in a world not dominated by class, perhaps – Fen would make a good living from his talents. As it is, he's always short of cash. He gives his charts and his readings away for a small lump of hash, or a pint or two.

The story of my New Year's Eve emerged in embarrassing dribs and drabs over a number of days. Every time I went to town I'd be cringing with each new revelation. I saw Kodan.

'What happened to you on New Year's Eve?' he asked.

'I don't know.'

'You were out of it. I saw you outside the pub and it was like all the lights were on, but there was nobody at home.'

'Were you at the Crow's Nest?' I asked and groaned.

'Me and Marion. We tried to get you to come with us, but there was no persuading you. You didn't even know who we were.'

'Didn't I manage to get a New Year's kiss even?' I asked.

'You were kissing everyone, it didn't matter what sex.'

I groaned again.

Later, my son asked me if I'd been hit.

'I don't think so,' I said, trying to put a brave face on it.

'Somebody told me you'd been hit by a woman and had fallen down.'

Kodan managed to piece the rest of the story together for me. Everyone knew some detail or another. After the pub, it appears, I'd actually been seen lying in the gutter, rolling about and groaning. After that I'd gatecrashed a private party. I was stumbling around, rolling against the wall, moaning fitfully. That's when Rick had found me. He was pretty pissed too, though not as bad as me. He decided that we should go into partnership. I remember none of this. We were lolling around in a drunken gaggle trying to stick our tongues into anything that moved. It must have been an appalling sight, to see me or Rick, dribbling and smelling of beer, lurching towards you saying, 'Gi's a kiss ... ' And at a certain point I lunged at someone, tried to snog her and put my hand on her breast. She simply knocked me down with a weighty punch on the nose. She's a well-built German with formidable biceps and fists like clubs. I went flat out, sprawled on the floor like a puppet with broken strings. 'We hadn't even been introduced,' she said. For weeks after she was going round town asking people whether they knew C. J. Stone. If they did she'd say, 'Don't talk to me about C. J. Stone.'

Later I went round to Rick's house. There was someone asleep on the settee. This was the girl in the Afghan coat. Apparently she was woken up to find me with my hand between her legs saying, 'I love you, you know, I've always loved you,' and trying to kiss her. I cringed when I heard that – not only because I'd woken her up by putting my hand between her legs (although that was bad enough), but that I'd tried to make out I loved her. It made the rude awakening even more rude. It was so tacky. I avoided her for weeks. When we did meet I said, 'I'm really sorry. I just don't remember what happened.'

'It's all right,' she said, giving me a cuddle. 'You were drunk and randy, that's all. I rolled you a spliff and you went out like a light.'

1 My First Rave

The sacred music and the splendour of the ceremonies aroused a strong tide of emotion that was shared by all hearts in unison and that awakened a consciousness of the common origin of all creatures.

I Ching 59: Dispersion

I went to my first rave some time in 1991. In fact I never considered I was going to a 'rave'. I thought I was going to a party. Which is what it was: a big party in the open air. The term 'rave' is something of a media invention. What's a rave? A sound system, some lights, some backdrops, people getting off their faces. Apart from the context – and, to some degree, the music – there's hardly any difference between a rave and a disco, except that 'disco' as a term has become profoundly unfashionable. Only slightly more unfashionable than 'rave'.

The party was taking place near Plumpton in East Sussex, site of some famous festivals in the early seventies. It was being run by DIY of Nottingham. There were six of us in the van; seven if you include my dog. Gem, Nik, Oz, me and two students: a quiet, gentle Asian with curly black hair called Hash, and a soft-spoken Irishman called Gordon, whose tendency to clip his words – a combination of hippie reserve and a heavy Irish accent – made him almost impossible to understand. Gem was my girlfriend at the time. Or rather – since we were always splitting up and getting back together – she wasn't quite my girlfriend at the time. But she's a very beautiful woman and I loved her then as much as I ever loved her. Gem was the reason I took up raving in the first place. Being younger than me – I was in my late thirties, she in her late twenties – she was always more in tune with what was going on, what was currently underground and therefore cool. If it hadn't been for Gem I'd still be wearing Marks and Spark's woolly jumpers. I was never one for fashion, even in my more fashionable days.

Nik and Oz run a sound system themselves – tVC – but in those days they were still experimenting with forms, just beginning to broaden their musical outlook. Oz is a northern working-class bloke turned radical philosopher. Six foot two of Geordie menace with pale, cold, sceptical eyes. People say he has eyes like a dead fish, but deep down, you feel, there's a softie struggling to get out. He likes the fluffiest of fluffy house music, all orchestral trills and swirling clouds of melody. Occasionally I would pat him on the belly and he'd respond to that. You'd see his eyes soften, like a cat being stroked. You almost expected him to purr.

At the time of the Plumpton party, tVC were justifiably famous in the small area around which they worked. Eclectic and thoughtful, they happily mixed rap with reggae, thrash with jazz, and had (still have) one of the most comprehensive record collections I have ever seen. But it wasn't until they discovered house music that things really started to come together.

House music, in all its disparate forms, is undoubtedly the cultural driving-force of the nineties. More so than punk in the seventies – which was simply rehashed rock'n'roll but played faster, and which was more about an attitude – house is brand new. House music takes apart all other forms of music and begins again. It is produced in the studio – it is fundamentally a producer's music – and you really don't need to play an instrument to compose it. Consequently, it is freed from the constraints of formal training. In a sense, anyone who has access to a computer can do it and it is based on what sounds good, what sounds 'right', rather than on any set of rules. It goes straight to the visceral heart of the musical body. It bends and shapes sounds like they were malleable objects, selecting sounds for their emotional quality rather than their intellectual content. Aural sculpture. Using sampling techniques the whole history, the whole range of music is at its disposal. Nothing is sacred, nothing is beyond its scope. It strips down, re-forms, reconceives, fractures, twists, speeds up, slows down, distorts and rearranges, selecting and reselecting, redefining music according to mood, and all to a hypnotically perfect – and therefore perfectly danceable – 4/4 beat. It is true that it owes more to sixties soul and to seventies disco than it does to Mozart (and it clearly defines itself as being in the tradition of black American music), but it can more effectively redefine Mozart in a rhythmical context than classical music can redefine funk. It's a magpie music: it steals samples from every era to decorate its musical nest.

Techno music has gone even further. It no longer depends on musical sounds at all. Its samples are street noises, factory noises and machinery, as well as pure electronic sounds. John Cale and Karlheinz Stockhausen would have been proud. Their conceits have finally developed into a full-blown popular music.

House music can be bold, it can be repetitive; it can be inventive, it can be derivative; it can be witty, it can be dull; it can be emotional, it can be dreary. But you can't ignore it. It is the music of our age.

How many notes are there in an octave? Eight? Well, there are twelve: there are also four half-notes in traditional Western music. But Indian music, particularly, allows for greater and greater subdivision: into $\frac{1}{4}$, $\frac{1}{8}$, $\frac{1}{16}$ and even $\frac{1}{32}$th notes. The greatest guitar players derive their emotional range, as well as their technique, from bending between the notes: twisting, curving, caressing the notes, taking us on the long journey between one note and the next. House music goes even further. Computer-generated sounds allow it to explore the infinity that lies between the milestone structures of conventional technique. It can organise sounds into pure form, chaotic rather than ordered – a jungle, not a garden – its very repetitiveness reminding us of the fundamental formulae that underlie the structures of nature. It is no accident that fractal images are its natural complement. Fractal images, infinity in a finite space, endlessly repeating, endlessly swirling computer-generated shapes, lead us down, down into a mirror-upon-mirror reflective universe (as above, so below) and are the very constructs of ordered nature in its mathematical purity. House music is fractal sound.

Oz and Nik were relatively new to the scene at the time. They still had a reggae set to fall back on, but they were completely sold. They were giving all their spare time, their money, their energy and their relentless organisational skills to this one thing, pursuing it like it was a new religion. Which it is, really: a non-organic guru, impassively perfect.

We arrived at the site some time in the evening. We had to drive up a steep chalk track rutted with crumbling water channels, the back wheels sliding and the entire back end skidding towards the precarious drop beside us. We'd picked up a couple of girls at the bottom without realising just how dangerous this climb would be, and they were chattering blithely about such-and-such a crew, and the size of the rig, and who was doing the lights. I didn't know what they were on about. I just wished they'd shut up. I was in panic mode, looking down a long tunnel to my possible death.

We made it to the top and the girls got out, giggling among themselves. We found a nice grassy spot where we could park up, and Oz and Nik could set up their bell-tent. Gem was ignoring me and giving me her hard-woman act. I said, 'I'm glad I came.' And she said, 'Well enjoy yourself, then. I don't want you saying you came for my sake.' Hash and the Irish guy had no money, just half a tab of acid each. So it wasn't all that promising at first. I didn't even like the music particularly in those days. I was into blues, jazz and heavy R & B. And what was this stuff? Just 'twiddle-twiddle, doink-doink, dum-dum-dum'. No lyrics. All you could hear from behind the screen of trees was the incessant thud-thud-thud of the relentless 4/4 rhythm and the occasional whoop from the crowd.

We walked down the main track lined with cars. That's where all the drug dealers sat, with disdainful faces and barely disguised sneers, car stereos blasting out. 'Fucking bastards,' I thought. I was applying it to everyone at that moment: 'Fucking bastards.' I just felt out of place.

Then we were in the field where the sound system had set up, in a perfect bowl of land like an amphitheatre, bounded by trees, and with fires and lights twinkling all around. Ten minutes later I'd swallowed an E. Half an hour later I was dancing amid the shimmering lights and cascading sounds while little winds bustled about my body, sending ripples of pleasure up and down my spine. There were a couple of hundred people dancing beside me: travellers with dreadlocks and nose-rings, fashionable clubbers with stack-heeled shoes; a Rastafarian who'd shaved part of his head and looked like a shaman from some ancient tribe; young girls with slinky skirts and sunglasses; black people, white people, Asian people; and at least one middle-aged ex-hippie still yearning for the revolution.

Above us the vaulted sky arched like a cathedral, sprinkled with stars. I stretched my back and raised my arms as all the tensions lifted, all the ancient aches and pains and minor worries floating away like incense into the cool night air. Everything inside me felt like an offering to some unseen but benevolent presence: my guardian angel. Dance is prayer. Movement in sacred space: non-verbal communication to the deity. The movements acquire a symbolic air, like some ancient form of wisdom. I took off my shoes to feel the cool grass tickling my feet. Nikki said, 'Look at you. You're a hippie.' I didn't care. Nothing mattered. I was warm and contented and in love with everyone and utterly, utterly alive: confident in my right to be there and to be as happy as I chose.

This was not the first time I'd taken Ecstasy. The first time was with Gem, on our own in her damp, cheerless bedroom, by an open fire in the middle of winter. And it was a disaster. Well, not quite a disaster. Gem had heard about this sexual drug and was looking forward to a long, sensual fuck. She got me to strip off while we listened to 'I'm a Man' by Muddy Waters. There was the whoosh of unfettered energy bursting in her loins while she fell back on the bed, whooping with joy. Only by this time my dick had gone quite flaccid, and it was shrinking smaller and smaller, till it was barely a wrinkled nub of a thing peering out from beneath my belly like a turtle's head from its shell. Ecstasy is an amphetamine. It has that effect. I was as nervous as hell in any case, this being my first time with a psychedelic drug since I'd let go of the things of youth and decided I was better off, after all, as an alcoholic; a good twelve years or more. But later we got into the sensuality of it all, basking by the fire and then moving into the cool depths of the room to feel the contrast. Later we went out to buy a bottle of champagne. We kept saying, 'It's our anniversary.' Which it was, just about. But it certainly felt like a special occasion. It could just as well have been Christmas. We went to the pub and noticed how beautiful everyone looked; how crystalline their eyes. It was as if you were looking through their eyes like a sparkling glass, directly into the personality beneath.

After that we started taking it fairly regularly. It's still a period I remember as one of the happiest of my life. Gem and I had just got back together after yet another temporary split, and I'd decided – at last – that I was going to have to commit myself to this writing thing or die an unsatisfied man. I was bouncing out of bed in the morning, full of plans. And I'd stopped drinking, for the first, and only, time in my life. Ecstasy was so much better. I felt clean.

It didn't last. Who knows how these subtle shifts in the atmosphere build up until one day, maybe, you're caught out in a full-blown storm? Ecstasy is a pure hedonist's drug. It encourages you to take other drugs with it. Cocaine and champagne are two of its complements: rich people's drugs. You always end up spending vast amounts of money. In the end, I was drinking beer on it too. This never worried me, despite the propaganda. I've always enjoyed a pint, and when you are on E you want to do the things you enjoy. But I began filling up with beer before it, and maybe a few while I was on it, then gallons and gallons the day after. There was a kind of inevitability about this. Your body is wrecked, but your mind is still raging. You need a drink to sleep.

Ecstasy is a mood drug. When you're happy and in love it makes you more happy, more in love. But whenever Gem wasn't with me, I'd find it just plain dull. The beer put the bounce back into me. It became as much a part of the trip as the Ecstasy. Sometimes I wouldn't bother with the E at all: I'd drink a reasonable amount of beer and, ignoring all the sneering remarks ('Here come the beer boys'), I'd dance all night just the same. That E-snobbery thing got on my nerves. Like they were proscribing my drugs for me. In the end – especially after Gem and I split up for good – the E just dropped out altogether and I went back to my old ways, mooching around in pubs and chatting to the old geezers, and smoking too many cigarettes. Well, at least you know what they put in beer. It's a natural process, as old as the hills. I drink Shepherd Neame's, which is brewed in a nearby town from the same ingredients they've used for centuries. OK, so it makes you feel like shit, but at least it doesn't make you feel precious.

Most Ecstasy simply isn't Ecstasy, in any case. Not MDMA. It's a cocktail: heroin, speed, acid, a variety of other chemicals. More often than not it's MDA – closely related, but far more dangerous than MDMA – and sometimes it is no more than caffeine. Even when you find a good source, they're obliged to sell you whatever they've got, just to make their own money back. At £15 a hit, it seems like a self-indulgent luxury. You can't share it. You can't pass it round. You can't buy someone a dose, like you can a pint, just to show them you're their friend. I've always felt that it was vastly over-priced.

I've nothing against MDMA. It's a lovely drug, when it's used properly. Once a month, or on special occasions. A good dance and a good hug. It can help you to re-establish your friendships and your relationship with the universe. If only you could be sure what goes into it. That's the problem of illegality: there's no way to control the quality of the product. Sometimes I'm inclined to believe that the government wants to keep it that way. Ecstasy is a dangerous drug; not necessarily to the individual, but to Establishment images of how we are supposed to live.

At this time – the night of the Plumpton party – I was still in the throes of my love affair with the drug. It was new and fresh to me. There's another thing about E. It gives you unlimited confidence, like you're the King of the World. Your back straightens and you rise to a regal posture. You feel that nothing can harm you. So that when Gem told me that she, Nik and Oz had all taken acid, well I took some too. Why not?

We walked back to the van with Hash in tow. He was tripping and couldn't see where to put his feet. He was tripping and tripping up at the same time. Every rise seemed like a mountain to him. We had to guide him over clumps of grass as if they were jungles. When we were back at the van, Gem suggested we make some coffee. We had a double burner and a large bottle of Calor gas. Only the pipe wasn't long enough. You'd rest the bottle on the floor of the van, but you couldn't put the burner down. There was nothing to stand it on. Gem was doing one thing while I was doing another and we were getting into a muddle. Then some stranger appeared, clucking over the van. 'A double-doored VW. I've never seen one like this before. It seems longer to me. Yes, I'm sure it's longer than usual. Whose is it? Who's the owner?' I was having an anxiety attack. I really didn't want to get into a conversation about VW vans at that moment. Then Nikki said something and it made no sense. It was like the whole world spinning out of orbit. Suddenly nothing made sense. Reality was coming at me from some elliptical angle. The acid had hit and I ran away.

I'm really not sure what happened next. I was in the woods. The trees circled me like a sacred grove. I remember hearing people calling me, but I ignored them. I think I may have clung to a tree. I even have the vaguest memory of climbing one. I was embracing the trees and talking to them. After that I was wandering round looking at the ground, completely lost. There was an entire landscape down there. My consciousness was being guided ever deeper into that unknown place by a will-o'-the-wisp spark. A rational portion of my mind said, 'Pouk-ledden,' and that explained it all to me. Pouk-ledden is a nineteenth-century Midland colloquialism. It means 'to be led by Puck'. I was remembering my researches into folklore, how sometimes people are led by mischievous spirits into a strange fairy landscape. That's where I was, in fairyland. Everything glowed with an internal light. It was pitch black, but I could see every detail in there. I realised that I wasn't going to be able to get out and just sat down on the ground. All of a sudden I was contented. I didn't have to go anywhere. I didn't have to do anything. Everything was natural and good.

At a certain point, my dog found me. She'd been weaving her way between us all night. She's a German shepherd. We were her flock. She snuffled me and I buried my face in her fur, immersed in her dogginess. For a moment – for a century – we were one being. Then she was gone.

There's something about acid. Something beyond the rational. I think that's why I find it so hard to take. At the heart of every acid trip there's an enigma. Maybe it's the same enigma that is at the heart of the universe. That's how it feels at the time. You are not what you think you are. The world is not what you imagine it to be. Nothing is real. Or reality is something far different than you've been led to believe. It poses this strange puzzle for you. A flat – no, a deep – contradiction. In the heart of the trip is a person who does not exist, in a place which is nowhere, from a time when there is no time. It's you. And yet it's not you. It's huge (as big as the universe itself) and yet it is contained in the smallest space imaginable. There's no words to explain it. Contraction and expansion. The Enigma. We are so used to the measurable flow of things that when we hit the immeasurable, it blows our heads apart. We regard time as like the gradations on a ruler: seconds ticking by, turning into hours, days, weeks, lifetimes. And all of a sudden you are swimming in it. It is an ocean. Past, present, future: they are all the same. Moments are merely drops merged into that ocean of time, and this reality is like waves lapping the shore. My measured mind cannot take it.

What acid does is remind you that words are not reality. My verbal mind cannot take that, either. It seems like nonsense. Maybe it's just none-sense.

Then, in no time at all, it was light again and I went back to the van. It was empty; cold and abandoned.

Nik and Oz were the first to return.

'What happened to you?' I asked.

Nik had been having a hard time of it. Oz had been nursing her. They were both tottering as they arrived, arm in arm.

'What happened to you?' they asked.

'I've been talking to the trees,' I replied.

I could still feel the abyss of madness out there. I was still suffering vertigo.

Nikki and I lay down in the tent. Every so often I would have to go for a piss, and Oz would go for a piss too. It was odd that it was always at the same time. There was something incredibly boyish about us standing there, pissing against our respective trees. An identity. I'd look over at Oz, looking down at himself, then at myself, looking down at myself. We were the same. Cartoon characters. Oz looked like Big Vern in *Viz*. Everyone appeared distorted, blotched and cartoony to me.

Really, I was waiting for Gem to come back. I kept calling out to her in my mind (as I had been all night), 'Gem, Gem, Gem!' Then, finally, she was walking towards us through the woods, a vision. She'd been dancing all the time I'd been in the woods. She was wearing a shiny black plastic coat and a slinky dress, and her dark hair was slicked back. Her skin was the colour of copper. A sleek, dark, burnished angel. I'd never seen anyone so beautiful in all my life.

She sat down near the tent. Hash was leaning out. They were talking in subdued voices and Gem was playing with his hair affectionately. There was something between them. I was watching them from some sorrowful void, absorbing the scene in front of me, quietly subdued. Eventually I asked her if she wanted to go for a walk. I was looking round frantically for my sunglasses, but couldn't find them. I was desperate.

Hash said, 'You're vain.'

I said, 'No, I just don't want anyone to see how furtive my eyes really are.'

The acid was coming and going in waves. Everything would be looking normal, then there'd be a distortion of some kind, a face twisted into an agonising shape. In the end I gave up my search for the sunglasses and we went for our walk without them. The world would just have to put up with my eyes. We were looking for water. We walked down the dusty path where the drug dealers were congregated. Gem took hold of me, in a line of trees beside the path, and started kissing me. It was like drinking from the Fountain of Life. A salty-sweet liquid merging. The Water of Life. Her lips were soft and pliant as they parted for me, and the slinky dress (which was really a slip) slid wantonly over her smooth skin as I pressed my hand to her belly. She was looking up at me with her dark, impenetrable eyes, like a woodland creature, full of trust and love, and all my troubles lifted. Here we were again, in love again.

I wanted to take her to where I'd been hiding all night, but when we got there the woods no longer looked like a grove and there was no fairy landscape. Only Gem. No perceptual distortion. Just a vision of beauty. This is how it had been from the second I'd laid eyes on her. No matter how the world wove and twisted, when I looked at her everything became trans-formed. Gem crouched down in the woods and lifted her dress to piss, and she looked me in the eyes as she did it, chattering blithely like she was in a shopping queue. But I knew she was doing it for me. I knew it was a privilege meant just for me. To see her in her intimate loveliness, performing this simple human function, it was like she was saying, 'This is yours.' What lay in there, in the Well of Desire, was mine. And in that moment the ocean of time drowned my rational mind once more. It was like I'd known this moment all my life. That it was inherent in the very fabric of the universe, a quiet, secret *déjà vu*, only waiting to be discovered again. I felt that we'd been in communication all night, both waiting for this.

The day wore on and the acid wore off. We ate some food,

and Hash and I went scrounging for cigarettes. Hash told me he'd slept with Gem, but that they'd not had sex. I wasn't angry. I knew he felt strongly about her. How could I be angry? I felt strongly too. Then he said, 'God, I was so out of it last night I could actually see fractals in the ground.' It was only later that I realised that that was because there *were* fractals. It was no hallucination. The light crew were projecting them. That's the trouble with acid: you can't tell your arse from your elbow.

At a certain point a police helicopter circled overhead like an alien intruder. Why didn't they leave us alone? Then a police car came skidding up the track, closely followed by a repair van. People were hanging on to the frame of the van and whooping, waving their shirts and letting their hair flow in the wind. And there were some people who were still dancing. There was one striking Asian girl who was swaying back and forth with her eyes closed, rolling her head so that her black hair billowed about her face like a curtain. She'd been doing it when we arrived. She was still doing it as we left.

After that night I started going to parties regularly. tVC began organising them. Sometimes they were ecstatic. Sometimes they were dull. I was never entirely sure what made the difference. There was a particular group of people I needed to see for the party to work, a bunch of women we referred to as the Mothers' Union. They're all in their early thirties with kids. Mostly they'd been involved in the club scene in the eighties. They weren't what you'd call ravers, by any stretch of the imagination. They liked to dance, that's all. And they'd dance whether they had Ecstasy in their systems or not. Ecstasy just made the dance last longer. Oz, Nik, Gem and I became firm friends: the nucleus of a tribe. If Oz and Nik weren't organising the party, they'd know where the party was. My age didn't seem to make a difference. Or rather, it was when my age made no difference that the party was good. I needed other people around me of comparable age. When it was only teenagers, I started having problems.

Other times I found myself in situations where I was simply out of place, surrounded by wealthy hedonists and bored-looking young model-girls who wouldn't give me a second glance. I began to recognise the drawbacks to the party scene. It was a rich person's game. They were taking Ecstasy, drinking champagne and working in the City of London as commodity brokers. It reminded me of the cocaine-scene of the eighties: over-priced drugs and undervalued humanity. That gorgeous unity was available only to those who could afford to pay. The working-class people who were there were either drug dealers or prostitutes. There was a terrible stench of decadence about the whole scene.

I remember talking to one tired-looking woman.

I said, 'Haven't you taken any drugs?'

'Yes,' she said. 'I've taken a flatliner.' Flatliner means death. 'I'm a deck widow,' she said. Her boyfriend was more interested in music than in her.

Driving home from Plumpton I had a minor revelation about the landscape. I'd see pockets of land in the hills around me and think, 'That would be a good place for a party.' I could imagine the lights and the sounds and the people dancing, and I had a clear impression of the earth as like a lover, longing for our attention. I felt that the land itself enjoyed the dancing. She was the Shekinah, the goddess, awakening to Jehovah's love. Or that's how it felt.

I'd been brought up on a diet of Wordsworth, of the poet wandering lonely as a cloud. Except that clouds aren't lonely, of course. They like to gather. I'd tried hard to feel all the proper romantic feelings. There was no engagement there, no connection. The land was 'out there', separate, distinct; and I was here, an observer in my fortress of solitude, bereft, lonely. Something was missing. What was missing was me. After Plumpton, the landscape took on a new aspect as a place of celebration. Every natural amphitheatre, every glade, every ancient oak became the scene of some imaginary party where the sub-bass heartbeat of the music ran in currents through the earth, in which I and my friends gathered in celebration of our lives. It was as if the land was opening up to me, awakening. In a way, this was the most revolutionary thought I've ever had. It wasn't a thought, it was a feeling. It wasn't theoretical, it was real – the knowledge that the land belongs to us, that the planet belongs to us, as we belong to her. It happened, that revelation, on some deep emotional level, like love.

Later that year, Oz, Nikki and I tried to repeat the experience. We went looking for a free festival at Cissbury Rings in Sussex. There were a couple of others with us, I'm not sure who. Rick was one of them. This was long before the Criminal Justice Act was even a twinkle in Michael Howard's eye, but the police were acting as if it was already law. We reached the site of the party and there were roadblocks everywhere. The police stopped us and asked everyone their names. I was obliged to answer, being the driver, but Oz announced from the back that the rest of us didn't have to say a thing. Nevertheless, Rick gave his name. He was overawed by the police presence.

We were sent on a wild-goose chase from one site to the next. In the end we were in a convoy of motorbikes, buses and beat-up old cars. In front of us was a Ford Cortina with a long-haired girl leaning out of the window, holding on to the roof and whooping. The police blocked all our exits and drove us on until we were out of the county. Once we got there, the next lot were waiting for us. They let us sleep in a lay-by, on the border between the two counties.

The following day the van was searched. The police were looking through the back, sniffing a bottle of washing-up liquid as if it were high-class drugs. I asked them why they were searching.

'You were acting suspiciously. You looked nervous.'

I said, 'Of course I'm nervous. I've got half a dozen policemen breathing down my neck.'

Fortunately, they missed the gram of speed that someone had stashed in the VW handbook. And the Ecstasy that was in Nikki's knickers. And the hash that was in Oz's top pocket. And ...

I drove off and threw a wobbly. 'I've had it, I'm going home.'

We stopped off briefly for a rest and something to eat. Rick had cooked some food: red cabbage and beans. It had been sitting above the engine in the back of the van and was starting to ferment. It smelled like sick. It was so repulsive that it made you gag just to be near it. The smell carried for about 300 yards. Rick was trying to get it out and he dropped it. The whole of the back of the van was smeared with this pink puke. Even my dog wouldn't touch it, but Rick ate a plateful in any case. He felt obliged to because he'd made it.

'Hmmm, it's lovely,' he kept saying, while the rest of us retched.

2 Everyone's Wally

I was talking to a friend of mine on the phone. This was some
time in February. She's involved in the free-party scene. She
heard what I was up to, writing a book about counter-culture.
'Have you heard of Wally Hope?' she asked.

Wally Hope, she explained, was the man who started the
Stonehenge free festival back in the seventies. She said that he
was later murdered; given an overdose of psychiatric drugs to
keep him quiet. This was the myth. He was part of a tribe who
all called themselves Wally. When the police came to summons
them for trespassing on the monument, they all gave their name
as Wally. As soon as she mentioned the name it resonated within
me, like some sort of symbol. Hope, yes.

My friend told me more of the story. More Wallies had been
killed. One of them was found tied to a tree in Epping Forest,
with a joint in his hand. Several others had disappeared. One of

them was Michael Fagan, the guy who had visited the Queen in her bedroom. According to him, my friend told me, the Queen is bald. She had to reach for a wig by her bedside before she could call in her attendants to get rid of him.

She added that, according to some people, the Queen is in fact the head of the Freemasons. She's one of the famed Illuminati, the people who control the world and all its doing by evil magic. This picture of a bald evil Queen controlling the world seared into my head, like a frame from some nightmarish cartoon.

I had a dream. I was at a Grateful Dead concert back in the sixties. It was a very modest affair, taking place in a church hall. People were scraping wooden chairs around, much bustle and movement, and the Grateful Dead were half-hidden behind their speakers, so you'd hardly know they were there. But I was intensely aware that I didn't belong. What was I doing in the sixties? I kept going up to people and asking them if they knew me. No one did. Once or twice I'd meet someone of my own generation, strangely disfigured by the time distortion. I'd say, 'I don't belong here. I'm not from this time,' and they would shrug and walk away. Eventually I walked out and someone followed me. I turned around and it was someone I knew from my own time.

'Do you know who I am?' I asked.

'Yes, I do.'

'So why am I here?'

He pointed up a slope to what looked like a derelict house on top of a hill.

'Up there,' he said. 'You'll find out up there.'

So I walked up the track.

There was someone coming up behind me, someone younger than me, dressed in hippie gear and carrying a rucksack. He was sliding around on the muddy track, his clothes caked in mud. We came to the door of the house and I said to the stranger, 'Take your boots off before you go in.' It was as if I'd been there before, as if I knew all the rules. The kitchen floor was tiled, and there was a long scrubbed wooden table in the middle and a fire burning in the grate. People were sitting round. It was obviously an early squat. I felt familiar with the place.

There were a couple of men with strange distorted faces. One of them was wearing a black monocle, or a pair of sunglasses with one lens missing. He was holding an umbrella or a cane, and had on a waistcoat with a watch chain. Neither of them was quite human. They were either angels or aliens. People were coming and going in the room. Everyone else was dressed like a hippie: cheesecloth shirts and flared jeans. I spoke to the two aliens.

'Do you know who I am?'

'Of course we do,' they said. 'This is your place. You created it. You taught us how to make a bender yesterday.'

I realised that I was passing between worlds – between the world of the sixties and the world of the nineties – and that things were pretty much the same. The people in the room were wearing fashions that were at home in either world. People's habits and inclinations were the same. The two worlds were coming together.

There was a girl with a fringed shirt. I felt a sexual tingle from her. I was shy, but it seemed to me that either we had already had sex, or that we would soon.

Everyone was smoking dope. The alien with the monocle handed the tube of a pipe in my direction, but I refused. 'I don't smoke,' I told him. 'I haven't done for years.' But there was smoke pouring out of it, in any case. It was pouring in my direction. I protested.

'Don't worry,' the alien said, 'it won't harm you.'

The room was filling with smoke. The smoke was billowing around like a steam-bath. White, white, white. I couldn't see anything but the white. Out of this blinding whiteness, images began to resolve themselves: a bookcase ... a table ... all lying on their sides. Until I realised that it was *my* bookcase, *my* table and it was me who was sideways, not them. I was lying on my side, in my bed, awake, in the pale light of my own room.

I drifted back to sleep. I was back outside that squat, only several years had passed, Narnia-like, in those few intervening moments. The squat was being closed down. There were police crawling all over the place. I bristled at the effrontery, stormed into the house and demanded to see the Chief Constable. I was very sure of myself, that I was in some sense the leader here. The Chief Constable turned out to be a black guy, wearing a checked shirt. (So this was definitely a fantasy.) He waited patiently while I ranted at him from my soapbox.

'Sorry,' he said, finally. 'Orders are orders. Sergeant, get rid of this man, will you!'

And I was thrown out.

There's a hymn we used to sing at school:

> God be in my head and in my understanding.
> God be in mine eyes and in my looking.
> God be in my mouth and in my speaking.

I hated that hymn. It sent shivers up my spine. Not only was the tune baleful and dreary, like a dirge, but the idea of inviting some alien creature into my head (and into my eyes and my mouth; the mouth sounded most repulsive of all) was, to a seven-year-old child, deeply unsettling. Never mind that this God-thing was supposed to be 'good'. It was something separate from me. Why should it be in my head? What if I didn't want it in my head?

I didn't understand any of it. We were always thanking God and asking God's forgiveness, and in the mornings, at assembly, we had to close our eyes, hold our hands together and talk to God. He was all around us, we were told. Everywhere. There was no way to get away from him. The headmistress held up a print of a pair of hands in the attitude of prayer and they looked agonised, not relaxed; knotted with anxiety. That's what prayer seemed to me at the time: a form of anxiety.

This was nothing less than ritual torture, an indoctrination. The God our headmistress was talking about wasn't an objective being out there in the heavens; he was society's idea of how we should behave. He represented authority, power, the State. There is no better way of supplementing the external power of the police force than by getting people to internalise that power too. 'God be in my head' is a perfect illustration of that process.

I told Kodan about my childhood anxiety about the 'God be in my head' hymn and he said, 'It sounds beautiful to me.' I guess that's where Kodan and I are different. I want to be responsible for my life.

So I was sitting in my local one Sunday lunchtime. Lyn was drunk. She's in her seventies and likes a drop of whisky. She always wants to talk to me when she's drunk. Which is all right, I don't mind. Except that she does tend to talk about the same things, over and over. Usually it's about kids or dogs. She says she likes kids and dogs, but that she doesn't trust adults. I say I don't like kids or dogs or adults, but that I trust bar stools. She throws me a puzzled glance at that one.

'You wha'?' she says.

'That's all right, Lyn.'

'Anyway, anyway, as I was saying, when my son's dog died – that's Barney, Barney is my son's dog – anyway, when Barney died the kids asked where he was and my son said, "He's gone to live in the country." He didn't want to tell them that Barney was dead. He thought it would be better for them not to know. So now the kids keep asking him, "When's Barney coming home, Dad?" And he has to make something up, like, "Oh, he's not feeling very well at the moment," or, "He's had to go away for the weekend." That's the trouble with lies,' she says. 'You tell one and it leads to a million.'

That's the trouble with God, too. One lie that led to a million. When you've told the same lie often enough, maybe it begins to seem like the truth. We've justified it to ourselves so often, repeating it over and over again. Then we start telling everyone else and they believe it too. Then they start telling it to everyone they know. It has become the truth, simply because it is shared by everyone. A million lies told a million times.

At that moment the fruit-machine hit the jackpot. £200. Ker-chunk, ker-chunk, ker-chunk, it went, on and on and on, spewing out £1 coins like there was no tomorrow. Which there wasn't at that moment. The bell had just gone for time, but in this bar it was drinks all round. I went up to the guy who'd just won. I'd never spoken to him before.

'It's funny how interesting people appear when they've just won £200,' I said. 'How about a drink?'

He laughed. 'No problem,' he said, digging into the weight of coins in his pocket. He slid a couple over the bar and I looked at these dense, dull coins like they were a miracle. Something for nothing. I'd come into the place with hardly a penny and, by a constellation of accidents, here I was getting drunk.

That's when it struck me. 'One lie leads to a million,' I thought. 'A million lies told a million times. God be in my head.' Money is just that sort of lie. It is a symbol. There's no objective reality there. It is something we lug around in our heads as certainly as we carry it in our pockets. If we all refused to believe in it all at once, it would be gone. Just like that. If we all refused to pay our bills, what could anyone do? If we gave all our money away, then wealth would circulate.

Money is the religion of the twentieth century. It has its churches and its theology. It has its rituals and its sacraments. It has its high priests and magicians. But it's a con, just like God. It doesn't really exist.

Here's a joke. It's a joke for which vast amounts of blood has been spilled, unfortunately, but it's still a joke. Columbus discovered America. Thereafter there were thousands of Spanish mercenaries crawling over the entire continent, 'pacifying' the natives – well, they were killing them. What they were after was gold. The Native Americans valued gold as a ritual object. It is malleable: perfect for forming into statues and beautiful objects. It never tarnishes and it glints like the sun. It is the sun's blood. They hung it at sacred spots to denote the points where the spiritual world and the material world meet: at the crossroads between the worlds. Thus the Spanish thought the natives were so unbelievably rich, they had so much gold, that they could afford to hang it from trees. So more natives were killed in the lust to find what was still hidden. The fact that the Indians didn't hide their gold didn't occur to the Spaniards.

But what happened to that gold which glistened from the trees, marking off the passages between the worlds? It is buried in storehouses, in places like Fort Knox or the Bank of England. It has disappeared. Gone, but not forgotten.

Now, here comes the punchline. Those ritual objects, the few that remain – those examples of early Mayan or Incan artistry, those statues of strange gods, those images from an ancient alien culture – are worth far more now than the value of the metal from which they are made. More, in fact, than their weight in gold.

Is the world richer or poorer for that?

Fen says that the hidden things will reappear, that what has lain beneath the surface will emerge, in the course of time; the good things and the bad things. I wonder if that includes all the Mayan gold, lying there in its secret vaults? Who knows? One day, maybe, we'll go back to using gold for what it's best at: ritual decoration. Imagine it: gold hanging from all the trees in all the parks of all the cities of the world, to mark off the passages between the worlds.

It was still February, near Candlemas. I hadn't started writing this book yet. I was just thinking about it. I went to a tVC party and took an E. You could say it was research. As usual, I left early. So I was sitting in my room in the pale dawn light, with the E still shuddering through my head, looking out of my back window. And I started to think.

There's a larch at the bottom of my garden. It looks like a lyre, or some kind of a cock-eyed angel with its wings raised. I put food out for the birds, who gather in its branches, twittering and scattering about, all chaotic activity, squabbling among themselves. There's a number of magpies who visit it regularly, and a blackbird or two who fix you with malevolent glances. And a robin. Jolly robin. It was out there now.

Do you know that you can train robins? They're the least fearful of all the wild birds. Leave food regularly in a trail to your window. Eventually it will wait on the sill. Then you can open the window and lead the trail indoors. Be patient. In the end it will eat from your hand.

Jolly Robin in the wood
Waiting for the gift of food.
Be he humble or be he bold
He'll turn a tumble, and then grow old.

I was thinking about time. I was looking at the robin and thinking about time. I was thinking of all the time that is gone. All those countless hours, what were they for? And all those days and months and years. All those centuries. All those aeons. An immensity of time. An ocean. We think we can count time, but how do you count an ocean?

I was thinking about reincarnation, too. Thinking about time makes you think about reincarnation. Not that I remember any of my past lives. Somehow I can't imagine that I was ever a pharaoh or a buccaneer, or any of those other things. I expect I've always been as I am now, the son of a Birmingham car-worker with a strange, speculative imagination. I imagine that all through the immensity of time I've always come from Birmingham, and have always been sitting here like this, looking out of my back window.

But when I think about reincarnation, the nature of the universe changes for me. It means I've been here for ever. That we've all been here for ever, since the beginning of time. That we are part of the process. That we are It.

It also means that Mozart is still among us. That he was always among us. And Einstein and Marx. And Jesus and the Buddha. And Ghengis Khan and Hitler. I expect that Mozart is sat in a bedroom right now, a weird genius with a DAT and a computer, making house music; altering our perceptions as he did the first time, messing about with our melody lines. And Jesus is a plumber living on a council estate in Staines, with a wife and five kids, keeping out of trouble this time round. And Ghengis Khan is a fast-food waiter on Victoria Station, getting confused about the orders and running round in an unhappy frenzy, at everyone's beck and call.

Reincarnation means that we all have to go on doing it till we finally get it right.

This is the third time I've tried to write this chapter. This was the worst chapter in the book. In the earliest version, when you reached this point, there was a section about the history of counter-culture. I tried to draw parallels between the counter-culture of the present age and the early Romantics. I talked about Dada. I talked about the beatniks and the hippies and what Timothy Leary said. I took note of the sixties. But somehow it didn't work. It was clumsy and uncomfortable, schematic and vague, and bore as much resemblance to real history as the Gold Blend coffee ads do to real love.

So I've changed my tack. I thought, 'What do I really know? Only what I remember.' So what follows is a personal testament. Maybe that's all any of us can offer in the end: personal testimony.

I was born in 1953, the year of the Queen's coronation. I'm a child of the second Elizabethan Age. I don't really remember much about those days. Except for one thing. We had a record player – a tiny little red and cream thing with a lid – and just one record. It was a dusty 78 of Fats Domino singing 'Blueberry Hill'. I loved that record. I would play it over and over before I went to school. It seemed ancient to me, like some archaic recording from the beginning of time, but I guess it was fairly new when I was playing it. Then one day it broke. The record player was much smaller than the bulky 78 spinning round on its deck. The lid fell, snapping the record in mid-chorus.

I guess there were still Teddy boys around. My mother told me that when the film *Rock Around the Clock* came out, everyone was so excited that they ripped out all the seats and danced in the aisles. Nothing like it had been heard in England before. The lyrics could be an anthem for the rave generation too. They show that the urge to rock 'till broad daylight' has been around for ever (or since the fifties, at least) and that what ravers are asking for now is no more than what Teddy boys asked for nearly forty years before.

Later I remember seeing the mods and rockers fighting on Margate beach. This was on the little black-and-white telly that sat proudly in the corner of our living room. My friend Keith Hart became a mod. He had a parka and wore brown brogues. And then I got a parka, so I was a mod too, in the end.*

I was about fourteen years old by now. But there was something new coming out of America: this strange new music, these strange new ideas. The newspapers and the TV were full of all this hippie stuff. We saw Timothy Leary saying, 'Turn on, tune in, drop out.' My mum and dad tried to make sense of it. 'Turn on, tune in ... that's drugs, isn't it? And then you become addicted and you die, and that's why you drop out.'

---

*I've been thinking about the mod style. They wore parkas, they rode scooters, and they were always trying to be cool. Eskimos wear parkas, they ride snow-scooters and they *are* cool. So there you have it. Another cultural knot unravelled by the razor-sharp pen of C. J. Stone. Mods were urban Eskimos.

Well, I knew that wasn't true. Even then I knew things my mum and dad didn't know. I used to go to the library, to a secret corner full of mysterious books about the paranormal, with pictures of mediums exuding ectoplasm from their noses and other strange phenomena. There were books on psychology and hypnotism. And drugs. There were books about drugs. So I knew that LSD didn't kill you. I read a book about it. It was full of case histories of the use of LSD as a clinical tool. I knew that LSD gave people strange experiences, sometimes religious experiences, but that it didn't kill you. The accounts of people's experiences with LSD in that book fascinated me. I knew that, one day, I wanted to try it.

This was 1967, the Summer of Love. I picked a flower and wore it in my lapel on the way to work. I was a delivery boy at the local grocer's. The shop manager said, 'Hey, what are you? Are you a hippie?' I saw a photograph of the Grateful Dead in a newspaper. They were wearing trousers cut so low that they clung to their hips – hipsters. I decided that that must be the reason they were called hippies, because they wore trousers round their hips.

In the following years, all my circle of friends got heavily into music. We used to go to a club in Birmingham called Mothers. I remember seeing Mick Farren and the Social Deviants (later just called the Deviants). They got so carried away that the drummer smashed up his drum kit. A lot of bands did that, as a kind of finale. It was like a psychodrama, the casting out of materialism. But this was on the first number, so they had to play the rest of the set without drums. It was radical.

None of us knew what to wear the first night we went. In those days people still went to dances on a Friday night to see big bands and do the foxtrot. It was customary to dress up, so we turned up at Mothers dressed in suits and ties. The band on stage looked at us in disbelief. 'Hey look, the straights are here,' they announced from the stage.

Over the years I saw Blodwyn Pig, Black Sabbath, Led

Zeppelin and Pink Floyd. Those were the days. Names really meant something then. It cost anything from 5/- to 12/6 to get in. That's from 25p to 62p. Black Sabbath were the resident band, being Brummies. They cost 5/-.

We went to the Isle of Wight to see Bob Dylan. He was crap. He was going through his 'Lay, Lady, Lay' crooning phase, pretending to be Bing Crosby. I was very disappointed and didn't play a Bob Dylan record for months afterwards. But there were all these hippies there, living in a rambling, makeshift underground shelter called Desolation Row, after the Dylan song. They all sported the Jimmy Hendrix frizzy-haired look and walked round barefoot. They were the first hippies I'd ever seen in the flesh.

Then – this must have been in 1969 – I ran away from home and went to live with the hippies. There's no reason to go into an explanation of this. There's hardly a sixteen- or seventeen-year-old on the planet that doesn't end up in head-to-head arguments with her or his parents. I was very independent minded by now and I was fascinated by the hippie cult.

I met a character called John Ellis. He was in his mid-twenties and had the customary frizzy hair. I was always jealous of that look, because my hair is so undeviatingly straight.

We went on walkabout. We travelled from Great Yarmouth to Devon around the coast, hitch-hiking all the way. We had a dog with us called Junkie. We slept in squats and derelict houses, and if we saw anyone else with long hair and a guitar on his back, we'd give them the peace sign. We begged, conned and stole for food, and addressed each other as 'man'.

I took my first drug. It was a cough medicine called Demerol. I saw visions. I saw a giant outlined along the houses. I saw gods and demons fighting their eternal battle down a back alley, and time distended so that a short walk seemed to go on for ever. Then we were in a café and there was a puppy on the table. The puppy fell off. I caught it without even being aware of what I was doing.

I travelled with John Ellis for about six weeks. We ended up in a town somewhere in the South West, in an abandoned old-people's home. The place was full of drugs, mainly opiates and pain-killers. I took huge quantities of them. One day I got a cramp in my back. I was nearly doubled over backwards, my back arched like a tightened spring, and John had to kick my spine to wrench it back into place. I stopped taking the drugs and felt better almost immediately. Those drugs filled your head with fluff. They made you stupid.

Eventually, the police raided the old-people's home and we were taken into custody. John had outstanding warrants against him, so he was placed in the cells. I was taken home by my uncle.

I continued to be fascinated by the idea of psychedelic drugs. None of the stuff I'd taken so far had been psychedelic in any way. It was all opiates and downers. I wanted to try cannabis. Most of all I wanted to try LSD.

I smoked my first cannabis that year at the Reading Festival. I hitch-hiked there by myself. My parents thought I was going with friends. I met a Dutch bloke who took me under his wing. He went into an off-licence to buy some beer. The man behind the counter said, 'Indulging your little vice, eh?' and he winked. The young Dutchman said, 'I've got four vices, actually: beer, cigarettes, sex and dope.' And he laughed. I was astounded at his openness. He didn't give a damn.

We all slept in a huge marquee. I watched one evening as someone filled a massive pipe with a pure grass and hash mix. He said, 'It's a better hit this way.' I was hoping that he would pass it to me, but he didn't. Eventually the Dutchman passed me a spliff. I puffed on it and got dizzy from the nicotine, but no more. I smoked a few more spliffs that he passed my way, but always it seemed to have no effect. I said, 'This stuff doesn't do anything to me.' And the Dutch bloke said, 'Well, I think you're stoned. You just don't know it yet.'

I carried on puffing and then lay down. All of a sudden I was overtaken by the most exquisite sensation. It was as if my body had disappeared. My body melted into the liquid earth. There was nothing in my head. I was completely relaxed. Despite all the noise and mayhem I was in some quiet, tranquil space. The only sensation I had was where one part of my body touched another, for instance, where my ankles were crossed, or where my arm was tucked beneath my chest. I was stoned.

Later that year I tried it again. We all used to go to a pub in Birmingham called the Alhambra. One day some one offered me a quid's worth. I bought it. It was wrapped up in silver paper, this finger of earthy-smelling, crumbly, greenish-tan substance. We smoked it the following week, before going to the Alhambra. I was the expert, having watched people making spliffs at Reading earlier that year. We were round Kevin Nurrish's house. It was me, Kevin, Robert Russell and Alan Greensall. I rolled the spliff and then heated up the hash as I'd seen the Dutchman do. The substance became suddenly soft as I spread it along the waiting tobacco in a line. We smoked that spliff and it did nothing. I had no idea how much to put in. So for the next spliff I put the whole quid's worth in. That was quite a lot of dope – about a sixteenth at today's prices. Then we went to catch the bus.

It was winter. The pavements were covered in ice. I kept losing my footing, but suddenly it seemed as if my body was giving way at the waist. I wasn't sure if it was the dope or the fact that I was losing my footing. I kept saying, 'My body's giving way.' They all thought I was putting it on. On the bus I had a terrible fantasy. I imagined suddenly crying out, right in the middle of the bus, and rolling on the floor like a baby. It seemed so real, as if it might actually happen. Unfortunately, no one else had been affected by the drug. I was all alone. It was my first paranoid experience.

I finally took LSD. It was with Colin Walker, a school friend. We took a tab of Californian Sunshine, the pure American acid that was still available in those days. The experience wasn't in the slightest bit religious or psychedelic. I simply didn't understand what was happening. I talked and talked, while Colin stayed perfectly silent. I was babbling away at him, while he just looked at me bemused. Nothing made any sense.

That's about as much as I ever got out of LSD, that nothing made any sense.

I left home soon after that to go to college. This was in 1971. I experimented some more with drugs and alternative lifestyles. I was never that successful. I wasn't that successful at college, either. I dropped out in the end, after several goes.

I used to visit a friend at a house where they smoked a lot of dope. People would loll around that house all night, blowing chillums and listening to music with their eyes closed. No one ever said anything. They just lay around on cushions in the half-light and blew chillums and looked cool. Unfortunately I was a bit of a chatterbox. I just used to talk. So one day I went to visit my friend and he had to take me to his bedroom. I'd been banned from the communal room.

I took LSD once and forgot who I was. I couldn't remember my name. I was paranoid that I might bump into someone who knew me. It's a terrible way to start a conversation: 'Excuse me, but do you know who I am?' Another time I took LSD and, as usual, I couldn't make any sense out of it. Maybe that was the problem. There wasn't any sense to be had. There were three of us. I'd say, 'I don't understand.' Someone else would say, 'What don't you understand?' The third person would say, 'There's nothing to understand.' And then there'd be a pause before I'd start up again. 'I don't understand.' It went on all night. 'I don't understand.' 'What don't you understand?' 'There's nothing to understand.'

One day someone took me to one side and said, 'Chris, you don't really get on with acid, do you? I think you should stop taking it.' But I couldn't let go of the idea that this was the drug to change my life. All those glowing reports in the case-history book I'd read as a youngster. Smelling sounds and hearing colours. And visions and hallucinations and communion with the spirits, and leaving the planet and voyaging through deepest space. But I was a very repressed person. I couldn't even look anyone in the eye when I was tripping.

I remember reading something which put the whole thing in perspective for me. It was about the early days of LSD-use in America. All the pioneers are sat around: Allen Ginsberg, Timothy Leary and Baba Ram Das, and a few of their acolytes. They're all tripping off their nuts. All of a sudden, one girl says, 'I've got it! I know what the secret of the universe is. I'm absolutely certain. I know the secret of the universe.' They all discuss whether it is better to know the secret of the universe, or whether it is best to remain in ignorance. Finally, curiosity gets the better of them. They want to know, but they decide that they will wait till morning, until they are all straight. So the girl writes it down, and puts the message in an envelope and seals it. 'It's true,' she says, 'it really is the secret of the universe.'

The following day, of course, they are all eager to read the message. They assemble in great solemnity, ready to have the message read out to them. The envelope is unsealed ceremoniously. The piece of paper bearing the message is unfolded. They wait with baited breath. Then the person who is holding the paper laughs. He reads out the message. The secret of the universe is:

'When I stand on my toes I can touch the ceiling.'

3 Nowhere Fast

I was warned. I knew it would be too much. You don't ask a roadside café cook to put on a banquet for the Queen. You don't ask a 1976 Fiat Camper with a leaky engine to take you to Glasgow.

But I wouldn't listen. The I Ching told me. I asked, 'Should I take the van to Glasgow tomorrow?' I got hexagram 62, Preponderance of the Small. 'Small things may be done; great things should not be done. The flying bird brings the message: It is not well to strive upward; it is well to remain below.' And again: 'The little bird meets with misfortune through flying.' The little bluebird in this case, as the Camper is a nice shade of blue. And everyone else told me. Even the man who sold me the van, just three days before, told me.

'It's an old banger,' he said. 'I don't want you ringing me up from Scotland saying I sold you a bummer.'

I said, 'I wouldn't do that, Dave. Anyway, I've got faith.'

So much for faith. It can move mountains, but not a 1976 Fiat Camper with a seized engine.

I knew something was wrong at the petrol stop just north of Birmingham. The entire back of the machine was splattered with oil. This wasn't just some messy old engine that smoked a bit too much – it was coming apart at the seams. Kodan chanted over it for me, as I added the last of the oil from the bottle I'd brought the day before. 'Sri Ram, Jai Ram, Jai Jai Ram,' he sang, which means, 'Glorious Rama, the fountain of all strength.' Or something like that. Even Kodan wasn't too sure, despite his years as a Krishna monk. It was meant to give the vehicle the power to undertake the journey. Only it didn't work.

Just north of the service station the engine began to smoke. I mean, really smoke. I could see it out of the side mirrors, pouring smoke, like a joint of beef that's been in the oven too long. Then the engine was rattling and the vehicle was juddering, and I just knew that this was it. I should've listened to the I Ching.

So we're sat on the hard shoulder, Kodan and I, on the M6 at Junction 21a, the Liverpool/Southport turn-off, waiting for the AA man to turn up. In front of us is one of those overhead gantries holding up the traffic signs. Someone has spray-painted graffiti across the length of the sign. This is what it says: 'Liverpool nil, BWFC 2. Manchester nil, Bolton 4.' It was Kodan who pointed out this out to me, as we huddled in the Camper sipping hot coffee from the flask my mother had made up for us: that someone is so fanatical for Bolton Wanderers Football Club – so mad, so unremittingly deranged – that he's climbed up a gantry, maybe in the middle of the night, in a buffeting wind, with traffic roaring and hissing by beneath; that he's shuffled his way along, clenching the scaffolding between the cheeks of his arse, hanging on to the thin metal of the signs as they bucked about in the wind, to construct a totally fictitious scoreline for his favourite, not very good, football club, against perhaps two of the most successful clubs in the world, two giants of British football; that he's risked life and limb for a futile fantasy, that he would die for the love of his team.

There's a lesson in there somewhere. Only I can't be bothered to work out what it is.

Later, Kodan and I are sitting in the back of the AA truck heading towards the M6 through Warrington. Warrington was the nearest town to where we broke down. We've scrapped the bluebird – oh, beautiful bluebird – for thirty quid cash, though there's still fifteen quid's worth of petrol in it. We've scrapped the bluebird and I'm kind of crying. Not about the money. I don't care about the money. About the dreams. All those little dreams tied up in a 1976 Fiat Camper. All those things I've already done in my mind. Those places I've been. Those people I've visited. The new friends I've made. Those drunken nights falling out of the pub and straight to sleep in the tiny little van with the lid up like a tent. And it doesn't matter, but there's still a lurch of regret in my solar-plexus region, like mourning for a long-lost friend, like making a promise to yourself that you failed to keep.

Actually, I'm lying to you. I did care about the money. Those things I've done ... those places I've been ... those drunken nights falling out of the pub ... they were as dependent on the money as on the vehicle. Always be wary when someone says to you that they don't care about money. They're on something.

The AA man says, 'Warrington is the fourth largest city in the UK.'

'Oh really?' says Kodan, as if he's interested.

'Yes. First London. Then Birmingham. Then Manchester. Then Warrington.' It's as if he's saying, 'Manchester nil, Warrington 4'. Warrington matters; it means something.

By now we're driving past an estate of brand-new houses, all candy-coloured brick with pert little windows like eyes, laid out in calmly curved streets in the midst of a bleak yellowed landscape of mutant grasses. There's not a sign of life in the whole place; just cars slumbering in the driveways and new white nets behind the glinting window glass. No pubs. No shops. No churches even.

'Could you live there?' I ask, pointing it out to Kodan.

'No,' he replies. 'It's got no soul. I wonder what they do with themselves?'

The AA man carries on about Warrington. 'There's a Lever Brothers. And new technology. And ...' – I think I'd asked him what accounted for Warrington's phenomenal success – 'they drove the M62 straight through Warrington Airport. Manchester and Liverpool saw to that, because Warrington Airport was challenging them as the foremost airport in the North West. And the United States used to lease the airbase here. See those houses there? 70,000 American Airmen lived here at one time. And ... '

But I'm hardly listening. Just looking out the window at the shadowlands outside, when a huge industrial/warehouse/shopping complex lurches into view, mile upon mile of prefabricated units in primary colours like plastic bricks, with names such as Toys Я Us and MFI.

'That must be what the people on those estates do,' I say. 'They go shopping.'

The AA man says, 'Yes. Today's a quiet day. You should see it sometimes, the queues go right back to that gas works over there.'

He's right. Even on this quiet day there are cars lined up on the exits to the motorway, lines and lines of people sitting motionless in cars, queuing for the industrial/warehouse/shopping complex; acres and acres of cars in car-parks. Cars sliding gingerly past each other in traffic-calmed streets of brand-new Tarmac. Shiny cars with catalytic converters and in-car entertainment, with quiet engines that purr unobtrusively. Cars full of families with grannies in the back. Cars lovingly tended and polished and vacuumed out once a week while the owner listens to Radio One or Radio Warrington or Radio Whatever, splished and sploshed, swished and shined like a champion prize pet on its way to Crufts, glorified shopping trolleys the lot of them. All these cars, all these people, all going shopping.

The AA man dropped us on a sliproad off the M6 so we could hitch a lift to Glasgow. He couldn't take us to the services, he reckoned, 'cos, what with these computers on board, they'd know what he was up to. 'It's a question of the mileage,' he said. 'I can take you to the railway station, or I can take you to the motorway.' So we opted for the motorway – an executive decision – just one more bad decision in a mad day's bad decision-making. And now we're here and the cars are sailing by, the occupants – or rather, the captives – hypnotised by the road; transfixed by the wily snake-line in the middle, like dumb poultry ready for the slaughter.

Kodan and I are making jokes about machetes and sub-machine-guns. We want to mow all of these people down. We want to slice them up and leave bits of them buried the length of our journey, like a bizarre, morbid paper-chase. Me, I'm looking like Charles Manson on a death-trip, Charles Manson on a particularly bad day, and no one in their right mind would pick us up, no one with a single functioning brain cell would take us into their nice little cars and run the risk of getting blood on the back seats – imagine trying to wash that off with a sponge and detergent. Anyway, most of them are going only as far as the shops. Suddenly it's spattering with rain and there's an eerie, dark cloud like an ominous thought, and ... Well, we turn on our heels and head the other way.

There's a town in the distance, with a bleak church spire

pointing defiantly at the heavens, and maybe we're hoping for a bus or a lift or something. Kodan is talking about cafés – eternal optimist that he is – and I laugh and say, 'On a Sunday? In a town the size of a postage stamp? You must be joking.'

So we come to a flyover carrying traffic into the town and start to climb the bank. At the top there's what looks like a possible way through to the road, but as we climb, the bushes seem to push us relentlessly towards the drop. Kodan is balanced precariously on the sloping concrete edge near the top, and there's a lurch in my stomach as I see the malevolent intent of those bush-triffid things and imagine Kodan flying off on to the road and under the wheels of the conspiring traffic. We've already spoken about this. Miles down the road, when the bluebird was still alive, spluttering its way between Birmingham and Warrington, we'd spoken about our mutual fear of heights, and how the fear is strongest when watching someone else. So here's Kodan now in front of me, being pushed relentlessly to his death by the machinations of these evil triffid-beings, paying us back for simply being human, for slicing down all their ancient brothers and sisters, to make way for yet more motorways.

What *is* a motorway? It takes you from A to B and back again.

It seems like a joke, only I don't think that the punchline is all that funny.

The little town is slumbering idly on a quiet Sunday afternoon, its church like a grim prayer, dark with the smoke of time. It squats on a green knoll, ponderous and worthy, a bastion of northern respectability and reserve. It's pissing down with rain now and there's three-quarters of an hour to go before the bus back to Warrington. Luckily there's a pub.

OK. Things are nice in here. This is what I like about British culture: pubs. Pubs are homes from home; places to be when the rain is washing down in great shifting waves like billowing curtains, warm like your own front room. And people are friendly or they're not, but you're always welcome in a pub. We drink a pint of Webster's each, eat a packet of crisps, listen to the rain rattling the windows, and talk about this and that, just being there, just enjoying each other's company. In this world, friendship is all. Friendship and pubs.

I like Kodan. He's one of those people I can talk to. I don't mean about the shopping, or what you're going to do today. I mean about speculative things. About the meaning of life, stuff like that. Right now, we're sat in a pub in the middle of nowhere and we're talking about time.

'See, time isn't linear, running from the past to the future ... It's lateral. Like this pub here is a frozen moment, containing an accumulation of time. The photos on the wall, the lamps on the ceiling, the people and how they're dressed, even their attitudes and states of mind, they represent a whole history of things present in this one moment.' And I talk about the I Ching and how it fits in with the view of quantum mechanics about time being like a matrix, weaving the universe into a unified web, where every moment is discrete and separate from the moment that follows it. 'According to the I Ching, if I kick a ball and then break a window, the two things are entirely separate. I kick the ball in one distinct moment, and the breaking glass is literally in another universe, wholly unrelated.' I think I'm probably attempting to justify trying to take an unfit vehicle on an over-ambitious journey. See, it has nothing to do with me. Starting out on the journey was an entirely separate moment to the one we find ourselves in now. 'Synchronicity' means 'at the same time'. It also means, 'Don't blame me, it was my *doppelgänger* wot did it!'

At this precise moment the barman calls, 'Time!' and someone wins the jackpot on the fruit-machine.

Eventually we're forced to leave. The manager locks the door behind us as we're cast into the blistering rain, while the rest of them – locals – stay in with the fire and the beer for the afternoon. Luckily there's a shop open, so I go off to buy something to eat. Just crisps, that's all they have. I get four packets and ask what time the bus is due. A man I'd hardly noticed, who's been lurking in the shop the whole time, says, 'It's Sunday, so there's no traffic, so the bus will be early.' He says this in a dour, flat northern voice, like he's reciting from Bram Stoker's *Dracula*, like he's making some horrible prediction about the monsters of the psyche, rather than reassuring me about the bus timetable. I turn around to glance at him, as he shuffles from one leg to the next, and his misery is almost palpable, like a dark cloak drawn around him.

'Are you catching it too?' I ask breezily. I can't think for what other reason he's lurking here in this shop.

'No, I live just up t' road there. I'm just goin' up t' hill.' This, too, has the air of some terrible admission, like he's telling me he murdered his wife last week and buried her on the moors, and God is dead, and the last tree on earth has just fallen, and there's no hope left for anything any more, we might as well top ourselves right now.

Well, Kodan and I share our crisps under a tiny shelter by a school. Kodan has tandoori flavour, and I have Canadian ham. His are nicer than mine. Then Kodan has Worcester sauce flavour, and I have beef. And his are still nicer than mine. While we're eating them the wife-slayer emerges from the shop, wrapped up in his black donkey jacket, and I point him out as he lumbers his slow, defeated way home, emanating misery and despair. Kodan laughs.

We caught the bus, and now, many bleak, damp hours later, we're back in Warrington, back where the AA man might have taken us, at the railway station, buying tickets to Glasgow. We had a choice of stations. 'Warrington Central' turned out to be a local station, so we had to walk again, three-quarters of a mile, to what sounds by its name to be a local station and is, in fact, the main station. As we arrived there was a train pulling out. 'I'll bet you anything that's the train to Glasgow,' I said. So I say to the man selling me the tickets, 'When's the next train to Glasgow,' and he says, 'It's up there on Platform 3 now. No, it's not,' he adds, after looking at the computer screen, 'it just pulled out.'

Why? Why are we doing this, putting ourselves to so much trouble, handing out money hand over fist – as if time and money were going out of fashion – getting damp and cold and miserable and nowhere fast? We're going to meet a prophet, and Kodan has a hankering after his mad, Scottish roots, and me, I'm on a journey to discover Britain, to find out what lies at the root of the British psyche. I might as well start somewhere, why not a pointless journey from the South to the North, taking in all the pointlessness in between?

Actually, I'm looking for Wally Hope. Not the man, the spirit. Wally Hope performed miracles, so they say, and I'm looking for evidence that miracles can still happen. Instead of which, I'm finding the exact opposite. I'm finding that everything can conspire to mess you around.

We settle down in the refreshments lounge and sip cups of strong dark tea, so infused with tannin that it makes your tongue cleave to your teeth, while we wait for the train. Then – at last – the train does arrive, and we climb on board and make our way to the back while the train draws out, to find the smoking carriage. Through the crowded aisles, edging slowly round people removing their coats and shifting their luggage on to the racks, knocking people with our rucksacks, through the buffet car and into the first-class carriages with their pale-maroon seats and headrest covers, right down to the guard's compartment at the end where the guard is preparing to make his announcements over the Tannoy.

'Lost?' he asks.

'We're looking for the smoking carriage.'

Then we realise it, and all three of us – Kodan, the guard and I – chant in unison, 'It's at the front.'

So we follow the same route back up the train, bungling down the long corridors again, crashing people with our bags again, as the train lurches from side to side, and we are thrown against the doors and the seats and the people sitting in the seats, right the way to the front, where we settle down and promptly roll a cigarette each as compensation. This is one cigarette we really do deserve.

I fell asleep on the train. I dreamed I was in a rock'n'roll band called The Miffed – like The Clash, only less confrontational. Not so much Rage Against the Machine as Slightly Peeved The Taps Won't Work. I was the drummer, only I didn't have any drums so I had to play the spoons instead. When I woke up the rattling of the spoons became the clattering of the train on the tracks and we were passing through Cumbria and the bleak hills were billowing plumes of snow in the gloomy evening light.

That's when I started writing this, on an InterCity 125 to Psycho Central, hurtling through the Cumbrian hills in the evening light, while snow like plumes of smoke billowed from the mountain tops.

We arrived in Glasgow exactly twelve hours after we'd started out. Birmingham to Glasgow in twelve hours. Kent to Glasgow in twenty-four. Coming out of the station I heard my first Glaswegian accents. Some blokes in a taxi called to their mates across the road, 'Ye wur fuckin' wreecked last nit, Patty, win't ye ... ' Or something like that. I didn't quite catch it. It sounded like a foreign language. Later, we're sitting in the Horseshoe bar near the station, with a pint of heavy each, and the people sitting next to me sound even more strange. 'I can't get the hang of this Glaswegian accent,' I say to Kodan. 'Sounds like German to me.'

We finished off our drinks and I went to the bar for some more. The odd thing now was that the man behind the bar was perfectly easy to understand, and so was everyone else leaning at the bar.

When I got back we'd been joined by someone who wanted to tell Kodan his life history. It's a northern trait, people who pick complete strangers to tell their life history to. Kodan told me later that the geezer'd walked up and down a number of times, sizing him up. 'Oh no,' thought Kodan, 'it's the Glasgow nutter. I hope he doesn't sit down.' At which point he did. His conversation was fairly innocuous at first, about work and the like. I had no difficulty understanding him either. He was dressed in workman's clothes, with a flat cap, and washed-out corduroy trousers. He's been all over the country, he told us, as his fingers stretched across his bulging paunch and he looked at us with these deep, ineffably sad eyes. Birmingham, yes. And Warrington. And Kent. Do I know such-and-such a place? Not really. He did a job down there once, fitting something or another at some factory or another. He's from the Highlands. I'm half-listening; sipping my pint and enjoying the luxury of knowing that – bluebird or not – at least I've made it to Glasgow. At which point he starts. Peter Ustinov is a nice man, he suggests. Yes, so I would imagine. He's fair. Maybe, yes. He always sees the good in people. Yes. Take Hitler, for instance. He built the autobahns, after all. And he brought full employment to Germany. This line of reasoning has crept up on us. From, 'Peter Ustinov is a nice man,' to, 'Hitler brought full employment,' in a few short, sweet, apparently harmless sentences. I'm not sure we didn't splutter into our pints. We ought to have. It was like someone selling you toothpaste, then when you clean your teeth with it, it turns out to be prussic acid. Well, the packet was nice. Pity your gums boiled when you used it and all your teeth fell out.

'Yes, he brought full employment,' Kodan says. 'and he kissed babies and he was a vegetarian. Nice man. Pity about the concentration camps.'

Trust us. In a pub full of people chattering about this and that mundane or pleasantly trivial subject – beer, girls, boys, fish fingers, mum, dad or the latest football results – we have to come across the only Nazi. We made our excuses and left.

Outside Kodan says, 'You know you thought those people sitting next to us sounded German? That's because they were German.'

4 Glasgow

This town has a fragrance, like eau-de-Cologne. You're coming out of a bar, or some other confined space, and it hits you: something fresh and sweet, like perfume or fresh-cut flowers. When I first smelled it I thought there must be some woman near by and looked around for the source. There was no one. I assumed that it was someone who'd recently passed by leaving a trail, and vainly looked up and down the road after her. When the same thing had happened two or three times I began to realise that it was in the air. The woman is Glasgow. Glasgow is a woman.

Really it's a small town masquerading as a big city. Even in the city centre you can see the hills circling in the distance, as if framing it. You never get the feeling – as you do in Birmingham or London – that the city goes on for ever. That's where the smell comes from: from the hills.

Kodan and I are in the Gorbals, visiting a friend of his. You can't see the hills from the Gorbals, just lines of tenements like concentration camps without the barbed wire. We've been in town for a day or two, relaxing and taking it easy after the madness of the journey. This morning we'd been to Paddy's Market to get some tobacco. We'd edged between the tat-laden stalls – there was half a packet of Tampax for sale at one of them – and into slimy railway arches like caves, that stank of grease and mould and ancient hot dogs, where we met a furtive man in a flat cap who spoke to us out of the corner of his mouth and gave us a cryptic message to pass on: 'Tell Big Mick Little Jimmy sent ye.' It felt like we were scoring drugs – which is what, I suppose, we were doing. I kept my mouth shut in case my English accent offended. When we found Big Mick, he sent us somewhere else. And so it went on until we'd found the tobacco. Paddy's Market is a measure of the poverty in Britain today. There's a place like it in every city.

Later we'd stopped off in the People's Palace, a large Victorian glass structure, full of plants and the smell of the tropics, where we'd had tea and homemade soup. I had lentil and tomato, Kodan had cheese and cauliflower, and his was nicer than mine. Then we walked to the Gorbals, into one of the tenements and knocked on the door. It was answered by Kodan's friend, dressed only in Y-fronts.

'Fashion victim,' whispered Kodan to me, after Danny had dressed himself and gone off to make tea. He'd put on a seventies brown Crimplene flared suit, with lapels the size of football pitches (probably bought from Paddy's Market), and a speckled shirt with a huge floppy collar. The sort of thing that nutters used to wear, back in the seventies, when this stuff had only just gone out of fashion, and all the rest of us were trying to deny that there had ever been such an era.

Danny is in his early twenties, with long greasy hair and a thin beard. Dressed like that, he could have been forty years older.

Later, we were walking back through town when we met another bloke dressed in a black plastic coat with a white polo neck, like some hip geezer from a jazz club in the fifties. Danny was slagging him off as he approached us and I thought, 'So this is what the youth get up to in their spare time: dressing up and putting each other down.' While we're talking I notice the Bluebird Café across the road, and now I'm thinking, 'So this is a significant moment.' Everything with a bluebird in it is a significant moment. Which probably makes this the last significant moment in the book. But Danny asks us what we're going to do tonight and he mentions the *Sunday Sport* Road Show which is taking place later. So we're standing here in this significant moment outside the Bluebird Café, me and Kodan, and a bloke dressed like a seventies nutter, and another one dressed like a fifties pot-fiend, talking about the *Sunday Sport*, and I think, 'Well, why not? It's as mad as anything else.'

We met later outside a supermarket. Our informant was a bloke called Woody, the very picture of a furtive pornography addict, with eyes that slopped round like wet oysters behind his thick glasses. He said, 'I'm just a pervy bastard,' and Danny told us that when they'd gone to Edinburgh together Woody had spent the entire time looking round the back streets for sex shows and the like. But he seemed happy enough with his drug. Unashamed.

I'm glad we went. It was a riot. Literally. It had a nerve calling itself a road show. It was a tit show. The room was packed with heaving, sweating, drunken Glaswegian men. The girls were dancing about and wobbling their breasts and doing various other things, and the men were barracking them and trying to get a feel as they walked by, and things were getting out of hand. The blokes were stamping their feet and clapping, and at one point the stamping got so fierce that part of the ceiling came down. There were guys standing there covered in ceiling plaster like flour, looking bemused. There were about twice as many people in there as there should have been, and fifty men for every woman, with everyone jostling for position, trying to get a look at the girls with their heavy make-up and huge silicone breasts. They were all still stamping and leering and shouting, and eventually the management shuffled the girls away. Then things got really wild. The men were in a frenzy. They wanted the girls back. There were still trails of plaster like dribbles of smoke coming down from the ceiling and now everyone was stamping in unison for the girls to come back – stamp, stamp, stamp – 'Bring on da girls, bring on da girls!' Then someone threw a bottle and someone else threw a table, and everyone started throwing everything, and there were fights breaking out all over the place. Glass was smashing with a melodic tinkle and it felt like the whole building would collapse. Then the police were called and everyone was thrown out into the cold Glasgow night like lost souls evicted from Paradise.

We were staying with a couple of friends of ours who'd just had their first baby, Daniel. He has orange hair, red cheeks and bright blue eyes. He's the most colourful baby I've ever seen. He's a psychedelic baby.

Kodan and I were supposed to be going over to the Pollock estate, the largest inner-city green space in Europe, where there's an anti-roads protest. I'd heard a few things about it: how the local people had got involved; how the school children had gone on strike and were spending their time on site; how one day a whole bunch of security guards had changed allegiance, given up their yellow jackets and gone over to the other side. It sounded fascinating. Only it started to snow. You could see the snow gathering in the air as we set out, swirling between the buildings like a wizard's cloak, before it hit, hard and stingingly cold. So we turned round and went home to a fire and a cup of coffee. 'Some revolutionaries we are,' Kodan said. 'First bit of snow and we're running home to mummy. Sitting discussing the revolution in bunny slippers over coffee and biscuits.' And here am I, contracted to write a book about counter-culture, and I can't make it to a road protest, but I can make it to a *Sunday Sport* Road Show. I'm not sure what that says about me, but it probably gives you some idea of where the book is going.

Later, we went to see a prophet. Here's a man who believes in miracles. We met him in Renfrew, just outside Glasgow, in someone's half-decorated kitchen. His name is John. John the Prophet. He was a brawling drunkard and petty criminal before he became a prophet.

John is genuine. He means what he says. He really is a prophet. And we're sitting here in a council flat on the outskirts of Glasgow with this compact, intense, athletic bundle of electrifying energy with sizzling blue eyes, telling us about visions of Christ and meeting the Pope and Pele and Muhammad Ali in the space of thirty-seven days, and punctuating his conversation with weird homilies like, 'Thoughts are things,' and, 'Imagination is the most powerful tool known to man,' and you can't deny there's something about him, if only that it's rare to meet anyone quite so audacious. 'I am returning to myself,' he says. 'An ideal world will be created through my eyes.' And he goes on to speak of his vision, of a world glowing like the sun, of a life beyond our wildest dreams, and how we all have the ability to create our own future. 'You can change the system. You can get an ideal world,' he says.

This is how it happened. He died and came back to life. He was sitting with some friends, when he turned grey and his eyes rolled back into his head (this is how his friends described it). 'I'm dying,' he said, 'I'm slipping away.' The two girls ran out crying. It was as if he was judging himself. He could see his life passing before his eyes, all these terrible things he'd done, and how he'd never lived up to his potential. He should've been one of the greatest footballers ever. He was already the greatest streetfighter. One hundred fights in fifteen years, and he hadn't lost one. Next he was rising up and up through layers of intense brightness, higher and higher, brighter and brighter, and there was a deep Presence near him, a being of light, a force.

'What the fuck's happening?' said John, speaking wordlessly from his heart. 'Who the fuck am I?'

'You should know,' answered the Presence.

'Am I John the Baptist?' asked John. (This had been his nickname.)

'Through time you will see.' And he was shown this vision of the world as it could be, resonant with the Presence and glowing like the sun. 'Go back down and sort that lot out,' he was told, and he came awake again in his body.

He was awake all night, gabbling insanely, while his friend tried to calm him down.

'I thought you were a gonner there,' his friend said.

'So did I,' said John.

This was 29 August 1989 – according to John, the anniversary of John the Baptist's death.

Then there was a roller-coaster of God-incidences, a sequence of events that conspired to confirm his new-found belief. Like the man who became obsessed with him, and took him to see the statue of John the Baptist at Carthain Grotto, and who then insisted that John should go to Rome to meet the Pope. John was reluctant at first – his girlfriend thought this bloke fancied him – but in the end he relented and the two of them went to Rome. They were at a Mass in St Peter's, the Pope was addressing the crowd in several languages, and John went into deep meditation. He was saying, 'I believe, I believe,' to himself, over and over again. Afterwards the Pope, coming out to meet the worshippers, walked straight over to John and did the sign of the cross on his outstretched hand. Coming back, they stopped off in Paris. When John went to look for the toilets he walked straight into Pele. They shook hands, John looked into his eyes and Pele said, 'God has made me a healer.'

Of course, all his friends took the piss. One day they were all off to see Lenny Henry and everyone was in high spirits, joking about.

'John, so ye're off t' see Lenny Henry now, are ye?' they said. They thought John would jump on the stage and announce he was a prophet.

John said, 'I'm no' fuckin' interested in Lenny Henry. It's Muhammad Ali I'm gonna meet.'

They turned the corner and there was a sign outside a shop saying that Muhammad Ali would be signing books there the following week. So he went to see Muhammad Ali too. He was the first in the queue. He shook hands with the great man and stared into his eyes and said, 'I'm a prophet.'

Muhammad Ali said, 'You're a prophet?'

'Aye, I'm a prophet.'

I've seen the photograph. Muhammad Ali looks startled and confused, as if he's backing off.

John stopped drinking on 18 May 1993 and that's when all of these signs became confirmed. He had a calling. An alcoholic before, now he was a Godoholic, a prophet.

Someone said, 'All that stuff was happening five hundred years ago.'

John said, 'Well it's no' happening five hundred years ago. It's happening now.'

John believes that the world is due for a cataclysmic change. The New Age is dawning, Christ's age at last. '1995, drugs are out of fashion. 1996, sex is out of fashion. 1998, money is out of fashion. Boom! Boom! Gonna blow them out of the ocean.' And he flicks his wrist in a quick dismissive gesture, as if by that gesture his predictions are confirmed. The Royal Family will fall, capitalism will fall, the international drugs and arms trades will grind to a halt, greed, violence and corruption will wither on the vine like diseased fruits, and the world will begin anew.

This is not the first time I've heard this. Fen says the same. It's millennium fever. What's 666 multiplied by 3? 1998.

John is currently the main spokesperson in an organisation called Renfrew United. It was his vision that led to its foundation. Their aim is to get people off drugs by using sport. They are going from strength to strength. There were fifty people at the first meeting; now, there are 350 involved. They have big plans. They want to transform Renfrew into the healthiest community in Britain, and hope to provide sporting and other activities 'seven days and seven nights' for the whole community. 'If someone wants to play the cello, we'll get a fucking cello,' says John. All free of charge. This is important. It's part of the 'big picture', as John calls it. 'Money is just power-tokens,' he says. 'People are addicted to money. We've got Alcoholics Anonymous and Narcotics Anonymous. We'll be needing Money Anonymous next.' He adds, 'This life is a vapour. Death is eternal life. The spirit comes from within you. Everyone is a prophet. Everyone has the ability to create their own future. If you expect to receive what you pray for, then it will happen.' The implication is, 'Who needs drugs?'

No one takes the piss out of him any more.

Kodan and I are on a train, lurching through the hinterlands of Glasgow, and outside is one of the most dismal scenes I've ever witnessed. Row upon row of grim tenements, windows broken or boarded, peering out at you dumb-faced from a murky sky. I'm genuinely disturbed by the scene. There are people actually living in these places. The poverty of the South is nothing compared to the poverty here. You can sense it: a relentless, dreary, aching poverty, like slow decay. You can also guess that the people brought up here will be as hard as nails, totally devoid of sentiment.

We're on our way to visit Kodan's dad, who's in prison for murder. He's done seven years of a life sentence, with a recommendation to serve fifteen. Kodan hasn't seen him for fifteen years. The old man had promised to keep in touch, but he never did. Kodan's sister is unforgiving. She says, 'He's got in contact only because of where he is.' Kodan accepts this, but is more inclined to be lenient. He feels sorry for the guy, wants to help him with the unimaginable burdens of life at Her Majesty's Pleasure.

Finally we reach the prison – a formal, undistinguished building on the outskirts of town – and ring the bell. We are delivered into what seems remarkably like a DSS waiting room, only more pleasant. There are a few magazines scattered about and a notice on the wall about domestic violence. The prison officers are lounging at a desk, playing with their keys and reading the Sunday papers. I wonder what their lives must be like, what 'job satisfaction' must mean for them. After all, they're in prison too.

Kodan is getting visibly nervous and has to go to the toilet. I reassure him, when he gets back, that his dad will be even more nervous. He'll have been thinking about this for weeks before and will be remembering it for weeks after. My guess is that prison is more relentlessly boring than anything else.

Finally, a door opens and a line of visitors from the previous session file out. The front door is locked ceremoniously behind them, then we are led out into the courtyard, through a locked gate in the high-security fence, and into a little room scattered with tables and chairs. The prisoners enter through a door on the other side, in two waves: pale men, some with slash marks on their faces. Kodan's dad enters with the second group, wearing a light-blue stripy shirt.

'Hello, Da,' says Kodan, as he jumps up to embrace the old man. I'm introduced, then go off to get a round of coffee while I leave them to their moment of terror. I take my time over this, stirring the coffee at a leisurely pace, while I watch from a distance the animated conversation passing between them, no doubt fuelled as much by nervousness as by mutual recognition.

Still, I'm happy to be here – not just as a witness, but as Kodan's substitute dad; to give him moral support in what, I guess, will become one of the seminal moments in his life.

I return with the coffee and Da makes a nervous appeal to me not to try to interview him. He knows I write for a national paper. He says that 'the Home of Lies and Corruption' – as he refers to the Home Office – take a dim view of lifers talking to the press. I assure him that I'm not here to question him and that I'll not identify him in the story I write. He's shaking as he sips his coffee. I take this as a sign of nervousness at seeing his son again after so long. He attempts to apologise to Kodan for not keeping in touch. Kodan answers him with one of his huge Bash-Street-Kid grins. He's only glad that he's here now.

Later we talk about the life sentence. I know the story. According to Kodan, it wasn't really murder, it was self-defence. A drunken fight between his dad and a best mate – over a woman, inevitably – at which knives were drawn. Da won and his friend died. When it came to the court case, the old man was suffering the ravages of withdrawal, having been an alkie for a number of years. He simply never argued his case. But I suspect that remorse was behind this lack of defence; really, he wanted to go down. This is confirmed later when Da says, 'I consider the sentence I'm doin' now' – you'll have to imagine the heavy Glaswegian accent – 'is not just for the things I did get caught for, but for the things I did'nae get caught for too.' 'So what were you into, Da?' asks Kodan. The old man tells us about a night at Tilbury Docks, when him and a few mates drew up with car carriers and carted off thirty-seven brand-new vans. 'The people living round about just thought the company was moving them,' he says, with a half-sheepish, half-roguish grin. 'No one twigged till morning.' The look on Kodan's face is one of unadulterated pride.

You can't help but like him. That grin is infectious. He's a wily rascal of the old school; pure mischief. A big, broad man, covered in tattoos, you sense a deep intelligence there that a better system of human relations might have made use of. Just one more wasted life.

The only thing that spoils the conversation is the old man's constant references to blacks. He turns out to be a racist. Kodan and I try to argue, but he doesn't pay any attention. In the end this is more irritating than distressing. We quickly realise that in Her Majesty's Prisons it's likely to be open warfare between black and white. I'm certain that the blacks give as good as they get.

Later, the visit over, we're back at Kodan's mum's place in Renfrew. I like her a lot. She's a warm, unassuming woman, quite happy to sit there with her teeth out. You sense that she's been an anchor in Kodan's life. Kodan loves her to distraction.

'Aye,' she says, a wry smile on her face when I ask about Da's leaving, 'he just went out for a pint one night and never came back.' Kodan took it more seriously though, she tells me. One day he was off school, but instead of saying that he had a cold (which was the truth), he said that his uncle was a train driver and had given him a lift down to London to meet his dad. Even a year later he'd lie in his bed expecting his dad to come home from the pub any minute. The effect it had on him is illustrated by the fact that he's six years out with his calculations. He thinks Da left when he was fourteen – fifteen years ago. His mum tells me he left when he was eight – twenty-one years ago – and that he'd only popped in for a day that once. It's as if Kodan has added another six years to the time he spent with his dad.

As we're leaving, Kodan embraces his mum and she asks what we're planning to do this evening. 'We'll probably get steamin',' he says, with a roguish twinkle. Just like his Da.

Kodan has a number of different names, depending who he's with, and where. In Kent he's known as Alan and he comes on like a fey hippie, all relaxed charm. In Glasgow he's Kodan, and exchanges insults and banter with his rave-scene friends. In Renfrew, his home town, he's called Big Ashie and he's a nutter.

How he got the name Kodan: When he was young he had a shaved head and everyone called him Kojak, but he hung around all the teenagers and he used to call them Hairy Dan, the Scottish equivalent of the bogyman. Then one day someone put the names together: Kojak + Hairy Dan = Kodan. When I first heard the name I thought it referred to his time as a Krishna monk. I thought it was an Indian name, resonant with spiritual significance. Sanskrit for 'many-petalled lotus chakra' or something. Instead of which I found out that it was a Glasgow nutter's name, meaning bald-headed bogyman.

He's six foot two and towers above me. We make a strange pair, us two: a tight, hunched, furtive little Brummie, and a gangly, expansive Glaswegian with a face like Plug from the Bash Street Kids. Or rather, he looks like Plug whenever he wants to tell me something truly spiritual. He draws his chin in so that it merges with his neck in a corrugated mass of fat wrinkles, rolls his eyes and waves his arms about. The look is meant to convey astonishment and awe. Instead of which, he just looks gormless.

In a way, Kodan is one of those people who have helped me to stay alive. We first met when Gem and I were still together, trying out our experiment in happy families: Gem, me, my son and her daughter, all squeezed together in a little terraced house getting on each other's nerves. It was a dismal failure. My son and her daughter were both too used to getting their own way, and Gem and I were just too uncertain about what love actually meant. It still puzzles me.

Kodan knocked on our door one Saturday morning in April or May. He was a complete stranger in the town and was looking for a friend of his. For some reason, he chose our house to make enquiries. It was an inspired choice. Gem and I knew his friend well. He was a friend of ours, too. We drank tea and chatted, then we gave him directions to where he might find his friend.

A couple of years later, he returned. He'd been in a Krishna monastery. His hair was cropped and he still had that dangly bit on the back of his head. Two years without drugs, sex, or even cigarettes. He started making up for lost time.

Gem and I split up. I went crazy. I started praying. There seemed little else I could do. The process was made even more poignant by the fact that, actually, I didn't believe in anything.

I bumped into Kodan one night and bought him a couple of drinks. I had some speed in my pocket. I invited him to my place where we shared out the speed and started listening through my record collection. I'd got to the point where I hardly listened to it any more. We listened to all those heavy blues and sixties psychedelic records I had stashed away: Howlin' Wolf singing 'I have had my fun, if I never get well no more', and Bob Dylan singing 'Sooner or later one of us must know that I really did try to get close to you'. It was all very poignant. I thought every word of every song was a reference to Gem. We nattered on about this and that all night, about God and the revolution, and the future of humankind. Kodan saved me. I felt I had a purpose again.

No one ever visited me in my home – a crummy maisonette on a run-down council estate on the edge of town – but it was exactly the sort of place where Kodan had been brought up. He was the first person I knew who was able to visit me without being intimidated by the air of poverty and depression.

It was also about this time that I began to realise how unreliable he was. A reliable friend, an unreliable business partner. We were going to start a magazine together. While I was busy writing, making plans and enquiries, negotiating finances and the rest, he was fazed out on cheap sherry, thinking about his penis.

He got a girlfriend, then dumped her unceremoniously. Then

one day I went to visit him and found him in bed with someone else's girlfriend. I walked into the room and saw the two of them naked in bed, and my heart did a sort of off-balance trampoline act. It leaped and plummeted, and I walked out apologising. I cried all the way home. This was barely a few weeks after Gem and I had split up and I was still feeling sensitive. Life seemed so unfair.

But who am I to pass judgements? Who am I to say what's right and what's wrong? The world is only the place where we work out our destiny. And we pay for everything in the end. Or I do, anyway.

All the time we were in Glasgow, Kodan was off his head on some chemical or another. It was codeine tablets at first, then poppy tea, and while we were in Renfrew staying with his sister it was Temazepam and beer. I got exhausted with it all and spent a couple of days in retirement while Kodan went out raving. He had a couple of Es that time.

Kodan never really got over his dad leaving him like that. He's always looking for some substitute, something to fill in the gap. If it's not chemical stimulation, then it's God. We met one of his Krishna friends selling books on the street in Glasgow. She was a gaunt Asian woman wrapped up against the Glasgow winter with a woolly hat and an anorak over her robes, with a fine, dark moustache and red-veined eyes that were nearly popping out of her head. She spoke in a curious whispering voice and there was something sickly about her. Too much fasting, maybe – self-mutilation in her grasping search for God – or maybe she was just ill.

She asked Kodan if he was still chanting. He said he wasn't.

'So what are you doing with your life?' she asked.

Kodan shrugged. 'Wasting it,' he said. We were on our way to get some beer.

Kodan bought her some carnations to spread at the shrine and they talked about the death of a guru. I think she used an expression like 'he's passed on' or 'he's left the body' – some such optimistic euphemism. They'd had to keep the body in the monastery for several weeks before it could be shipped back to India for cremation on the Ganges. The devotee's huge lidded eyes were shining and Kodan looked down at her with an indulgent expression. But the other-worldliness got on my nerves. I couldn't help feeling that it was just another form of self-indulgence.

We got to the pub and the smell of beer relaxed me.

I said, 'I wanted to ask her, didn't the body smell after all that time.'

Kodan said, 'I'm glad you didn't say that. She'd have been offended.'

We started talking about Kodan's life. In fact, one of the reasons he'd come to Glasgow was to meet the ex-girlfriend I'd found him in bed with that time. They'd moved back to Glasgow for a while, until Kodan had taken up with his drugs habit again and turned into a seriously dangerous nutter, injecting heroin and running about with the small-arms-toting drugs set. She'd dumped him. Kodan had returned to Kent and was now with a new girlfriend, Marion. I had high hopes that this one was going to work out for him. We were discussing how he could make sure that he kept this one together.

Kodan said, 'I'm glad you're my pal, because you take my life seriously.'

We caught the overnight train back to London. We had a few drinks in a pub where spectacularly beautiful young Glaswegians vied for each other's attention, and no one looked at me. Then we bought a bottle of whisky and caught the train.

The guard said, 'Change at Preston,' when he saw our tickets. We were only supposed to go as far as Warrington.

'We know,' we said. We drank our whisky, then fell asleep.

We woke up in the pale dawn light in Milton Keynes. It was rosy-hued. But it didn't matter where we were. All places are the same when you wake up cricked and cramped in a train seat after a bottle of whisky. At least we were nearing home.

On the train to Kent the guard said, 'Tickets please.'

Kodan looked at him. 'We haven't got any,' he said, staring him straight in the eyes.

'That'll be ... ' started the guard, fumbling with his ticket machine.

'We haven't got any money, either.'

Again the man looked at us. I told him about the bluebird and the returns to Warrington and the money I'd lost. He paused sceptically, looking first at Kodan, then at me. You could see the wheels clicking over in his head. Is it worth arguing with them? Are they telling the truth? Then he smiled wryly.

'If the inspector comes,' he said, 'tell him you were hiding in the loo.'

5   Naff Brigade are in the Area

'Valerie Polaris says ... ' said Kodan.

'Who's Valerie Polaris?'

'You know, the woman who wrote the *Scum Manifesto* ... '

'Valerie Solanas. Polaris is a missile.'

'Same thing. Anyway, she says that whenever men speak they're showing off,' said Kodan. 'And, you know, I've watched them and it's true.'

'Well, you must have been showing off when you said that,' I said, showing off.

This was the plan. Kodan, Marion and Rick were going to set up a puppet show and we were going to drive round the country in the bluebird, visiting all the festivals and looking for Wally Hope. Kodan would write the script, Marion would make the puppets, Rick would collect the money, and they'd all perform. I'd just keep my weather-eye open and write about it. They were calling themselves Pan's Puppets. 'Sort of Merry Pranksters on chip butties,' said Kodan, and he blushed. He always blushes when he says something clever.

Marion is Kodan's girlfriend. She's a bright, vivacious eighteen-year-old, with an expansive personality and a bosom to match. Rick is a devotee of Pan, and is looking more and more like an old goat as the years go by. He likes beer and LSD, preferably in combination. He lurches round in a strange chemical daze like some dishevelled devil, grinding his jaw and sweating, and leering at women. I've always described him as a friendly psychopath, because he believes that whatever is going on in his head is true for the whole world. Which may well be true, who knows? It would at least explain why the world seems so utterly crazy at the moment.

After we got back from Scotland, I gave Kodan some money to be getting on with the puppet show. We'd got a date set at the Labour Club on 1 April, in about a month's time. I bumped into him the very morning we got back, still reeling from the whisky and the journey, and he had four cans of Tennent's with him. Later I called round and he was opening a bottle of red wine. A couple of days later he was round at Rick's place brewing up poppy tea, using dried poppies he'd brought from the flower shop. That's how he spent the entire month leading up to the their first gig. Red wine, beer, opium tea, crack cocaine, cough medicine, LSD, Ecstasy, sweet tea and vitamin C tablets – anything he could stick in his gob, or up his nose, or into his lungs. Kodan thinks you can beat addiction by changing your drugs every day. He's like some monstrous baby with an uncontrollable dependency.

He said, 'I wish there was such a thing as a pushchair for adults.'

I said, 'They're called wheelchairs, Kodan, and you'll be in one soon enough.'

The Labour Club is an old haunt of mine. It occupies a couple of railway arches under the main line to London. You'll be sitting there with your pint when there's a rumble like thunder and all the glasses on the tables rattle. 'There goes the 9.27,' you'll say, and imagine yourself on some flight to freedom. Except that at the other end is only London, and there's no freedom there – not without money.

I'd set up this date before we went to Scotland.

'Just a few people doing a few turns, you know, like a cabaret,' I said.

'How many people do you expect?' the barman asked.

'I dunno, maybe fifty.'

I made him enter it in the calendar to make sure. By the time we got back, he'd changed his mind.

'That puppet show,' he said, 'we have to discuss it some more.'

'What's to discuss?'

'We'll have to see.'

'What will we have to see?'

'We'll have to see.'

In the end we got it sorted out and the puppet show was due to go ahead.

The afternoon of the show, Kodan and Marion came up to see me. Kodan was still writing the script and Marion was typing it up for him. This is two hours before the show was due to start. I lent them my word processor while they squabbled their way through the last pages. Neither of them had had any sleep the night before, and they were tetchy and ill-prepared. I left them to their devices.

When I got down the club later that evening, Rick was still fixing the puppet show together with screws and brackets, and other people were running about preparing this and that. It was a shambles. When Rick finally stood the flimsy structure on its end, it was clear that he'd fitted it together wrongly. It was as if he'd imbued it with his own personality. It was reeling lopsidedly, like Rick on a binge, but there was no time to take it apart and put it back together again, so it had to stay as it was. Then Marion had to wrap the sheeting around it. She'd hand-painted some material in purple and yellow, with horned faces. She stapled it to the drunken structure. Unfortunately, she'd forgotten to leave a gap. The entire structure was shrouded in cloth, with no space for the puppets. They quickly cut a ragged hole and hung a picture frame over it. Meanwhile, people were beginning to turn up. They were sitting at tables watching the chaos as if this were part of the show. You expected them to clap as each part of the set was erected, as the puppet show was placed on the stage like a symbol of our shot-away times.

Someone was coming through the door while I made my escape to the bar. 'Naff Brigade are in the area,' I said. Later, I extended the analogy. 'Remember the Angry Brigade, whose finely-honed anger was like a knife to the heart of capitalism?' I said. 'Well, we're the Naff Brigade, whose overripe naffness is like a squelch under the foot of capitalism. I need a drink.'

Finally the show was under way. Kodan, Rick and Marion disappeared into their lopsided coffin.

Pan popped his wrinkled head over the edge.

'Before the show starts,' he said, 'which is our version of the teddy bears' picnic, I have to tell you that unfortunately Pink Bear's run off with Madonna. However, Emu's prepared to step in at last-minute notice.'

It was Rick, putting on a quavering voice to represent Pan. And Pink Bear hadn't run off with Madonna, they'd just not got round to making it. And Pan wasn't a puppet, he was a battered old doll that Rick had wandered around with at Glastonbury the previous year, off his tree as usual, and taunting people with the strange loopholes of his logic. You could see Rick's fingers clutching the doll from behind. Still, we were suspending our disbelief.

'So,' continued Pan, in his thin, quaking voice, 'without

further ado I present you with ... Pan's Puppets,' and he slipped behind the curtain.

There was a pause. A long pause. A very long pause.

'With some further ado,' Rick added, after which you could hear Marion mutter, 'What puppet am I?'

There were three of them squeezed into that cramped, teetering space. You could see them struggling in there, elbows and backs pressing through the material, as the whole thing rocked and jolted like an archbishop's cassock with a choirboy beneath. Rick was holding the script and shaking, and Kodan was hissing, 'Keep the fuckin' script still, will ye?'

Finally, the teddy bears appeared. Red Bear and Punk Bear and ... yes, Emu. You could tell Red Bear was Red Bear because it was red. You could tell Punk Bear was a punk because it had a dog-collar round its neck. And you could tell Emu was an emu because it was an emu. Only you didn't notice it because it was staring abstractly into the corner most of the time, keeping its back to the other two. All you could see was its mouth.

Red Bear: This, my dear chaps, is what I call a beautiful day.

It was Marion, sounding drippy.

Emu: Yup. Oh, to be in England in the summertime.

This was Rick, using the same voice he had for Pan.

Punk Bear: Ay, England. Home of the brave, land of the free. But it'll soon be buried under concrete.

This was Kodan, sounding like Kodan.

Red Bear: Cynical nihilistic bastard, this is our land, we can wander as we please, just so long as we love the earth, no harm will come to her.

Punk Bear: Wander as we please? Three miles from here there's a fuckin' army base, ya numfty. Just try wanderin' over that telling them you love the earth. If they don't shoot ye, they'll fuckin' cart ye off to the loony bin.

Red Bear: Yeah, I take your point, but surely you see that there's the beginnings of a global consciousness which will sweep away the oppressor under a tidal wave of love and truth, and give the land back to the people.

Marion's drippy voice was getting the most laughs. She pronounced 'love' as 'lurrrrve'.

Punk Bear: God, you're an innocent bastard, in't ye? Haven't you noticed that most of this country has fenced itself off intae wee Barratt house estates? But the fences aren't just made of wood, they're made of fuckin' fear and suspicion and the fuckin' myth of ownership. What do you think the Criminal Justice Bill's all about, eh?! Why's nobody trying to stop it except the sad bastards that it dispossesses? It's 'cos the fuckin' nine-to-five wage slaves fear us and hate us, man. They agree with the Act. They want us done away with 'cos they're envious of us and our freedom.

Red Bear: So what do you think we can do about it, then?

Emu: Well, we've got to come together, don't we!

Punk Bear: Yeah, yur starting to get it. The mistake they've made with the Act is that they've marginalised too many of us, and most of the groups they've picked on are getting radical. Guys, we're teddy bears, our two greatest weapons are our numbers and our joy.

Emu: Revolution, beginning in your Reeboks. . .?

Rick had no idea what this line meant. You could tell by the way he muttered it with a question mark at the end. No one had any idea what this line meant. It was obviously the product of Kodan's blighted imagination.

Red Bear: Yeah, party right on!

Enter **Wizard**.

There was another long pause, and more rustling and shifting about. "'Scuse me while I turn the page,' said Kodan, as Kodan, and the Wizard appeared, a wide-eyed papier mâché puppet with dreadlocks.

Wizard: Did I hear someone say party?! I hope you kindly young bears don't mind if I plonk my tired old ass down by ye! I've been on the road a long time and I'm in need of some relaxation and a bit of the crack. It's so nice to see some youngsters enjoying our land, before it's all swallowed up in what they call progress. Ye'll get used to me, I do go on a bit. I hope I haven't interrupted your conversation, my dears.

This was Kodan too, also sounding like Kodan. The Wizard was meant to be Irish, and Kodan can do a fairly decent Irish accent most of the time. Only he was so carried away he forgot. You'll also notice by now that Kodan has all the best lines. In fact he has all the lines. Well, he did write the script.

Punk Bear: Naw, naw, not at all, mucker, sit you'self down, have a cup of tea. We've just been discussing the CJB.

So that's Kodan talking to Kodan. Two characters, same voice. It was perfectly impossible to tell who was talking to who, or why, even.

Red Bear: Yeah, I heard you mention being on the road, so I guess that'll affect you quite adversely if you've been travelling.

Wizard: I'll tell you, young bears. The government have drawn the lines now, and when the shit hits the fan everyone better know which fuckin' side they're on. And there have been serious fuckin' developments in fuckin' government legislation. I'm sure you've heard the latest fuckin' policy to come out of Westminster and the fuckin' Home of Lies and Deception, or the fuckin' Home Office as they call it.

By now Kodan was completely carried away, swearing

constantly. Suddenly the barman marched in, dressed in his red sweater. 'Oh no,' I thought, 'he's going to put a stop to it.' I had no idea why he would want to stop it, except it's the kind of thing he was likely to do, just exercising his power. Instead of which he slipped on to the stage and joined the others in the teetering booth. You could see him pressing into the already overcrowded space, with just his buttocks sticking out. Everyone began laughing, including the puppeteers. The man was obviously deranged. Maybe he wanted a part in the show. Then Rick's voice erupted from the booth. 'Francis Green's mother wants her urgently,' he said. The barman added, coming out to address the crowd, 'The baby wants her.' So Francis got up and was putting on her coat. 'Bye, Francis,' everyone said. Someone else added, 'Is that in the script?' Then it was Kodan's turn, still from behind the booth, but being Kodan now, which was exactly the same as being Punk Bear or the Wizard. 'What d'ye think,' he asked, 'should we give up now instead of embarrassing oursel's?' 'No! More!' everyone shouted. They wanted them to carry on embarrassing themselves. So they started up again.

Punk Bear: What have the bastards come up with now? It can't be more Fascistic or ludicrous than the CJB.

'He's not speaking, he's speaking,' added Kodan, indicating by jiggling the puppets around. You couldn't tell. Punk Bear was flopped over the edge as if exhausted, and Red Bear and Emu were just stuck there without lines or anything to do. Occasionally one of them would move and you'd hear Kodan hissing, 'Keep the fuckin' puppets still when they're not talking.' The three of them were sweltering in the confined space, Kodan doing all the talking, with two puppets on the end of his hands, trying to read the script over Rick's shoulder, while Rick was shaking like a leaf. 'Keep the fuckin' script still,' whispered Kodan, frantically, the very model of the Fascists his characters were railing against.

Wizard: You think not, my angry and idealistic young bear? Just consider for a second the mass outbreaks of revolutionary violence and civil disobedience that have gone down in this fair land of ours over the last couple of centuries. How have they been dealt wi'?

Someone shouted, 'Violence!', and Frank Park, who'd climbed up on the stage, said, 'Yeah, violence.' Frank is nine years old, and he started punching Red Bear, who thought it was Punk Bear and hit him back. Red Bear was supposed to be the drippy hippie, remember, full of lurrrrve and optimism and global consciousness, and here she was belting Punk Bear full in the face. And Punk bear hit Red Bear, who hit Punk bear who hit Red Bear, while someone in the audience, obviously carried away by the realism, let out little stifled gasps of pain every time a blow was landed. She thought she was watching an Arnold Schwarzenegger movie. Frank said, 'Isn't it a bit unsafe in there? Just don't fall over.' Everyone was cracking up at this. Meanwhile, Kodan was manfully trying to get on with the script. He couldn't see Frank Park up there on the stage. He thought everyone was laughing at the confusion in the script. Finally he walked out in a huff, a monomaniac with a wizard on one hand and a punk teddy bear on the other. By now everyone could see that it wasn't going to work, and clapped. Rick brought on the Fascists, a cardboard cut-out regiment on the end of a stick with swastikas painted over them, and wiggled them about a bit. And that was the end of the puppet show. I went off to get more beer. So did a lot of other people. Everyone was in need of beer that night.

I've seen the script, by the way, and it's good. A bit of work, a few more jokes, a few less lines for Kodan and a few more for the others, and it would have been all right. A bit of rehearsal, too. The main contention involves the government surrounding

Highbury at the Arsenal–Millwall game, force-feeding both sets of fans with strange drugs, giving them uniforms, weapons, ammunition, amphetamines and Special Brew, and then letting them loose on the rest of us. A plausible scenario, I feel. They're already here. They're called security guards.

But anyway, here I am, gloriously drunk by now, and in despair; vanless, penniless, puppet-showless, and, finally, witless and deranged, and not a sign of Wally Hope within a thousand miles. Wally Hope, remember, pulled off that first Stonehenge festival on a shoe string, with no more than a battered old Ford and a vision from God. We can't even pull off a puppet show.

A number of people who were at the puppet show have read this account. They think it is too negative. They say that, in fact, we all had a good time that night. And we did. We had a laugh. But it was in spite of the organisation, not because of it.

Rick was so pleased with the show that the following day he went off with the video they'd made of it to show to Michael Eavis, in the hope that they'd get a slot at Glastonbury. They didn't get a slot at Glastonbury.

So anyway, at the end of the evening I said to my friend Anne, 'Is it true what Valerie Solanas says, that all men are always showing off when they talk?' I was showing off as I said this to her.

'Yes, it's true,' she said, 'but I don't agree with her conclusions about what we should do about it – you know, the violence and all that stuff. Actually, it's quite endearing.'

6 Where's Wally Hope?

You'd imagine the house to be black. There's an image of Crass: screeching lyrics over a relentless backdrop of screaming noise; uncompromising black-and-white graphics, stark pictures of pain, death and decay; anger bordering on hysteria. Instead of which, you walk into Paradise.

We sat in the garden. There was Pen, Gee, Steve (all from Crass) and Paul, who was my contact. I was there to interview Pen. He was the drummer. A middle-aged man with long faded-blond hair and quiet eyes, wearing shorts, sandals and a T-shirt, you realise immediately that he's a hippie. Always was; always will be. The punk image was a front for some highly evolved anarchist political agenda.

I said, 'I always thought that Crass were very worthy and I loved the lyrics, but I must admit I hated the music.'

Pen said, 'Yes, so did I.'

Pen's stage name was Penny Rimbaud, after the French poet. 'Penny' as in 'half a penny' as in 'Arthur'. His real name is Jeremy.

We're sitting on wooden benches in the shade of an over-hanging tree. It's the first of May – Beltane – and the sun beams down on us like a long-lost friend. All around Nature cascades. It frolics. It tumbles. It dances in the radiant sunshine. I've always believed that Paradise is a garden, the interaction of the human with the environment. And here we are, in Paradise's garden at Pen's commune home: Deal House.

I'm here to talk about Wally Hope. Pen knew him and was involved in the organisation of both the first and second Stonehenge free festivals. Behind the enigma of Wally Hope there's a man, a person. Pen knew this person and, in some ways, Pen is responsible for the myth. He wrote a pamphlet which was given away with one of Crass's albums. It was called *The Last of the Hippies* and is the source of many of the conceits which have built up around the life and strange death of Phil Russell, a.k.a. Wally Hope. Pen says that while he was writing it, he knew that he was engaged in iconography.

The story that most intrigues me, only briefly touched on in the pamphlet but repeated over and over again by anyone who met Wally Hope, is that he performed miracles. Pen says that he did. He says that during the time that Wally was planning the first Stonehenge he was coming around a lot, irritating them all with his relentless enthusiasm for this idea. Pen and the others were sceptical. They thought he was living in a dream world. They'd always know when Wally was arriving because he'd chant out, 'Wal-ley!' like that, in two distinct syllables, with a rising tone.

So there's a few of them sat in the back shed one day, when they hear the customary war cry. It was a day very much like today: warm and sultry, with no clouds. May or September, Pen's not too sure. Wally dances out backwards from behind a bush. He's weaving his fingers in a magical pattern and there's a strange grin on his face, like some jester-fool from a demented tarot. 'Watch this,' he says, winking, and he dances back out of sight. When he reappears he's dancing backwards again out of the bush, but this time accompanied by a snowstorm. The snow is lashing about in the still, warm air as Wally's arms are twisting and jerking. The sight is so incomprehensible it sends their minds reeling. The people in the shed look on astonished while the snow is swirling and spinning, and Wally's arms shift around in the middle of it, stirring it up. Then Wally winks again and dances back behind the cover of the bush, taking the snow with him. Finally, he walks out normally as if nothing has happened. It's no longer snowing.

He created rainbows too, Pen told me. He'd be sitting in the back garden at a table, after five or six solid hours working on the Stonehenge project, and he'd throw his arms into the air which would become scattered with prismatic light, like colours tinkling on the surfaces of a chandelier.

Another day, Phil and Pen were in the garden. This was before the work on Stonehenge had begun. They were standing by a fire which had died down and Pen began tapping the logs with a stick to see the embers swirl. This was some time in the evening and there was no one else around. Phil took a stick and began tapping too. The embers scattered in the half-light like doomed fireflies, dancing about, then flickering out, as Phil beat a convoluted tattoo on the logs. Then they were both tapping, one after the other, like a conversation. Pen says that he began to be aware that it *was* a conversation. A dialogue. That they were speaking to each other ritually by ESP in an acid-religious ceremony without drugs. This went on for an hour and a half. By the time they'd finished, Pen knew that something had happened, that the idea had been formulated. Stonehenge. 'What the fuck!' Pen thought. He didn't believe in the idea, but now he was part of it. He decided to let Phil use the facilities of the commune.

According to Pen, Wally was an English shaman. He was an animist and, like all those involved in magical processes, his life was characterised by massive self-discipline. The only drug he took was acid, which he saw as a sacrament.

'He wasn't like you and me,' Pen said. 'Everything in Wally's world had life. There wasn't anything that wasn't something. He moved through a symbolic universe where things had inherent meaning, moving in constant tension from one set of meanings to another, part of and yet driven by the world in which they exist. He didn't choose to do things. Things were done to him.'

By the time he met Phil, Pen had been living in this commune for a number of years. This would have been in the early seventies. There was a small hippie presence in nearby Ongar, where Phil lived with his guardians, and the news must have spread about this experimental community on their doorstep. It was natural enough that Phil would come to visit.

By the age of sixteen, Phil had 'ceased to be at school', as Pen put it. He was sent to therapy sessions and various reports were written on him, so perhaps his peculiar belief system which could be easily interpreted as madness was already inherent in him. He was from a very wealthy background and was due to inherit a fortune at the age of thirty. Meanwhile, he lived on a small allowance that left him free to do what he liked. By the time Pen met him in 1972, when Phil was in his mid-twenties, he was heavily under the influence of a group called the Dwarves, a kind of Notting Hill version of the Yippies in America: a joke-prankster group. He'd travelled a lot – to America, where he became enthralled by Native American culture, and to Cyprus. He was also fanatically enthused by Gadaffi and wrote to him regularly. These were revolutionary times, just after the 1968 uprising in Paris and the anti-Vietnam demonstrations in America. If you weren't supporting Mao Tse-tung, then you were chanting 'Ho Ho Ho Chi Minh' through the streets of London. Phil walked the tightrope – common in those days –

between the demands for revolutionary change and a deeply conventional respect for traditional British values. He wanted change, but not at any cost. In reality the whole thing was simply a jest to him, a jape.

Pen says he had the Stonehenge vision in Ibiza. This was another of his regular haunts. There was a café in a fishing port where all the hippies would meet. Phil went there one day and took some acid. Later, he sat on rocks overlooking the harbour. It was a natural enough conclusion to reach, Pen feels. He was into the sun and the land. The sun was his God and he loved anything to do with the Arthurian legends. The vision involved the idea of taking Stonehenge – a sun-temple – back from the State, for people to worship at. 'He was sitting on a stone, stoned, and he thought of stones,' says Pen, smiling. There's a certain mad rationality in this.

The preparations for the first Stonehenge free festival involved writing to world leaders and others whom Phil admired, and inviting them along. He wrote to the Beatles, to the hippies of Kathmandu, to the Pope, to the Dalai Lama, the Duke of Edinburgh, Allen Ginsberg – a range of disparate personalities, and for no other reason than his admiration for them. He wrote to Ursula Andress because he liked her figure, to the air hostesses of BOAC because they represented his ideal of the compliant woman, and to Gadaffi, of course. He always wrote to Gadaffi.

Pen says that Phil had no political awareness whatsoever. He was a libertarian royalist. He was drawn to Ted Heath rather than Harold Wilson, because he respected personal integrity over party politics. He also had no problems with the notion of privilege. He never questioned his own wealth and good fortune. He was no saint. Had he lived, he would have been Thatcherite and he was an old-fashioned male chauvinist. There was a particular image of a prostrate woman from a soft-porn magazine that he carried round with him. Hence his love of air hostesses. He had a girlfriend called Mon, whom he referred to as 'the Mother', who stayed at home while Phil pursued his high-flown plans. She was the moon and he was the sun. She embroidered him a shirt that became his trademark: a riot of spectacular colour with the eye of Horus in the middle banked by a rainbow, across which was emblazoned the word 'Hope'.

Pen was not my only informant about the first Stonehenge festival. A few weeks earlier I'd met Penny Mellor of the Festival Welfare Services, an organisation which has been promoting safety at festivals since the mid-seventies. She'd also known Wally Hope.

The first festival was a quiet affair, she told me. This was summer solstice 1974. Maybe five or six hundred people at the most, and one band: a synthesiser combo called Zorch. They built geodesic domes from twigs collected from the woods near by; lived, ate and slept communally. Some of these early free festivals were less pop concerts, more exercises in communal living, an attempt to create a blueprint for a better world.

They were mad, optimistic times. There were endless meetings, endless discussions about ethical and philosophical matters. It was all very serious and, at the same time, very naïve. There was a discussion about whether or not acid should be given to children. There was one couple who were giving their small children acid every day, as they thought it was the religious thing to do, and the others at the festival discussed the ethics of this. The question was whether the individual freedom of the parents overrode that of the children. When Penny told me this story I almost retched. It summed up everything I hated about the era. The idea of giving drugs to small children is not one I find either reasonable or romantic.

Penny became defensive at this point. She's spent over twenty years engaged in dreary bureaucratic exercises for the protection of other people enjoying themselves. She's developed a certain dry cynicism, but underneath it, I could tell, there's still the old

84

idealism that led her to this job in the first place. She was moved to tell me about a scene she'd witnessed at the time which had affected her. A couple had got up on stage at one of the Windsor festivals. They'd declared their love and – in an act reminiscent of the marriage ceremony – exchanged acid tabs. It was a very romantic moment, she said.

I also asked her about the miracles. Was it true that Wally Hope created them?

'Yes,' she said, 'it seemed so at the time.' She said he'd be talking in his usual animated way when he'd suddenly point to a cloud formation. 'Look,' he'd say, 'that cloud agrees with me.' They'd all look, and the cloud would certainly seem strange, as if it was signifying something. 'It seemed important at the time,' she said.

The festival over, about thirty to forty people stayed on. They were all called Wally. There was Phil Wally, Arthur Wally, Chris Wally, Wally Egypt, Wally Moon, Sir Wally Raleigh and Wally Woof the Dog. As Wally Hope put it in a 1974 *Windsor Festival Newsletter*, 'I look to the revolution to rename every citizen with one sound and the composite name of all citizens to be the analogue of the deepest terrestrial vibration so that when we are all called we will all hear.'

There's some debate as to where the name Wally came from. Some say the Isle of Wight festival 1969 (Bob Dylan was playing), where a sound engineer called Wally had gone missing and the sound crew were calling out over the PA, 'Wally, come to the stage immediately.' They kept calling out for Wally, then the crowd took up the chant and from then on it became a regular festival phenomenon. Others say it was a missing dog at another festival. The owners were traipsing round the site calling out plaintively, 'Wally, Wally, Wally,' and the rest of the crowd were trying to put them off by echoing the call. By the early seventies, it was the festival joke. Every festival had its Wally-chant, a few moments when the cry 'Wally!' would circulate like a mad, mundane, meaningless mantra.

In any case, when Department of the Environment officials went round the Stonehenge site some time in July or August 1974 to find out who was living there, they were met by a bunch of Wallies.

They were taken to court in August, during the so-called 'silly season', and made front page news. They cited God as their witness and gave their address as 'Fort Wally, c/o God, Jesus, Buddha, Garden of Allah, Stonehenge monument, Salisbury Plain' (*Daily Telegraph*, 13 August 1974). They were all in fancy dress. Phil himself was resplendent in the full dress uniform of an officer of the Cypriot National Guard (*The Times*, 13 August 1974). They argued that as the monument was given to the nation, not to the Department of the Environment, they therefore had a right to stay. They also stated that the department had not followed procedures correctly in that it had not taken reasonable steps to identify every person occupying the land. The fact that no one answered to anything but 'Wally' was obviously a problem in this respect. When the court found against them and ordered them to move, Phil came out and announced to the press: 'These legal arguments are like a cannon ball bouncing backwards and forwards in blancmange. We won, because we hold Stonehenge in our hearts. We are not squatters, we are men of God. We want to plant a Garden of Eden with apricots and cherries, where there will be guitars instead of guns and the sun will be our nuclear bomb' (*The Times*, 13 August 1974). The press loved it. The Wallies returned to Stonehenge, hopped over a fence and the whole procedure had to begin again.

Later they all trooped off to the fourth Windsor free festival, which was attacked by truncheon-wielding Metropolitan police. There was a fuss in the national papers over the affair and accusations of police brutality. Then the Wallies returned to

Stonehenge to take up residence. They held on till Christmas Eve. Some of them opened a squat in London Road, Amesbury, which became the focus for more Stonehenge-related activities.

Phil went off to Cyprus for the winter. He returned in early spring, ready for the next round of Stonehenge preparations. More letters. More posters. More leaflets. Hours and hours spent at the table in the sunny Deal House garden, making plans, writing, thinking, talking, getting on everyone's nerves. He drove a brightly painted Ford Cortina with a rolled-up, half-sized tepee on top, and travelled about the country spreading the message. He was a prominent figure in the underground, hanging round in Portobello Road, dressed in his Hope T-shirt, with his close-cropped blond hair and his lithe, athletic body, like a sun-worshipping warrior, handing out leaflets and talking to anyone who would listen about his vision and what it meant. It was all very amusing and enjoyable. One Big Joke. He didn't want to cause trouble. He was completely unaware that anyone would mind. He saw the underground movement as the true inheritors of the earth, and himself as the pinnacle of this movement. Pen sometimes wondered how much of this was just for the greater glory of Phil Russell.

In early May 1975, having done all that he could do, he set off to the south coast to await the coming time. Pen sensed that something was going to go wrong. There was an uneasy feeling as Phil left. A dark premonition.

Phil stopped off in the Amesbury squat, on his way to Devon or Cornwall, and the police raided. They were looking for an Army deserter, they said, but this excuse didn't seem to make sense. It was the local police, not the military, who burst in that night, and there's no such thing as a deserter during peace time, so in fact they were looking for a squaddie gone AWOL. However, it just so happens that desertion is the one crime for which the police don't need a search warrant. As Pen put it, ironically, 'Of course they didn't notice the brightly painted

Ford Cortina with the tepee on top parked out the front.' The same Ford Cortina seen around Portobello Road and all the other underground haunts for months now, and driven by a man who had so grievously humiliated them in court the previous year.

There was no Army deserter. What they found was a small quantity of acid in Phil's pocket. Even the details of this are in dispute – somewhere between a half and three tabs of acid. Others say that the drug was planted and that Phil pleaded guilty only so he could get out in time for the impending festival. He was taken into custody and there are no witnesses to what happened next. No longer bolstered up by the support of his Wally friends, Phil's elliptical self-justifications may well have sounded like madness. 'God told me to do it. I'm the son of the sun. Acid is a sacrament given to us by God.' By the time he appeared in court he was blocked out by Largactil, a brain inhibitor, and completely incoherent.

The first Pen heard about it was when Phil's guardian came over to inform them that Phil had been sectioned. The excuse was that he was refusing to wear prison uniform, saying that it brought him out in a rash, but even this is peculiar. He was on remand, so he was not required to wear prison uniform. He was sent to the Old Manor in Salisbury, a psychiatric home. Pen says that he was administered an anti-psychotic drug in large doses.

The people at Deal House tried to contact him, but were blocked. Pen asked the consultant why Phil had been sectioned and was told that it was because his favourite book was Aldous Huxley's *Island* – he was sectioned because he believed in an ideal world. Later they arranged for a solicitor to contact him, but his way was blocked too. Eventually, they decided they had to visit him.

Only close relatives were entitled to visit, so Gee (Pen's lover) went down posing as Wally's sister. She'd never been in a psychiatric institution before and it terrified her. Phil shuffled round to see her, walking like a zombie. Only weeks before he'd been the picture of health, lithe and tanned and in control of his faculties. Now he was pale and bloated, his tongue swollen and lolling round in his mouth like some mutated slug. Gee suggested they sit in the garden. He led the way, walking stiffly, his arms and legs at odds with each other.

In the garden, Phil shuffled into the shade. He couldn't stand the sunlight. A sun-worshipping warrior, afraid of the sun. The other inmates seemed to have been taken straight from a nineteenth-century etching, cameos of madness. As she was sitting there, terrified, she glanced up to the modern extension overlooking the garden and there were four or five men in white coats watching them intently. The whole time she was there, those men never took their eyes off them. Perhaps this was Gee's nervousness, but she was insistent that this was the café.

When she got back to Deal House she announced to the others that they had to get him out. They conceived a plan to help him to escape. They would take him to Holland by boat, but it all depended on his compliance, and when she returned to the Old Manor to tell him their plan she found him thoroughly institutionalised. 'I'm appearing before the board next week,' he told her. It was as if he had some part to play in a film and he was relishing his role. Gee was aware that he was about to be destroyed. He said, 'No matter what they do, they can never take the little spark of Jesus from my stomach.'

Pen believes that Phil took a decision there. He likens the garden of the Old Manor to the Garden of Gethsemane, and recalls a conversation he and Phil had had in their own garden some months before. They were talking about principles, about vision.

'You and I have a vision,' said Phil. 'But what happens if that vision is threatened in any way? What happens if we realise that there is no way of fulfilling it? Would you be willing to die? Would you join me in falling on the sword?'

They had a long discussion as to whether it was better to die with your vision intact, or whether it was better to continue to fight for the vision, even when the odds are against it.

'Will you do it? Will you do it? Will you fall on the sword with me?' Phil urged.

'Yes, I will,' said Pen, 'only I'd let you go before me and I'd veer away at the last second.'

This is exactly what happened. Phil died with his vision intact; Pen went on to found Crass, to carry the fight forward.

Pen says that Christ's decision in the Garden of Gethsemane was a cynical act. In that moment he condemned others to suffer the torture of guilt. He led others to his own murder and, in the moment he took the decision – to die rather than to compromise – he was transformed. He was no longer the man, Jesus; he was the icon, Christ. It was the same with Phil. By making the decision, by conspiring in his own death, he too was transformed. From the man, Phil Russell, he became the icon, Wally Hope.

Gee, on the other hand, regrets that she didn't just knock him out that day and drag him to freedom.

The 1975 festival took place while Phil was still inside. It was a resounding success. Thousands attended and danced in the sunlight for two weeks or more, gloriously hedonistic. Pen did a bread run and the Krishnas provided free food. There were many bands, appearing on two stages, and the quality of the acts was sometimes very high. Pen remembers falling asleep only to be woken up by these inspirational sounds drifting up into the ether. 'Fuckin' hell, Jimmy Hendrix has turned up,' he thought. Only what he saw on the stage was this unbelievably stoned band, so far gone they were nearly falling off the stage. Yet it was as if they were calling God down to join them in a jam-session.

The police kept off the site, but had set up roadblocks half a mile down the road, where they were busting people for various offences. There was a collection for the farmer whose land they were occupying and a substantial amount of money was raised. The farmer came away satisfied and there was a massive clear-up afterwards. Everything was done properly, with the best will and organisation imaginable – Phil's vision brought to life.

The only thing that marred the whole thing for Pen was the fact that Phil was still inside. It was like a dark shadow in the back of his mind and he was angry that the other Wallies were not trying to help in any way, that no one had even been to see him. He sensed a fear in them, some sort of backing away, as if they were worried that they might be next.

Two days after the last van had pulled away from the Stonehenge site, Phil was released. He was 'cured'. Somehow he managed to drive the hundred and fifty or so miles from Salisbury to Epping. It took him two days. He was forced to stop every twenty minutes to sleep. When he arrived at Deal House he was in a complete state, as bad as when Gee had seem him at the home. He shuffled along like an automaton, his arms and legs still stiff and moving in the wrong order. His face was mask-like, puffy, with no signs of expression. All his well-toned muscles were gone. He was flabby, fearful, pale and confused. Gee and Pen put him on a diet, with ginseng and other curative herbs, and he did improve slightly, but it soon became apparent that his condition was permanent. Worst of all, this once self-sufficient son of the sun was still afraid of light. He would sit in a darkened room all day, brooding, sobbing, unable to do anything to help himself, a creature of the shadows. Gee had to teach him to walk. She spent hours coaxing him, getting his arms and legs to move in the right order.

Some of the organisers of the Windsor free festival had negotiated with the government for a replacement site, Watch-field, a disused Second World War airfield. This was the only time in history that the government co-operated in the organisation of a free festival. Phil wanted to go; the others didn't think he was up to it. It was August, near the bank holiday. They were trying to hold him back, but he insisted. As he stepped out of the door there was a tremendous thunderclap and a downpour, and a bolt of lightning struck the vegetable patch, like an image from a picture book. It was the last time they saw Phil.

He died at his home, soon after the festival was over, choked on his own vomit on the kitchen floor. Not on an oriental carpet; on the lino. I asked Pen why he'd written in the pamphlet that Wally Hope had died on an oriental carpet. Pen said, 'It was symbolic. It was meant to be a magic carpet, you know, taking him on a journey,' and he looked away, mildly embarrassed. I said I thought the irony of him dying on a kitchen floor was far superior: an extraordinary event made more so in being framed by the ordinary. It makes more sense, not least because it's true.

After this, things really started to get out of hand. A coroner's inquest was held at Brentwood. It was adjourned for lack of evidence. Then another inquest at Epping was again postponed. By the time of the third inquest, all the evidence had been destroyed. Something very strange was happening. In the first report, there had been a mention of needle marks on his arm. By the third, Phil's body had been cremated. The psychiatrist who'd administered the anti-psychotic drug had been posted to Australia and his place taken by another specialist, who told the court that the records had been lost. He was not cross-examined. When asked to assess Phil's mental state, a police officer witness had said, in an off-hand, almost joking manner, 'Well, he thought he was Jesus Christ, didn't he?' It was clear that no one was taking any of it seriously. As a representative for Phil, they found someone who'd met him at Watchfield only a few months before and who had no knowledge of the background. This was Steve Hurman, who later became Crass's guitarist. Steve felt that Phil must have killed himself. Pen and Gee, who were present throughout the proceedings, felt that there was a whitewash. Something very peculiar was going on.

Pen began his own investigation. He spent a year and a half researching for a book on the subject.

There was a second death. Another of the Wallies was found tied to a tree in Epping Forest with a joint in his hand. There were links between the Essex police and the Brighton underworld, a whole network of murky dealings and unpleasant goings-on. It was like biting into a crisp apple and finding the inside writhing with worms. Two policemen turned up at the house one day and mentioned that they knew Pen was writing a book. It was like a warning: 'Watch out!' Pen became frightened. He stopped sleeping out in the garden, which had always been his habit when the weather allowed. As a result, Pen burned the manuscript and all of the evidence.

It is too easy to doubt Pen's theories regarding the death of Wally Hope. It is also too easy to accept them uncritically. Hardly anyone knows what really happened to Phil Russell in those few short months. Conspiracy scenarios are a lot like mystical experiences: they're down to the individual. In the end, you can neither deny them absolutely, nor prove them. What is certain, it seems to me, is than Pen experienced something profound in that time which lived with him and shaped his life afterwards.

I'd put a note in one of my *Guardian* columns that I wanted to know about the early history of free festivals, and Wally Hope in particular. This was how I'd contacted Pen, but I also had a letter which, in part, confirms some of his assertions. It was from the solicitor who he'd contracted to investigate the allegations.

Dear Mr Stone

In the early days of the festivals I was a weekend hippie/ weekday solicitor. I attended many of the early festivals and got to know a few people involved. It was through my festival contacts that I was instructed professionally to make some enquiries into the circumstances surrounding the death of Wally Hope. It was a time of paranoia and suspicion of the authorities and those instructing me were convinced that Mr Hope had been 'done away with by the Establishment'. It is unfortunately a long time ago. I do, however, recall that at the time when I started my enquiries I thought that those instructing me had over-fertile imaginations, but I later changed my mind and would have liked to have investigated further ...

From my recollection the authorities were anxious to stop the Stonehenge festival taking place. I cannot now recollect the exact year, but I remember that Mr Hope and his friends were announcing the festival was on and the authorities were saying it was off. Shortly before the festival was due to commence, Mr Hope was arrested after a raid by the police and was accused of being in possession of half an LSD tab. I believe he denied possession of the same and wished to plead not guilty. He was, however, told that if he did this he would be remanded in custody until after the summer solstice. Wishing to be out for the festival and not anticipating a custodial sentence for such a small amount, Mr Hope decided to plead guilty to the possession charge. This was, however, a bad move on his behalf as the court committed him to a psychiatric hospital. This would appear to have been an unnecessary and draconian sentence for such a small amount. I also believe that this was done upon little if any medical evidence and I also believe that Mr Hope was not legally represented.

The conspiracy theory put forward by his friends was that when in custody in the psychiatric hospital, Mr Hope was involuntarily given certain tranquillising drugs and that the dosage given was many, many times the normal dose. As a result, when eventually released, Mr Hope was a completely broken man and a vastly different character than he was before his arrest. I was told that Mr Hope then had a very unhappy life until he later committed suicide. It was in fact suggested to me that there were also suspicious circumstances regarding his suicide ... I never followed up this later theory, but I do recall that there was certainly some suspicion regarding his treatment and the drugs prescribed while he was in the psychiatric hospital.

I hope the above may be of interest to you.

Yours faithfully

Trevor Helm

Later, Trevor Helm rang me up. I asked him what had made him change his mind about Pen's theories. Why had he wanted to investigate further? He said that he'd written to the Old Manor and that they'd as good as admitted that Phil had been overdosed on psychiatric drugs. He also confirmed Pen's paranoia. He'd been to visit Pen and the others at their commune home, and he'd seen some people literally crawling round in ditches, keeping an eye on the house. He said that he wished he could show me the letter to confirm what he'd been saying. 'But the files have all gone missing,' he told me. 'We're a firm of professional solicitors, we keep meticulous records, but there's nothing in the files. I've looked. Make of it what you will.'

The third Stonehenge free festival was even larger than the second. Phil's vision had become enshrined in the national consciousness. Pen managed to get into the stones for the solstice on a press card. Meanwhile some of the other festival organisers were trying to pull down the fences. Pen persuaded them to come in by the public entrance. He'd made a box in which Phil's ashes were placed. It was a small, simply made wooden box, on which was inscribed the words 'Wally Hope, victim of ignorance'. Hundreds of people were in among the stones and a film was made of the proceedings. Syd Rawle (one of the Windsor organisers and self-proclaimed 'King of the Hippies') was chanting. Someone read a poem, which was burned. An Army helicopter came over very low. It was like a warning: 'Behave!' They opened the box and each person took a small handful of the dust and scattered it over the stones. The wardens, who were standing near by watching the ritual, said, 'You can't do this,' but they carried on anyway. Someone was dancing on a tarpaulin covering one of the stones. 'Come on, get off the stones,' the wardens pleaded. There was an argument. 'I'm not on the stones, I'm on a tarpaulin.'

All of a sudden the cameraman started shaking and cried out. Pen went over to see what was the matter. The man was deathly pale. 'Look through here,' he said, indicating the camera. Pen looked. The camera was focused on a group of people standing round, just watching. And between them, quite clearly Pen says, he could see Phil, an ethereal body dancing in and out of the stones. He just danced back and forth, into and out of one of the stones. It was a deeply moving moment. Wally Hope was still with them, still there, an eternal presence in his beloved monument. Pen wondered what the film would show. In the end, it showed nothing.

Later, there was a confrontation between Pen and Syd Rawle back at the tepee circle. Pen wanted Wally's box burned. Afterwards he learned that it had been kept as a memento. Phil mistrusted and disliked the extremist hippies who had run the Windsor free festival, and now here they were claiming his inheritance. They'd blocked Phil all the way on the foundation of this festival, saying it diverted attention from Windsor and Watchfield. They were into political confrontation, whereas Phil was into peace. Yet now he was dead, they were taking an unhealthy interest in the iconography of Phil's life. Pen had helped Phil put into operation this dream, in making it come true, but somehow all that was forgotten. He didn't ask for thanks; just some acknowledgement, some recognition. He felt like a stranger here. He'd come to this place as an act of homage to his friend, to pay his last respects, and yet no one seemed to care about him. He wasn't even offered a bed for the night. He had to crash out under a hedge by his bike. As he was leaving, a woman approached him smiling. His heart rose to see that warm human face coming towards him. He felt that she was going to say how sorry she was that he'd lost his good friend and wish him luck, perhaps touch him lightly to show she understood. 'Before you leave,' she said, 'have you got a fag?' He got on his bike and drove off, crying.

He stopped in the first Little Chef along the way, with all its plastic falsity – the kind of place he would normally scorn – and the woman behind the counter said, 'Hello, dear, what would you like?' She was so down-to-earth, so human. He felt her ordinary presence as a contrast to the self-indulgent mayhem of the festival people. He had a banana milkshake.

Pen says that Phil's death was the turning point in his life. Phil died at the end of a wonderful era, his death represented the end of a cohesive and workable dream: a better world, a better future. The circumstances of his death made it clear to Pen that what they were up against was no longer simply ignorance or stupidity; it was manifest evil. Crass were formed to combat this evil and to present the case for which Phil had died. In a very real sense, Pen said, Crass was Phil's band. Not only Pen and Gee, but Steve Hurman, and Steve the singer, all had some connection with Phil Russell, and they were consciously fulfilling Phil's famous axiom: 'Guitars the tommy-guns, drums the missiles, sun the bomb.' Rock'n'roll as a revolutionary vehicle.

One more irony. Crass played Stonehenge in 1982. Phil's band had returned to play at Phil's festival. The bikers, who by that time had a large presence there, were incensed at what they saw as a take-over. This was 'their' festival. Pen feels they felt threatened by the appearance of the punks. There was a riot at which anyone with spiky hair was beaten. It went on all night. Many threats. Many bruises. Many broken bones. One tribe against another. One generation against another. Divide and rule. That way the Establishment always wins. In that long night of violence, Phil's dream finally came to an end.

We had many other conversations on that long, bright day, as we sat in this sunny paradise and drank endless cups of tea – Pen loves his tea – or ate bread and cheese and hummus in the shade of the overarching trees. One I remember in particular was about motorways. We'd been talking about the road-building programme and I'd told him of the road-protesters' theory that the motorways are, in fact, a way of cutting the ley-lines, conceived by the higher Freemasons to extract the earth-energies for themselves and turn it to whatever dark energy they themselves worshipped. Pen said – these aren't his exact words, I wasn't taking notes at this point – 'I sometimes wonder if we're right in doing what we're doing. Don't get me wrong,' he added, 'I'll go on doing it, I'll go on fighting to my last breath for what I believe in. But as I get older, sometimes I start to think that maybe I'm on the wrong side, that maybe the road-building programme represents some sort of signal. Who knows? Who knows what the builders are up to, what the overall plan is? Maybe the M25 is a kind of hieroglyphic design meant to communicate something. Maybe the motorways are a magical design representing positive energy and we just don't know it.'

I baulked at this. It's mad enough to begin with trying to imagine the road programme as a conspiracy to cut ley-lines. And I'm none too sure of that. But then to start putting forward the idea that it might even represent some sort of positive magical force – it was way beyond me. Magic is just a myth in my mind – like gravitational fields or morphic resonances – it's just words; it has nothing to do with my daily life.

But Pen assured me that he wasn't saying it was true. It's just that he sometimes wondered. Maybe there are things we don't understand, and that all of this is part of some overall plan meant to bring the world on to a higher plane.

I also told Pen about my dream, about the squat, and the distorted aliens. When I came to the bit where I spoke to the young hippie and told him to take his boots off, Pen and Steve exchanged a significant glance.

'That was the rule here,' Steve said. 'For years there was a notice on the door saying "Take your shoes off before entering".'

He rolled on to his back on the lawn, singing the theme tune to *The Outer Limits*.

'Spooky!' he said.

7 Tepee Valley

It's like a Wild West town. The streets are brimming with drunken squaddies, lolling over each other and shouting, the pubs are heaving, loud music is spilling out on to the road like an amphetamine heartbeat, and there's military police in full uniform posted on the street corners watching the proceedings with stern, manly expressions, weapons at the ready. You could get killed in a town like this.

Amesbury in Wiltshire, the nearest town to the Stonehenge monument. Somehow that fact explains the frontier atmosphere. Maybe there is a war on.

I drove in at about 10.30 p.m., parked up in a huge sprawling car-park and walked into the town centre. You can tell a squaddie a mile off, even in their civvies. Maybe it's the uncompromising haircut, or the obscenely muscle-bound physique. It could be the air they give off of slightly dangerous schoolboys on the rampage. But it's not. It's the moustaches. They've all got moustaches. It makes you wonder what motivations they have lurking in their unconscious that makes them all want to look like Freddie Mercury. They're swaggering about and playing manly games with each other, play-fighting, wrapping their arms around each other's necks and slobbering in each other's ears, slapping each other on the back, wrestling, play-punching just this side of a ruptured spleen, ruffling hair and pinching cheeks, obviously in love.

Amesbury is the town where Wally Hope was busted. I'm on my way to West Wales to visit the tepee people. They have Wally's box over there and I've been promised a meeting with one of the original Wallies. I thought I'd stop off here on the way, check it out. There are deep roots here in the Wally Hope story, and its connection with the great festival is obvious. A lot of the festival-goers must have shopped here and I'm certain the off-licence did a roaring trade. I don't know what I expected to find: a sleepy little country town? A place steeped in ancient myths and atavistic customs? Who knows ... Instead of which, I end up in Dodge City.

I was dying for a drink. I pushed my way past a bunch of people gathered in the doorway of a pub. The men were as muscle-bound as the squaddies, but clearly local. They had long feather-cut hair and wore cap-sleeved T-shirts.

After my pint I negotiated a bed and breakfast, then went for a walk about the town. I soon decided it was far too dangerous. Squaddies are notoriously tribal and I was clearly not one of them. Why else would it be that even the locals have to sport mounds of muscle-fibre, and military police look on sternly from every street corner? The smell of testosterone and aftershave oozed from every pub. I went back to the hotel.

I started chatting to a man leaning against the bar. I was trying to work out which drink to buy. I wanted something local. He offered advice and then asked me why I was here.

'I'm looking for Wally Hope,' I said.

'Wally who?'

'Hope,' I repeated, and went on to tell him what I was up to.

'Oh, the festival,' he said. 'It was the worst thing that ever happened to this town ... the festival being closed down.'

I was surprised at this statement. 'I'd've thought you locals would have hated it.'

'Not at all,' he slurred – he was very drunk – 'lots of money.' He told me that his dad had pitched an ice-cream van there for the full ten years that the festival had run. 'He used to get all sorts. People coming up to him bollock-naked, buying an ice lolly. Didn't bother him in the slightest. They were all nice people. Best little tax-free earner he ever had, that ice-cream van.'

The people around the bar began to join in. Opinions were divided. The monument had to be protected, some of them said. Otherwise some little oiks might try to carve their initials into it. There was a degree of thieving in the town, too, during the festival period. Apparently the Co-op was at the head of the anti-festival lobby, while the off-licence wanted it to stay. 'So what?' said the ice-cream man's son. 'The Co-op lost a bit of stock, but think of the money the rest of the town made. As for the damage,' he added: 'I've got a bit of the monument myself. Strangest thing. No matter how hot the weather is, that stone is always ice-cold. One of the security guards sold it me.'

I asked about the underpass the DoT were planning to build. Wouldn't that damage the monument too? What were people scared of?

'That's the most dangerous stretch of road in the country,' someone said. 'People are belting down the dual carriageway at eighty mile an hour when at the self-same moment they hit a single-lane road and catch sight of Stonehenge. And, of course, they just look at it. Drive along, craning their necks and braking, saying, "Ooh look, it's Stonehenge!" And people wonder why they crash. Something has to be done about it.'

The conversation went on for hours. Everyone had something to say on the subject. The landlady of the hotel said she'd bought the place in 1986, after the festival was banned, but every year the solstice became a running battle. 1988 was the worst. It was like a prison camp. The locals all had to carry ID cards. Police and roadblocks everywhere. Cars were stopped coming into and going out of the town. It was a nightmare, she said. And although everyone agreed that there had been some problems associated with the festival, particularly in its later years, when there was a lot of heroin going about, they were all in agreement that the police reaction was excessive. 'You couldn't hope to meet a nicer bunch of people,' said the landlady. 'They may have been scruffy, but they were always polite.'

The following morning I went looking for the site of the squat where Wally Hope had been busted. It was on London Road, up a hill, I was told. I cruised about the town trying to find it, but ended up on the road to Stonehenge. 'Oh well,' I thought, 'maybe Stonehenge is calling.'

When I got there I tried to walk in but a security guard stopped me. There were already people in there, shuffling about among the stones, carrying posies of flowers and polished brass bowls and a range of other incomprehensible implements.

'It doesn't open until 9.30,' the security man said.

'I'm on my way to Wales,' I said. 'I haven't got time to wait. Anyway, there are already people in there.'

'It's been booked,' he told me. 'It's the Sahaja Yoga people doing a ceremony for peace,' he added, with a faint smirk.

So I got a cup of coffee instead. There was a heat haze rising up over the bleak, strange plain, and a dirigible ambling about in the still air like some Heath Robinson flying saucer. Families sat around on the benches eating sandwiches and drinking tea from flasks. Children played. Everyone was dressed in smart-casual gear – not a hippie smock or a nose-ring in sight.

By now, the Sahaja Yoga lot were floating out in twos and threes, wafting their posies about and looking smug. One couple passed me and gave me a look of complete contempt. 'They just don't understand,' one of them said, smiling like one who did. 'What do they think this place is? A cafeteria?' Sahaja Yoga people don't drink coffee. They drink raspberry-leaf tea.

Despite all the efforts at normality – the visitors' centre, the car-park, the wire fencing, the atmosphere they've tried to create of some sort of a historical theme-park – Stonehenge continues to exert a fascination. There's a wildness in the stones, a presence. You really sense that each of the stones carries a personality, and you know that you are face-to-face with something ancient and mysterious. They draw you to them. They call out to you. You feel that you are truly on the threshold of another kind of space – the dreamtime – as if the monument was a stepping stone across the dimensions. Giants doze here, murmuring and stirring in their sleep.

I arrived in Tepee Valley around 2.30 in the afternoon. I'd been given instructions how to get there, and the further I'd pushed into this landscape, the thinner and windier the roads became, the more entangled the tree-cover, the wilder the outlook, the greener and sweeter the view over the rolling hills, so that I really began to feel like an explorer in a new territory. The final instructions were very detailed indeed. There was a little sketch-map with a gate and a stream drawn in, and a little rectangle with a triangle to represent the tepee, which was marked 'Jim's garden'. Fortunately, I didn't have to follow any of this. By the time I'd arrived at the track it was clear I was in Tepee Valley. There were ramshackle buses scattered about behind makeshift fences, and vans and cars and trucks. Barefoot kids grubbed about on the dusty tracks and you could see the tepees pegged out along the valley, peeping through the tree cover like weird sculptures. I pulled up and asked if anyone knew Jim and, sure enough, there he was, emerging from a car. He'd just returned from shopping in the nearest town. He got into my car and we followed the rutted track down to the parking place.

Jim's garden was a revelation. Another little Paradise. Neat vegetable plots laid out in reassuring squares. A gurgling stream skipping beneath the overhanging trees. A few well-built structures like garden sheds and workshops. And two tepees, standing like inverted ice-cream cones, across from one another. But that image isn't quite right. Certainly, they are shaped like ice-cream cones, but the picture lacks dignity. There is a sentinel-like quality to these creatures. They seem almost alive. And the spread of poles at the top, ranged like antennae, with the canvas smoke flap fixed like a satellite dish, gives the impression of a giant receiver of some kind. GCHQ for the New Age. Earth funnels, as Jim calls them.

Jim and I sit on logs by the fire, in a dusty patch crowded with pots and pans, and buckets and bowls, and plates and cutlery and chopping boards, all sheltered with a loose canvas covering secured by ropes. The kitchen. Jim is preparing lunch. He's in his forties, with short greying hair and a thin beard. Lunch is salad and chips. The chips are fried in a heavy cast-iron frying pan, blackened by smoke. After they're cooked Jim throws the oil into the fire, which sizzles and leaps. Much care is taken over the fire. It is clearly the living heart of the garden. Three logs with glowing charcoal ends are placed around a skillet made of horseshoes, under which the fire dances. Dry sticks are fed into it from the side in a constant stream, and the bubbling, hissing frying pan is periodically turned to get an even spread of heat. The complexities of open-fire cookery engender a kind of meditative concentration: Jim's movements are practised and concise, a domesticated Tai Chi, as he snatches one hot pan from the fire and replaces it with another, then feeds more wood into the flames and stirs the ashes with a stick. Kitchen yoga, as ancient as these hills. We eat lunch from wooden bowls, served with pan-baked bread tasting of yeast and smoke and grain. Absolutely delicious.

By this time, Jim's lover has arrived to share lunch with us. She's like some strange pixie, diminutive and hunched, with her front teeth missing. She's wearing only an orange vest and a pair of wellies. Every time she bends down I get a view of her fanny, like some pink winking eye through dark bushy brows. I'm starting to have trouble knowing where to look. She gives me these sidelong mischievous glances, and there's something unfathomable and disturbing about her. Not that she's unpleasant in any way. It's just that I have a sense of an ancient, almost mythic way of life manifesting itself here. She's like a creature from some Scandinavian saga: not quite human. A witch, a wild fairy-creature. I feel certain that she casts spells.

She tells me her name, but asks me not to use it. I can call her 'Black Pearl' she says. At first I thought it was some sort of sexual innuendo (which only goes to show how my mind works). It's not. It's the name of a particularly powerful strain of skunk-weed. They smoke dope here almost constantly. It has almost universally replaced alcohol as the social drug. There's a lesson here, I feel. Currently most of the people in Tepee Valley have to sign on. But given their dedication to hashish as a sacrament, and their skills at gardening, I feel sure that, if hash was legal, they could easily become self-sufficient.

It's strange how comfortable I feel here. I'm a townie at heart, more at ease with the hiss of traffic than the twittering of birds, more in tune to the romance of the supermarket than the rhythms of nature. I like the sight of decaying factories, the smell of carbon monoxide, the sparkle of streetlamps on wet pavements. The Great Outdoors is too disordered for my punctuated mind. Yet here I am, crouched over an open fire in Jim's garden paradise, beneath the shade of a flapping tarpaulin, and I am – I'm happy.

There's a steady stream of visitors, lured as much by the smell of fresh coffee, no doubt, as by the prospect of passing the time of day with some townie journalist. I remember the faces, but not always the names. There's a guy in a sarong with a nervous voice and long dreadlocks snaking down his back. He's in his late forties at least. His shin is wrapped in a handkerchief which he takes off to reveal a deep, yellow wound. He burned it while attending a sweat-lodge, a matter that later was to attain great significance for me. I advise him to see a doctor. I'm none too sure if these people ever see conventional doctors. There's something endearingly childlike about the man, a kind of innocence. And it's no exaggeration to compare Tepee Valley to Eden before the Fall: lots of Adams and Eves wandering about, naked, tending their vegetable plots in the sunshine.

I met a woman who took an instant dislike to me because I am a journalist. She said she'd been interviewed by a *Guardian* journalist last year who'd described her as having blackened teeth and matted hair. It was an entirely gratuitous description. She'd been deeply hurt and insulted by the article.

There's another bloke who insists on being called Finn, after a character in *2,000 AD*. Tight, thin body and jet-black dreads. Army boots. This one has the air of a latter-day crusty traveller, rather than the hippie crew that mainly inhabit the valley. Which is what he is. He joined the movement after the Battle of the Beanfield. He's ex-Army, like a significant number of travellers. He says he left the Army after an incident in Northern Ireland. A kid pointed a toy gun at him and said, 'Bang, you're dead!' Only he meant it. Finn could see the hatred in the child's eyes, like a nuclear-tipped, armour-piercing shell sluicing it's way through his defences. In that moment he knew he was on the wrong side. He cried. There and then, a British soldier on the streets of Belfast: he cried. In a sense, you feel, he's been crying ever since.

Finn is boiling over with the mythology of the movement. He says that Stonehenge was originally a moon-temple, orientated towards significant lunar events, before the heel-stone was shifted to its present site. It is its transformation into a sun-temple that is at the root of the current malaise. The shift from goddess-worship to god-worship is at the heart of the shift in consciousness that marks out the modern era, a fact which also explains our dislocation from the world around us, our fundamental lack. He says that the power of Stonehenge exists only at dawn on the 23 June: summer solstice. Then the energies whirling round the monument bend matter. At other times it is inert. This explains why English Heritage have placed a ban on Stonehenge only at that precise time.

He says that he has always been a soldier. Throughout time, through countless lifetimes, he has lived and died by the sword. He says that he has never lived beyond the age of twenty-one. (He looks to be in his late twenties or early thirties.) This is the first lifetime in which he has ever survived beyond that age.

As he talks – almost oblivious to the people gathered about him sipping coffee and smoking spliffs – you get the sensation of some deep wound: like the other bloke's leg, but far more painful. The subjects spill out of his mouth with unsystematised abandon. It really is as if he's boiling over. He's in a state of excited reverie, not really caring who is there with him. Maybe he cares, maybe he doesn't; but that catch in his voice, that faint warble of emotion, indicates a sort of generalised love. He does love. He is love, though a peculiarly lost and abandoned kind of love.

He's talking about his wife and children, and life on the road. He'd been going mad. Too many people in too small a space. His wife had packed his stuff and told him to get out for a while, to get himself back together.

He's talking about that time in 1988, just after he'd left the Army, when he was leading the campaign to organise the festival, cutting fences and securing site after site all over Salisbury Plain. Small festivals here and there, niggling the authorities. People gathering and moving on, and always pursued by the police and the Army. He says that they knew who he was. He says they always keep a track on 'their' boys. He was using his specialised survival skills – given to him by the Army – to another end. A spiritual end. He describes the travelling community as his tribe.

I cannot remember the order. There was no order. He talked, as if talk was his only defence against a reeling, mad universe, on and on and on. And all of it was fascinating and weird (in the original Anglo-Saxon meaning of the word): fatalistic and fated, tempered in a strange mythic fire.

He talked about being in the Army. He says that the essence of Army-life is love. I recognise this. I've noticed that emotional timbre in the voice of soldiers before. The root of all relationships in the Army is not the battalion or the squadron or the company, or any of the other levels of organisation the Army groups its recruits into: it is the 'buddy system'. The word 'mate' comes from Army-life. It is used by working-class men to denote work-fellows or friends or men they like. And yet, of course, its root meaning is 'sexual partner'. Your buddy, your mate, is like your lover in all but that one sense. You are absolutely dependent upon him. Until recently, on the streets of Northern Ireland – as in any combat situation – one soldier walked forwards while his mate walked backwards. They 'watched each other's backs'. They placed their lives in each other's hands. Total readiness. Each is willing to die to save the other. This is indeed love. A poisonous love, a strange love. A psychologically crippled love: love attained through fear and oppression. This is the secret at the heart of the Army. Not the weapons. Not the strategies. That they have psychologically stripped the human being to his base components and that they use these raw emotions to power their particular ends. Love. Love more total – and more disturbed – than any known in civvy life.

I've said before that a significant number of travellers are ex-servicemen. I cannot give you exact figures on this, but in my experience this is true. They represent the reverse – the underground – of the Establishment. Men whose contact with war has twisted and maimed them. The functional essence of the State is war. War is its meaning, its purpose, its very heart. These men – these soldiers – have come face-to-face with the coercive nature of the Establishment machine. As a rogue soldier – as a soldier who would no longer obey orders, who thrashed around in his pain and confusion, hitting out blindly at the figures that taunted him and had power over him, the sergeants, the senior officers – Finn was locked up, bullied, beaten, tortured and humiliated and, finally, cast out.

All armies depend on brutality. They depend on force and on obedience. They strip away all symptoms of individuality. They deconstruct the human machine, paring away the sense of personal identity, removing all rogue elements, until the fleshy exterior is no more than a seething bag of raw instinct. Then they reconstruct it again: as an instrument of war. They work on what is most primitive, most basic in the human psyche. And if, in the process of creating these psychological monsters, these lunatics inured to evil and to the evils of war, there are also times when they create the opposite, then that is but a psychological side-effect. At the heart of the human process, perhaps, lies the struggle between good and evil. If evil arises, so too does good, in answer to it.

I came to Tepee Valley looking for counter-culture, for the underground. The underground is not the same as trendiness, which alternates from generation to generation (flares–drain-pipes–flares); nor is it rock'n'roll rebellion, so easily absorbed into the Establishment; it is not the same as youth culture, which simply disappears with age. The underground encompasses a range of ideologies. From free parties to road protests to hunt sabs. From hippies to punks to ravers. From violent anarchism to non-violent direct action. From primitivism to high-tech sound systems. From travellers in trucks to travellers in horse-drawn carriages to travellers on filthy, mud-slimed sites, off their heads on Special Brew and heroin. From occultists to cultists to followers of earth-lore magic. From atheists to monotheists to polytheists. From computer-generated music and fractal imagery to penny whistles and drums around an open fire. What distinguishes it from the Establishment is that it also absorbs all the suppressed elements from above. We all take drugs. But only pharmaceutical and commercial drugs are allowed in the overground. So the underground is crowded with those whose chemical inclinations are different – the dope smokers as well as the heroin dealers.

Here in Finn, I felt, I was closer to the heart of what is meant by underground than ever before. The underground is like the unconscious: the repository of failure and a well-spring of creativity. Finn typified this for me: a failed soldier – deeply wounded by his contact with the inhuman force at the heart of the system – yet born again, enlightened as it were, by his contact with the tribe. The travelling tribe, not allowed to travel any more. Skills that are of no use in civvy life become extraordinarily important on the road. Camping skills. Survival skills. Love and loyalty. What use are they in a city?

His initial statement about what is wrong with the earth – about the moon-temple Stonehenge being turned into a sun-temple – provides the other key to what motivates the underground. The overground worships power, authority, masculinity. It worships Jehovah. The underground worships the goddess. It is the revival of that most suppressed of all religions: worship of the female principle: Shekinah. It doesn't matter what you call her – Gaia, Mother Earth – she is the missing element in the equation, and the reason why the Establishment god is mad with grief.

*

In the afternoon I met Chris Wally. He'd been one of the Wally tribe. He was very drunk. Chris Wally doesn't live in a tepee (he doesn't even call himself Chris Wally any more); he lives in the only house in the entire valley: a grim, grey cottage, devoid of light. He talked a little about Wally Hope. He thought it was no wonder that Phil had been certified back then. He must have sounded mad with all his strange declarations: 'I am the son of the sun. Acid is the sacrament.' All that stuff. And he pooh-poohed the idea of using any kind of conspiracy theory to explain the motivations of the powers-that-be. Their motivation is profit, that's all. They don't need to get together in secret meetings. They share the same motivation. It's an understanding. Events like Wally Hope's death are the accidental side-effect of this, not intentional: a conspiracy of accidents. His death was brought on as much by his own intransigence – and by their failure to understand what he was trying to say – as by any dark machinations.

He was talking very loudly. It was a declamation, not a conversation. He wouldn't answer any questions. His drunken armour was impenetrable. I had the feeling of a cover-up. Not a conspiracy, you understand, but an understanding with himself. He was one of the people who had been in the house when Wally Hope was busted. He was one of those who'd got on with the 1975 festival, oblivious to Phil Russell's fate. Of course he'd never meant him to die. He wasn't guilty in any way. He'd have been very young at the time. All that was gone. If he'd ever believed in Wally Hope's miracles, now it had no meaning for him. He was sticking doggedly to the facts. Too old for youthful fantasies, he was simply trying to get on with his life. What else was there to do?

I recognised a bitterness in his tone. It wasn't that I disagreed with his analysis (personally, I'm both drawn to and suspicious of conspiracy theory). It's just that he seemed too forceful in his argument, too quick in his rejection of what has come to be a mythology of the movement. How did Wally Hope die? Well, he died. And he left all of his friends behind.

While we were talking, I noticed a scurrying in the hedgerow. It was a muscular brown rat with an obscene pink naked tail, slipping into a hole beneath the bank. Jim told me that he was planning to kill it. He believed it was already breeding. Despite his vegetarianism, despite his pacifism, despite his back-to-naturism, he still saw the need to kill a creature he recognised as an enemy of humankind.

In the evening I went and bought some beer. I was feeling left out as the rest of them were rolling spliffs constantly and I don't smoke. Everyone to his own poison, I say. Dope makes me feel self-conscious.

We sat around the fire and chatted as the sun went down. They told me of their continuing battle with the authorities. Apparently no one had gained planning permission for any of these structures and the local council were trying to remove them. This land was designated as arable land; it wasn't meant to be lived on. It struck me as revealing how the planning laws always seem to be used to stop poor people doing what they like. You rarely hear of a road programme or a supermarket being stopped. Apparently, though, the valley had been inhabited once, up until the sixties. For some obscure reason the farmers had left and now they were all living in council estates. Jim told me that it cost £200 a year to build and maintain a tepee. How much does it cost to live in a council house?

I had one surprise during this conversation. It seems that everyone here does the Lottery. I couldn't understand it, mainly because I'll have nothing to do with it. I think the whole thing is an exploitative con. But these hippies, for all their alternative lifestyle, their goddess-worship, and their temporary housing, they all did the Lottery. They were talking about what they'd do if they won, like everyone does on a Saturday night in the

British Isles. Finn said that he'd buy some land which all travellers would be free to use.

Peopled drifted off to bed. I felt very calm, very peaceful. Finn and I retired to the spare tepee, where a fire had been lit in a little wood burner in the centre of the circular room. It was warm and comfortable. The floor was covered in reeds and scattered with sheepskins. The walls flapped slightly in the breeze. The atmosphere in there was one of calm meditation. Finn continued talking about Army-life until I asked him to leave. As I lay down to sleep I could feel the earth shifting beneath me, rumbling on some subatomic level, stirring to its depths.

I was in Tepee Valley for two days. Initially I was going to stay for a third, but then Jim told me he was going to build a sweat-lodge.

The following day we started its preparation.

What's a sweat-lodge? Well, it's a kind of outdoor sauna. They heat limestone blocks in a huge fire, they take the blocks into an insulated bender, and everyone sits around in the darkness, while they sprinkle water on the stones, and sweats.

I'd confided to Finn that I was a bit nervous about the sweat-lodge. He'd said, 'Yes, it's the place where you confront all your fears.'

Ulp!

Black Pearl and I were going to cut some reeds for the floor. She was still dressed in her orange vest and her wellies. As we drove by, she was calling to everyone, 'Sweat-lodge tonight.'

'Trying to fill it up with men, eh Pearl?' someone replied, looking at me pointedly.

I asked Jim for more details. He said, 'We all sit around by the fire chanting and drumming while the rocks are heating up. Then we carry the rocks into the lodge using poles. After that we all enter in a procession, chanting. But it's all right. If you have to get out, all you need to do is shout, "Door!" and the flap will open and you can leave.'

Pearl and I built the sweat-lodge between us. The framework for the bender was already there: a network of hazel coppice secured in the ground, and bent and lashed into the shape of an upturned bowl. It was about six foot in diameter, and four foot high. We took blankets and duvets and wrapped them over the frame, then covered the whole thing in tarpaulin. Layers and layers and layers. We were passing by each other as I brought wheelbarrows full of material down from the shed to the bender. She said, 'Sweat-lodge tonight,' with a strange little snicker, and one of her unsettling sidelong glances. It sounded like a threat.

We went to visit someone further down the valley. When we arrived he was in his garden dressed only in a headband. His whole body was pinkish-brown. He was squatting in his vegetable patch, plucking out weeds. He was accompanied by his seventeen-year-old daughter.

He turned out to be the son of a South Wales miner. In the early days he'd been a revolutionary, he told me. Now he was content to dig his garden.

He turned on a small transistor radio. It was *Gardener's Question Time*. A familiar Radio 4 voice was saying, 'I think you should chant over the plants at full moon wearing only a loincloth.'

Later, we went to see Rick the Vic, an ex-Church of England vicar turned hippie. He had Wally's box tucked away – the box that Pen had made for Wally's ashes, which Pen had wanted burned. I looked it over. It was just a box. It smelled of damp and age. Rick asked me if I wanted to attend a dance camp that summer.

'What's a dance camp?'

'It's a place where we all gather to camp and dance. All kinds of dance: African, Thai, Tibetan ... '

I had a sudden realisation. I could picture them there at their camp, all these fey, twee folk, practising their African dance movements with concentrated looks on their faces. I could imagine them in serious conversation: 'I just can't quite get the hang of that twirl, you know.' It wasn't dance they were on about, it was therapy. These were the people the punks had called Boring Old Farts. Meeting Rick the Vic opened up an ancient wound for me, the memory of the precious, middle-class hippies with their crystals and their drums and their chants and their therapies and their philosophy of personal growth. Well, back in the seventies I was a working-class lad. I licked my spoon. I had no grace. I liked pie and chips. At the time, that philosophy had damaged me; now I was going to have to sit round a fire with them, naked, and ... chant.

I bottled out. I drank some beer and fell asleep in the afternoon. When I woke up it was to the clear realisation that I really didn't want to sit around a fire with a bunch of naked hippies drumming and chanting. Nor did I want to enter a confined space with them with red-hot flesh-sizzling rocks in the middle, in utter darkness, and sweat. I simply wasn't ready for it.

I left as soon as we'd eaten dinner. I drove off into the sunset with a huge sensation of relief.

I thought about them all as I slid along the dusky motorway in the deepening evening, the sun like a huge raw wound slashed across the sky in my rear-view mirror: Jim and Pearl, and the woman who hated journalists; the man with the wounded leg; Finn; Chris Wally; the ex-revolutionary and his daughter; Rick the Vic. 'Was it a cop-out,' I thought, 'hiding out in this gorgeous piece of countryside playing Adam and Eve? Is this the way to change the world?' Well, no, obviously not. They are simply getting on with their lives the way the rest of us do. Not doing any harm – doing a great deal less harm than the majority – trying to do good by example.

I thought about the council estate where I live. The people

there share something in common with the Tepee Valley residents: everyone signs on. There's a major difference, though. The people in Tepee Valley are happy. I'd mentioned this to Jim and he'd said, 'Yes. We have everything we want here. We eat well. We work hard. We sleep like logs. It's the perfect life.'

The way they dealt with their own shit was a revelation. They compost it. There are four compost bins. The first is filled with a mixture of shit and organic matter from the hills and the garden: bracken and leaves and reeds from the sweat-lodge floor. The second is filled with worms. As the decaying matter goes down the line, it breaks down more and more until it is pure, clean compost. You could pick up the rich, loamy, crumbling humus in the last bin and smell it.

Jim said, 'The way we deal with shit is to grow food from it. It's natural. Lead into gold. No alchemist could do better.'

8 VE Day

The world is even madder than I thought. Our town already has a bypass. So they're going to build another one. Which makes the second bypass a bypass to bypass a bypass.

Fen can't stand it. There's a special place he's been going to ever since he was a boy. Fen's sacred field. There's an ancient oak called the Flat Oak, which Fen describes as the reservoir of memory in the landscape, saying that it's like the anchor knot in a pattern, the focus around which the landscape weaves. Behind it trails a thin strip of woodland called Convict's Wood, and around it a little brook swaggers self-confidently, chuckling to itself, and serving as the gathering place for the local non-human subculture. There's water voles, moorhens, coots, ducks, pheasants, foxes, rabbits, squirrels. Fen is a wood elf. He sits in his tree and plays the penny whistle, and afterwards he returns to his dingy council flat and he's at peace again. And now they're about to build a seven-lane motorway right through the middle of it, put the stream into a concrete tube, and cut down the Flat Oak, in order to save a possible two minutes' travelling time in the rush to get from here to there. Is beauty and peace of so little value: two minutes for an eternity?

The first time I ever spoke to Fen it was about the motorway. I offered my help in organising a protest. Fen rejected it airily, saying he would meditate in the field and create a psychic barrier. Well, he's mad – mad, but good – and he knows now that it will take a lot more than psychic barriers to stop a motorway. For the last few months he's been frantically pouring out material about the road, designing posters, painting signs, talking to anyone who will listen. He's changed his name to Jo Oak (which is a joke) in honour of the tree, and he's talking about revolution. This is something Karl Marx never envisaged: revolution for an oak tree.

He organised a gig to raise money and wanted to throw a party afterwards, but the local sound system backed out. The sites were unsuitable. They'd been shown around a derelict farmhouse, along the route several miles further on. When they pointed out how dangerous it was – imagine all those drunks staggering around in a derelict farmhouse – the person showing them had said, 'Yeah, but when the police come we've got all these bricks as ammo.' Brick 'em, Rick. He used to be in the SWP.

So, by the day of the party we'd got one dodgy amp, a couple of rattling bass speakers and a piece of tarpaulin the size of a handkerchief. We were in the nearby city trying to hire a generator and all the hire places were closed for the weekend. By now I was getting hysterical.

'Don't worry, man,' Fen said, 'I'm telling you it's gonna happen.'

Just then we bumped into Nik and Oz, the sound-system stalwarts. Half a minute later we've got a thousand-watt rig, a marquee and a clutch of the South East's finest DJs at our disposal, and the party was back on, in Fen's sacred field. The shift was so sudden, so surprising, I was almost inclined to believe Fen's assertion that the land itself has a magical and transforming effect. Fen reckons it's not him organising the party, it's his field.

Later on we're easing through a creaky gate and along a bumping track, one car and one van with a paranoid driver, nuzzling through the darkness with our lights low, and the excitement is mounting. Fen has hopped on to the back of the van and is holding on with fingers and toes. As we come to the stream he leaps off and is belting along like a lanky spider, all arms and legs, to guide us. As we come to the bank of the stream we rev up and slide in the mud, just making it to the top. Then we're passing through another gate and across a wet field to the oak tree. We unload the vehicles and everyone is breathless at the beauty and the atmosphere of the place. 'We've pulled it off,' I say to Fen, grinning, and give him the thumbs-up while he grins back at me. That's the wonder of these parties: one of life's last adventures.

Afterwards, Fen, the paranoid driver and I headed back into town to collect a table to put the decks on, leaving Nik and Oz to and their crew to put up the marquee. Only when we got back to the gate the driver said, 'This is boring, I want a drink.' We dumped the table in a field, went back to town and proceeded to get roaring drunk. By the time we finally arrived, the party was full-on with the decks on the floor and Oz moaning. So Fen and the paranoid driver stumbled off into the night to collect the table and everyone was happy. They said it was their Arthurian quest: not to get a Round Table; to get a square fifties kitchen table with tea stains and scratches like cabbalistic symbols.

The police turned up at about 5.30. They were tiptoeing gingerly through the stream when Fen spotted them. He loped barefoot across the field to greet them and grinned merrily.

'How you doin', man?' he said, holding out his hand.

'What's going on here?' they asked.

'What does it look like? It's a party.'

'How did you get in?'

'Through the gate.'

Just then, one of the party-goers broke in. 'Hi, I'm Athie. Aren't you impressed that we've found somewhere so remote we can express ourselves without disturbing anyone?'

'You might disturb the people over there,' they said, indicating the distant farmhouse.

'Yeah we might, mightn't we,' said Fen. 'Have we then?'

Silence . . .

'So what's the problem?'

'We think you're all on drugs.'

They wandered around the site asking questions. When they spoke to Oz, who was DJing at the time, and asked him what his name was, he said, 'C. J. Stone.' So I get the blame for everything. After that they woke the farmer up to ask if he'd been disturbed. He stood in his doorway, bleary-eyed in his pyjamas. 'Well, I wasn't until now,' he replied.

Later, the local press arrived.

'What's the point of this?' the reporter asked.

I told him it was the first act in our war against the road. 'We've planted a psychic bomb here,' I said. It's like a psychic barrier, only more volatile. Fen's madness must be catching.

This took place at the end of April, just before I went to see Penny Rimbaud at Deal House. The paranoid driver is called Paul. He was with me on the trip to see Pen. He's a cadaverous south London bloke, with severely cropped hair and an aggressive manner. Between the three of us – Fen, Paul and me – we managed to set up this anti-road campaign.

Paul had been a punk. At the age of seventeen he'd helped to set up a band which attained a brief notoriety. They were called Conflict and were part of a community of bands (including Crass and the Poison Girls) who'd taken the anarchist message to the world. Paul had believed, with all the fervour of youth, that punk would never die. That was his slogan: 'Punk will never die!'

They were heady, violent days, of streetfights and running battles with the Fascists ('Boneheads!' as Paul calls them), of squatting and drinking beer, of dancing and sheer exuberant joy. Youth, energy and idealism: a potent mix. He lived a life of nomadic luxury. There was a community of punks, followers of the cause, who they'd stay with, who would feed them and look after them wherever they went.

Then Paul began to fall out with the lead singer. Everyone involved in Conflict lived well: there was beer, food and lots of fun, but never any money. Meanwhile, the lead singer was being a rock star. He was singing about anarchy and the revolution, but living a different life to the rest of them. It began to seem as if these were empty slogans, that anarchy was simply a means to an end. Conflict meant business. Then one day Paul took an acid trip with some of his school friends and he became aware that there was a whole world out there, outside the punk ethos; that it had been ticking by, oblivious to their tribal concerns. He was meant to be going over to help out at the new Anarchy Centre in Wapping. He was meant to be designing Conflict's new album cover. He was meant to be doing all sorts of things. He did none of them. The lead singer saw him afterwards and said, 'You let us down.' Paul replied, 'No, *you* let *us* down.' He gave up punk and the punk style, got himself a job, and tried to live a normal life. This lasted for about eight years.

In 1987 he got into the New Age ethos. He went to Glastonbury town and immersed himself in mystical speculations. There were people from all over the world gathered there that year, awaiting a major spiritual/occult revival. People were talking about a shift in consciousness, about the old order collapsing. Within two years the Berlin Wall had come down, so in a sense their beliefs came true. People were beaming out happiness all over the place. Paul felt sure that there were advanced spirits among them.

Paul's earliest memory was of being in a hospital. Outside he could see gnarled dark oaks creaking in the breeze, twigs like fingers almost brushing the window-panes. They seemed like old men murmuring incessantly to themselves. This was Oxleas Wood, between Eltham and Welling, not far from his home. Later, during his teens, when his mum and dad were splitting up, he'd go camping in the woods with his friends. It was a place where he could hide from the storms gathering in his life and just have fun. He found a place, right in the middle, where even the drone of traffic couldn't be heard. Then, one day, years later, he discovered that they were going to build a road through it. This was just after Twyford Down had hit the headlines. He knew that he had to do everything in his power to stop this destruction.

Between them, the organisers of the Oxleas Wood campaign managed to secure 3,000 pledges from supporters saying they were willing to take direct action against the bulldozers if they moved in. The DoT caved in. To this day, the Oxleas Wood campaign is the only road protest that has actually stopped the bulldozers.

So Paul is an ex-punk, a New Ager, and a seasoned anti-roads campaigner (later he went to Twyford Down, then got involved in the M11 campaign). You can't get much more counter-culture than that. And he is paranoid – at least when it comes to driving his father-in-law's van without a licence or insurance. These days he has a wife and a child, and collects hats as a hobby.

The day after I got back from Tepee Valley there was a tree-dressing ceremony up at the Flat Oak. What's a tree-dressing ceremony? Your guess is as good as mine. Mainly it involved writing little notes to the contractors, telling them why they shouldn't damage the countryside, then hanging them from the tree. The old oak was fluttering with these little notices. It looked very jolly, very festive, like a sacred shrine.

It was VE Day. So we were there not only to protest against the road, but also to celebrate peace and the defeat of Fascism. We were remembering the sacrifices which had been made in the struggle against the political philosophy of evil, and hoping that – in our own small way – we could continue the struggle. Fascism never dies; it only finds new clothes to wear.

Fen had been camping up there ever since the party, hidden away in a little clearing in Convict's Wood. People had been bringing him supplies of water, food and dope, and – occasionally – setting up camp with him. There were about three or four of them up there by the time of the ceremony, mostly the young dope-fiends of the town. Fen was their spiritual guru. They had a nice little open-air dope-session going on most of the time.

When I arrived, Athie was sitting in the Flat Oak smoking spliffs. I had a couple of bottles of red wine with me. I opened one and climbed the tree to join her.

I'd met Athie at a party. It was Hallowe'en and we were all in fancy dress. Someone had told me about a woman who had some E, so we went into a room – I was dressed as a priest – and Athie handed me my little package. Something struck me about her immediately: a startling candour in her eyes; a certain poise; a sense that she's at ease with herself and her world.

After that I'd bump into her at demonstrations against the Criminal Justice Bill and was struck by her joyous collision with life. I'd seen her confront burly policemen head-on and laughed as they actually ran away. I'd heard her husky voice ringing out over the crowd – a proud warrior, a fearful opponent and someone definitely to be noted – and I'd wondered where this powerful spirit came from.

She had not always been like this, she told me. Although her early life was idyllic – she grew up in the wilds, in a tiny cottage without electricity or running water and with no roads for miles – her teenage years were fraught with confusion. This was after her mum and dad had split up and she'd moved back to London. She was taking drugs by the time she was fourteen, bunked off school and got herself expelled, fell out with her stepdad. Then, after she'd been forced to move in with her dad, she fell out with her dad's girlfriend too. She was tossed from here to there like a burning coal, too hot to handle, and a messed-up kid became a messed-up adult in a messed-up world.

Athie was a very negative person. She believed that the human race was done for, finished, pegging out its last days in a mad ritual of despair. So what was the point in working for anything? She saved up her money from her first job, jacked it in, then went off to Goa.

It was there that things began to change. There was a new thing happening. It was happening in Ibiza, too, and in Amsterdam. By the time she got back, it was happening in London. A mad new music. A revelatory new drug. A new spirit and a new hope: acid house. It was beautiful for a time.

'For the first time ever there were situations where there weren't any barriers. There'd be Rastas and skin'eads and punks, and everybody was just partying together and there was this amazing feeling of strength and unity, and people were really starting to communicate.' As she speaks her eyes are shimmering and there's a tone of relish in her voice. This was 1988/89, the Summer of Love.

After that, she hit a bad one again. She thought, 'But this isn't gonna get anywhere, just living it up, never doing anything,' and after two years of solid E-ing: the inevitable depression. A negative worm was eating at her insides. She spent one last weekend over-the-top partying in a deliberate attempt to do so much she'd never want to do it again.

On the Sunday morning she's fumbling about in a shop, spaced-out, when this bloke comes up to her and says, 'You know today is Earth Day?'

She's confused. Why does he want to tell her it's his birthday? 'No, *Earth* Day,' he says.

She looks at him sceptically and says, 'Look, I really think we've done irreparable damage, so let's just get on and enjoy the last bit.' On the word 'irreparable', she can see that he's agitated.

'You know any junkies?' he says.

'Yes, a few.'

So he goes on to tell her about a smack-head, how he's at death's door and all his friends are sat at his bedside thinking this is it, he's had it now; and how, three years later, he's kicked the habit and this guy is a healthy, happy human being, with a kid and a future. As this story is drilling into her, she realises he's not only talking about a junkie, he's talking about the earth.

Later, she's labouring up a hill. She can feel these thoughts zooming in from somewhere, from some secret space in the universe, and she rushes home and writes: 'Athie: three things. 1) Do not try to justify your existence, merely exist. 2) Goodness is everywhere, you only have to look for it. 3) Any form of energy never ceases to exist.' She says to me, 'In the end, whether we survive as a species or not, it's all right. If we don't, it's because it's best for everything else and, anyway, energy carries on.' Ever since then, she's been a positive person.

Well, this is her life and it means something. Athie is the product of a new culture. Her dad was a hippie and she's a raver, and it's not the drugs (she saves them for special occasions), it's the lifestyle. She went to her first festival when she was fourteen and was amazed that such a place could exist. The sun was shining and everybody was relaxed. No police presence and yet people seemed to get on. Later, after the post-acid house

126

revelations, she took to the road herself, moving from festival to festival all over the country during the summer months, doing a tea stall. 'What a way to make your money and survive,' she says. 'Freedom. People living as they choose instead of being dictated to. Community. People caring for each other without being scared because of the barriers they put up.'

Well, the Criminal Justice Bill is now law. It exists, in part, to stop this lifestyle, to stop travellers and ravers and road protesters and animal-rights activists. It is an attempt to suppress nature, she says, just like the road-building programme. It wants to cover our feelings in Tarmac and chop down our dreams. But it shows the government's fear. It shows their desperation. You can't legislate against the spirit, she says. All it has really achieved is to unite the disparate groups against it.

So it's New Year's Eve. Two and a half thousand people at a party, in a warehouse so huge she thinks she's in the open air, until she looks up and sees the roof-arch like a firmament disappearing above her. She speaks to no one, but she doesn't have to. A certain something. An indivisible spirit. The music is saying it. She's hearing it in the lyrics, and in the relentless flood of sound and rhythm. People's eyes are saying it, in the startled realisation of their common humanity. People's movements are saying it, in the joyous expression of dance. We all come from the same source. We all have the same aims, the same hopes, the same fears. And in the sweating mêlée of their mutual joy, they all seem to be having the same thought too. This is the time of change. Spiritual time. Revolution time. Not an end; a beginning.

Athie was telling me about a party she'd been to over the weekend. It was a small free festival, held outside an airforce base. Athie was tripping and there was some sort of scene. One of the travellers was beaten up and his bus trashed. The story was that he'd ripped people off and was only getting his due, but later the bus was brought round to the front of the stage, like a centre-piece, like a symbol, and systematically dismantled. It was like a scene from a Mad Max movie. There were naked traveller's kids smashing up this van, traipsing round in bare feet amid all the broken glass.

'It's starting,' Athie said to me, her green eyes startlingly clear and bright.

Athie believes that the spiritual revolution is on its way and that things will have to get worse as they get better. We're emerging into a new time and there will be a price to pay. 'We are getting down to the core,' she said and looked at me with such fierce intensity it made me shiver.

Later, I went into the woods and met Fen. He showed me where he'd been camping these last few weeks. We stood by the circle of fire and Fen told me that he'd spent lifetimes in this very spot, watching this very fire.

'Sometimes I'd be standing here staring into this fire and know that there was another being, on some other planet, watching another fire just like me, and that we were in communication.'

He told me he'd been waiting his whole life for this moment, this road protest. It was his destiny. He'd been coming here since he was a boy. Later, he'd had all these strange experiences – on acid usually, but they still defied reason. He said he believed that the land itself had chosen him.

I knew about his strange experiences. He'd told me about them before. One night I'd sat enthralled while Fen had woven magical tales out of the air, casting us both back into a mythic time before rationality had measured out the world into ordered little packages. The world, as Fen described it, was full of portents, messages. It was mysterious, visionary. It knew no bounds.

One night he and two pals were up here, sitting in the woods by a fire. They'd taken some acid and were waiting for it to come on. Fen noticed that the smoke from the fire, instead of diffusing, was gathering like a fog. It was a full moon. He asked the others if they could see it too, but they said no, they couldn't. They sat in an unnatural silence for about five minutes, while fear began to take a grip in Fen's mind. The smoke was gathering and gathering, blotting out the moon. It was eerie. Then Fen couldn't stand it any more. He let out a yelp and started to run. He ran and ran, until he was out of the woods and up on a rise overlooking them. His friends had followed. They turned to look back when, suddenly, the fire leaped out of the woods and into the sky. It somersaulted and let out a piercing screech – whee, whee, whee! – before it dived back into the trees. Everyone saw it. It had the air of some malevolent spirit which had become entangled in the fire and which was now revealing itself. It was a perfectly clear night, except over the woods, where a razor-edged cloud brooded like an alien presence.

Another time there were two of them in the field near the Flat Oak, tripping as usual. It was just starting to get dark. Suddenly they saw beams, like ultraviolet light. They were free-flowing, independent beams, wriggling through the air like fishes. There were thousands of them. They seemed to be sweeping the area, searching for something, and there was something palpable about them. Fen could feel them passing through his body like a shiver. This lasted for about ten minutes, during which time the beams zeroed in on the two trippers. The lights were vibrating with a peculiar intensity. One minute it was twilight, the next it was utterly dark. They found themselves on the same spot, only now they were sitting down. Some time had passed, though they had no memory of it, and around them, at about half-mile intervals, there were what looked like several floodlights. Fen knew that something had happened to them, though he couldn't say what it was. The lights winked out, one by one, until there was only one left. It seemed to be indicating to them, so they followed it. It led them home.

Once they were back in Fen's flat, they looked at the clock.

Five hours had passed since their disappearance. 'I was abducted by aliens, I'm convinced of it!' Fen said, and he told me that when he got home the tea made itself. 'I went to boil the kettle, but the kettle was already hot. Then I looked in the teapot and there was already tea in it, and there were cups there with milk and sugar already in them.'

I said, 'Oh, come on now. Surely you just forgot you'd made the tea yourself. You were tripping, after all.'

'No, I'm telling you: the tea made itself.'

It's events like these that Fen cites to justify his stance against the road. He believes that the land itself harbours spiritual forces, which he has picked up on. He was brought up on a ley-line, the same one that passes through this very spot. Ley-lines are like the neural network of the planet: they connect all the spiritual centres around the globe. Historically, the dark forces have wanted to take the power that courses through these lines, to keep the power for themselves. They do this by cutting the lines, or by building on the focal points along them. 'Pathways of consciousness' Fen calls them. He says that they belong to the common people, that they are our historical inheritance, and that if ever the people gained access to these energies, then governments would fall. This is his version of revolution.

Later on, everyone was sat around a fire by the oak tree. There were about twenty people gathered, chatting away, getting drunk and stoned.

Athie was sitting across from me. Suddenly she announced, 'Right, I'm moving in up here.' She'd decided to join the road protest. She was in the middle of her finals and was giving it all up to stop this road. Athie has a slogan. It consists of one word: 'Strive!'

Fen was talking to a couple of women. They seemed very impressed by his rhetoric. He invited them back to his tent in the woods and they followed him. It was his lucky night.

9 The Road to Nowhere

I said we'd planted a psychic bomb. That was true.

Within a week of the tree-dressing ceremony my life was changed beyond all recognition; blown apart, fractured into a million pieces, exploded into shrapnel.

If you want to know why this book is such a shambles, look no further. It was the road protest.

Even now I get an attack of anxiety every time I think about it. I'm anxious now, as I write these words.

So on the Friday evening I was composing my account of the Tepee Valley weekend. I'd finished the section about Amesbury and was pretty pleased with it. Afterwards, I went to the pub where there was a road-protest party. Fen was there and a few of the others. We had a few beers and everything was cool.

The camp at the Flat Oak was going strong. I'd been to see the farmer who'd not exactly discouraged us in our activities. When

I asked whether we could camp in the field he'd said, 'Well, I need the crop in the top half of the field.' He seemed to be implying that he could dispense with the bottom half. There was a ramshackle tepee there by now, made of rough branches and bin bags, and about twenty people camping. Word had gone round to other road-protest groups around the country that this one was about to kick-off, though no one had turned up yet. It was the calm before the storm. Almost everyone was at the pub with us.

Suddenly Athie burst in. Athie, with all her sizzling, green-eyed intensity.

'The diggers are coming. They're going to start this week. They've already laid out the markers. We've got to do something now.'

'Do something? Do what?'

'Something. We've got to do something.'

I can't remember if we did anything or not. I think a couple of us may have driven up to the site and glanced around. We may have laughingly talked about sabotage. That's about it.

The following day there was a phone call.

'We're trying to get over to the road protest. We've hitched from the West Country. We've just walked about twenty miles and we're fucked. Can you come and pick us up?'

I agreed. I drove over – three-quarters of an hour there, three-quarters of an hour back – to find them in a Happy Eater just outside a little town on the main south coast road. This was Simon and Andy.

It was obvious who they were as soon as I walked into the café. Andy is about six foot five, built like a radio mast only thinner, and dressed in combat gear, with a morose face and long, snaking dreadlocks. Simon is a diminutive ex-merchant seaman, covered in tattoos and with multiple body piercings, including one through his tongue. They stood out in the Happy Eater like two exotic dancers at a church service. In that pristine, plastic interior, their grime-streaked faces, their ragged clothing and their lively, gesticulatory manner seemed to dominate the room. They were already on first-name terms with the staff.

I took them to the camp via Fen's house. Fen came out to greet them.

'Welcome on board,' he said. 'There's some gorgeous countryside out there.'

When I left them at the camp they were already tying themselves into their climbing gear. It looked kinky to me, like bondage, and Andy was giving lessons in tree-climbing to all the wide-eyed trainee eco-warriors who looked upon these two as the epitome of anarchist revolutionaries. Which is what they must have been. They looked the part.

The following evening we had a meeting round the fire. There were maybe about thirty people there: supporters from the town, campers, and some of the new people who'd begun to turn up. There'd been a communal meal, cooked on the open fire. It was dark by now, the firelight flickering around a mass of contented faces. We passed around a rough hunk of wood, introduced ourselves and each made a short speech. We called the rough hunk of wood 'the talking stick'. No one was allowed to interrupt you when you had it in your hand.

Simon had told me earlier that he was going to lose his temper. He'd said that the organisation was a shambles. 'What do this lot think they're up to? This is a road camp, not a holiday camp. Everyone's just sitting round smoking dope, doing nothing. Well, they've got to work. Otherwise, what's the point? I'm gonna let rip, man. I'm gonna blow. And when I lose my temper, man, you should see it. Everyone will just have to listen.'

When it came down to it he was as gentle as a lamb. He muttered a few kindly words about how glad he was to be here. And that was it.

I said that we had to define our roles and stick with them. I said I'd been working full-on all day (which I had, driving

133

round, buying food and equipment, chasing about here, there and everywhere) and that all we'd asked people to do was to dig a fire-pit, which had never got dug. I said that we had to rely on people to do what they said they were going to do. This is what Simon had said he was going to say. So I said it instead.

Someone else said, 'I'm Tom and I believe in revolution,' then passed on the stick. Athie whooped at this and a couple of people clapped, while the eco-warriors looked on with puzzled frowns. You'd think they'd never heard the word 'revolution'.

But there was one speech I remember very clearly. It was from a relaxed-looking bearded guy wearing a woolly hat with a spray of plastic sunflowers attached. He was lying on his side, resting his cheek on his hand. He said, 'My name is Sun-Flo-Wer.' He said it like that, in three distinct syllables, the way you might talk to a toddler, enunciating the sounds with careful precision and emphasising the 'w': Sun-Flo-Wer. 'I was at the land occupation at George's Green. There were two police officers there. One of them said, "What's going on here?" and the other one said, "I don't know. We have very little intelligence."

'You'll have to excuse me,' he continued, 'I do go on a bit. I thought I was on my way to the West Country. I got in a van to take me down there, but we decided to pay you a visit on the way. Now I've decided to stay. I believe in magic moments. When I was a kid I was always bird-watching and I always wanted to hear a nightingale sing, but I never got the chance. So this is a magic moment right now. Listen.' And he paused, enough to let us hear the bird-song echoing from the distant woods. 'A nightingale.'

That speech blew my head apart. That's the nature of love: it blows your head apart. Love cannot be kept in a box. It is the most dangerous thing in the universe. It's possible for one person to say one thing to you which can change your whole life. It was like being in love with an idea. Like being in love with a thought. Like being in love with a whole group of people all at the same time. I was lost in the atmosphere. All of these people, all hugging each other, all bonded by the same cause, intense in their belief that this really meant something, that they could transform the world. Real camaraderie. Real intensity. Real power.

Fen's stuff about the land having a power of its own seemed to be true. When you live within the landscape, framed by it instead of framing it, breathing the air, hearing the breeze bustling through the trees, sleeping under the stars, cooking food on an open fire – acting out this ancient, almost nomadic way of life – something happens to you. It's as if the spirit of the land enters you. It fills you up. You become the landscape. I'd never felt anything like this before. I'd never felt so at one with my surroundings. My revelation at the Plumpton rave – all of my talk about the spiritual revolution – seemed to be coming true. Everything I'd ever believed in. Everything I'd dreamed about. Everything I'd hoped and prayed for. It was happening, right now. Nothing else mattered. Not my home. Not my work. Not even this book. The road protest was everything. It took me over.

I went to bed that night in a tent which had been pitched over the roots of a tree. I curled my body so that it seemed to mould to the roots. My body fitted snugly into that weaving, curling web. I went to sleep to the sounds of the young dope-fiends blowing pipes and giggling.

The following morning Fen woke us all up. He was panting with exhaustion. He'd run the whole distance across the fields.

'They've started work,' he said, between gasps.

We could see the digger about a mile away across the fields, ripping up the hedgerows, dodging backwards and forwards, and letting off little puffs of black smoke from its exhaust. We marched over in a line, following the edge of the fields to avoid damaging any of the crops. We were spotted and the digger tried to make a run for it. Simon managed to catch up and was soon perched by the cab, making small-talk with the driver. The driver's name was John. He was startled at first, but soon warmed to Simon's particular brand of disarmingly friendly warfare. They were soon chatting about John's kids and their future. It must have taken a bit of getting used to, being brow-beaten by a laughing midget with jet-black hair and a stud through his tongue. He was very intense, was Simon. He seemed to be looking at you from a point on his forehead.

Eventually the contractors agreed to stop work for the day and we all traipsed back to the camp. Only once we were gone, they started up again. They were panicking like crazy. They barged through a fence with a £25,000 stallion behind it. Simon recaptured the stallion and fixed the fence for the farmer.

By the following day, even more people had turned up. There were a couple of Italian girls and a Belgian girl. Lots of dreadlocks and pink Mohicans and nose-rings and flares. Lots of woolly jumpers. One of the Italian girls shook my hand and looked deeply into my eyes. She had curly hair and dark, hooded eyes. Her name was Miriam. I was instantly in love.

Fen had decided that he wanted to get arrested. Fen, Simon and three more people climbed up on John's digger and refused to get off, even when the police came. They were all arrested, under section 63 of the Criminal Justice Act. Fen was the last to come down. He held on to the piston-arm of the digger, all the muscles of his arms straining, his jaw set with determination, his teeth clenched. It took two policemen to haul him off. They handcuffed his arms behind his back and dragged him down, but at the bottom they momentarily let go. Fen was off like a hare, loping across the fields, almost bent double, with his handcuffs rattling behind his back. It took them about five minutes to catch him. He was dodging about between the trees, while everyone laughed and clapped.

Later in the afternoon I went back to the camp. There was a TV journalist there. He was chatting to Rick. I was supposed to be the press officer and I tried getting a conversation with him, but he ignored me. He was interested only in Rick. He was being far too chummy with him – suspiciously so.

That evening we had our weekly meeting at the pub. There was an intense atmosphere. The air was charged with electricity. Fen, Simon and the others walked in, after eleven hours in the cells. The atmosphere broke. Everyone was clapping and cheering, while they raised their fists in salute. The return of the heroes. We loved them.

Fen told me that Simon had gained a convert at the police station. One young officer had been so entranced by Simon that he'd spent the whole day sitting next to him on the floor of the cell, discussing the earth and the future and the road programme and all of Simon's beliefs. The young officer was hanging on to Simon's every word, as if this was John the Baptist himself sitting next to him, in a police cell, in a small town, on the South Coast of England.

The following day we held another demonstration at the construction site. Only this time we had TV crews and press there. Banners were floating and Miriam was playing the drums, and people were chanting and singing and stamping on the digger. Everyone was dancing fiercely, like pagans at an earth ceremony. The whole atmosphere was like a party.

Someone had decided that anyone of us who spoke to the press or the police was to give their name as Ted Dance. It was quoted in the papers later: 'Spokesman Ted Dance says . . . '

Athie called me from the top of the digger.

'How you doin', Ted?' she said.

'I'm not Ted, I'm Wally,' I said.

'Oh yeah, Wally. So how you doin', Wally?'

'I'm all right, Ted, and how are you?'

The police turned up in strength. There were a couple of sinister-looking figures with a camera. This particular sect have been a prominent feature at demonstrations ever since the

Criminal Justice Act was first put forward as a bill. They dress in black military-type uniforms, without numbers: black overalls tapering down to black boots, black anoraks, black baseball caps. They look like something out of a bad science-fiction movie. They carry an unusual-looking grey camera, and wear earphones and small microphones obtruding from their combat jackets, which they talk into as they film.

They were filming everyone very carefully. They'd stand in front of you and pointedly run the camera down, then up, pausing on your face. I grinned at them and did a 'Hello, Mum' wave, but I wouldn't let them film anyone else. I'd keep moving in front of the camera. They warned me: 'If you continue to block our view, then we'll be forced to arrest you for obstruction.' I stepped in the way again. They were becoming exasperated. The one not holding the camera would drag me away physically, then I'd step back into view.

'Who do you think you are?' I asked.

I'd not liked the look of these people from the first moment I'd laid eyes on them. To me, it seemed a sinister development in policing. It was as if they were trying to get the whole counter-culture movement on film. Maybe they took stills from these films and there was a database somewhere with everyone's photograph on file.

By now, they were getting very angry. Someone had joined me and was dancing around and waving her T-shirt in front of the camera. If it wasn't me, stepping in front of the camera in my cheap grey suit, it was her with her T-shirt.

'I'm warning you,' the one not holding the camera said, but they seemed either powerless or unwilling to make an arrest.

'What do you think you look like dressed up like that?' I asked. 'You look like Fascists to me.'

'And what do you think *you* look like?' they asked me in return. 'You look like a prat.'

The suit had cost 50p from a jumble sale. It dated from the

138

seventies. It had slight flares and huge lapels. And I had on a purple and red polka-dot tie and a purple and red shirt. So I suppose they had a point there.

A high-ranking officer came over to talk to me. I pointedly ignored him. The drums were crashing and pounding on top of the digger and everyone was going wild, whooping and screaming. The atmosphere had become deranged. You couldn't hear yourself think. It was like a war dance. The officer kept saying things to me and I kept turning my back, refusing to hear. I thought that if he wasn't able to warn us, then he couldn't arrest us.

One of the protesters came over and everyone went quiet to listen to him. He said that there was an animal sanctuary near by and that the animals were becoming distressed with all the noise. This is what the police officer had been trying to say to me. We agreed to continue the protest out on the road.

While the majority of us were meekly filing out on to the road, the police swooped on four people who'd been left behind. Athie was among them. She was frog-marched to the waiting van and was roaring at the officers who were holding on to her arms. They were looking sheepish. I didn't envy them.

Out on the verge, the media circus was performing. There were TV cameras, TV journalists and sound-engineers with huge boom mikes like dead dogs on sticks. There were radio journalists with microphones, and local newspaper journalists with pens and note pads scratching out their observations in shorthand. And there were photographers with cameras slung about their necks, kneeling down and looking for the unusual angle. 'Look over here, deary, that's right. Now raise your fist. Make out like you're really angry. That's it, love. Perfect.'

Everyone was having a wonderful time. Nothing like this had ever happened in our little town before.

Rick was being interviewed by the TV journalist he'd met the afternoon before. After the interview the interviewer was slapping Rick's back and putting on a show of chumminess. Rick and he were on first-name terms. He was called Mike or Dave or something equally down-to-earth. He kept calling Rick 'mate'.

Afterwards, Rick and I got involved in a conversation with a local police sergeant. Sergeant Pat. He's a nice man. Obviously graduated at the *Dixon of Dock Green* school of policing, rather than *The Sweeney* or *The Bill*.

He said, 'I see my job as much keeping the young officers in line as dealing with the public. Some of the youngsters can get too cocky.'

Rick said, 'I believe in revolution, myself.'

Sergeant Pat listened patiently. You could see that he was concerned to keep everything above board and peaceable.

I spoke to another bunch of officers leaning against their squad cars in the compound. The protesters were coming out to tell me about a certain amount of rough handling. The officers were looking at me sternly as I approached them. There was a WPC among them.

I said, 'I just want to make sure that we're allowed to go about our protest peaceably.'

One of them replied, 'I don't think you should be allowed to protest at all.'

'Tell that to your WPC,' I said. 'If the suffragettes hadn't protested, she wouldn't have the vote now.'

'I don't know about that,' said the police officer, glowering.

I went home that night to watch the news reports on TV. It was appalling. The whole thing was a set-up. The voice-over kept referring to the new road as a 'road-widening project'. Who's ever heard of a road-widening project taking place two miles from the road it's supposed to be widening? And the reason for Down-to-Earth Dave's mateyness with Rick became clear. The interview had been a set-up with Rick as the patsy. The journalist had specifically chosen Rick for his shambolic style. At this point in time, Rick had his head shaved patchily on

140

one side, while the hair on the other side dangled in greasy rat-tails. He was wearing baggy, ripped clothes that looked like he'd found them in a skip. And Rick is never articulate at the best of times. When the reporter asked, 'And what exactly are you objecting to?' Rick replied, 'This is the only bit of countryside between here and the woods,' indicating with his hands. It didn't make sense. Aren't the woods countryside too?

The way Rick came across fitted in perfectly with everyone's prejudices about road protesters as messed-up hippies, even though, in fact, he had never been on a road protest before. We had barristers and professional people on our side. People in suits. Smart middle-class people that the general public would have paid attention to, but Matey Mike (or whatever his name was) had chosen someone who couldn't even button up his shirt in the right order. The whole thing had been constructed to make us look like a bunch of idiots. Rick had suddenly become the official face of the road protest.

The phone rang. Fen told me that there had been four more arrests that afternoon: thirteen arrests in two days.

I can't even begin to describe the intensity of my feelings over those few days. I was eating, sleeping, shitting and dreaming road protest.

People were approaching me on the street to discuss the issue. They were either for us or against us. Either way, their tone was aggressive.

The kids on my estate crowded round me when I came home the following day to get breakfast.

'We saw you on the telly,' they said.

'Oh yes? And what was I doing?'

'You were telling a policeman what to do!'

They'd seen the bit where I was arguing with the man with the camera. The idea of people being able to tell policemen what to do seemed almost magical to them.

Simon rang me up. 'Listen, I've got something amazing to tell you,' he said. 'You know we were charged under section 63 of the Criminal Justice Act? Well section 63 is about organising an illegal rave. We've been charged with organising a rave on top of a digger!'

I burst into hysterical laughter.

Then Simon said, 'I've got to talk to you. There's something I've got to tell you.'

We arranged a meeting that afternoon.

I drove over to Athie's house with Fen, and Simon and I went for a walk. He told me he'd been out and about when a stranger had approached him.

'I'm warning you,' the stranger had said.

'What are you warning me?'

'We don't normally talk to people. We break legs, but I'm being kind in your case. I'm warning you first.'

'Who are you?' asked Simon. 'Let me see your badge.'

'And we don't answer questions, either. We know who you are,' and he recounted Simon's entire history. 'And we know who the ringleaders are.' He mentioned my name.

Simon asked me what my middle name was. I told him.

'That's right,' he said. 'The geezer knew your middle name.'

I'd been having strange phone calls for a day or two now. The phone would ring and there'd be no one on the other end, or whoever it was would hear my voice and hang up immediately. I hadn't really thought about it. Now it seemed to be more insidious.

'Who do you think he was?' I asked Simon.

'Dunno. MI5. Don't say anything to anybody though, will you? We don't want to upset anyone.'

I drove back home with Fen and told him what Simon had said. I felt I needed to speak to someone about this, despite my promise to keep quiet.

Fen said, 'If they know your name, then I'm bound to be on their list.'

'Fen, it was my name they mentioned, not yours!'

'I know, but I started this road protest, and I was in the woods before anybody else. I'm tellin' you, they must know I'm the leader.'

I was regretting ever having said anything. I didn't want to make it sound as if I were more important than him – I'm not – but it was irritating me that he seemed to want to claim some kind of glory for any danger that I might be in.

'Fen,' I said, 'I'm a nationally known journalist. I organised a march and rally against the Criminal Justice Bill last year, and gave my name and address to the Metropolitan police force. I've been a member of the Advance Party, which is known in government circles for its opposition to the bill, and I've written several articles making clear my opposition to it. I'm worried. A complete stranger approaches Simon and mentions my name. It was my name, not yours. I've been getting weird phone calls. I wanted to talk to you because you are a friend of mine. No reflection on you, but you've never done anything like this before. I wish I'd not told you now.'

Fen's professional paranoia had been worrying me for some time. He always seemed to want to blow things out of proportion. One day he'd announced that the archaeological dig taking place on the hill overlooking the Flat Oak was a front. It wasn't a dig at all. It was a way of keeping an eye on us, or a way of sneaking machinery in without us noticing. Just then I'd seen Tim, an old archaeologist friend of mine, emerging from the dig at the end of the day.

The following day we went to visit Tim at the archaeological site. He offered us tacit support in our endeavours. He said that the police had been using the site (which was prominent, on top of a hill) as a vantage point to observe the protest – at least some of Fen's suspicions were true – but that when the policemen had tried to disparage us, Tim had said that he agreed with what we were doing.

Another time, Fen had seen someone working on a roof near the line of the proposed road. 'They're dismantling that building by stealth,' he announced, with a tone of absolute authority.

I went over to take a look. It was a builder friend of mine.

'Are you taking the building down?' I called up to him.

'No! I'm fixing the roof,' he said, looking hurt.

Fen has an arrogant streak. When he believes something, he believes it with absolute conviction, and no one in the world is going to change his mind. It's quite endearing when you're discussing philosophical matters. He comes up with so many weird notions, then argues his point with such absurd conviction that you end up laughing. However, on operational matters it could be dangerous. He was likewise equally convinced that a set of diggers over on the golf course had been put there for reasons of stealth. When I argued with him he started ranting. Later, Fen's view became the prevailing one and the diggers were immobilised. Thousands of pounds' worth of damage. As it happens, they were there only to construct new greens for the golf course. The golf players, who'd previously been indifferent to us, became our enemies overnight.

I'd been sleeping at the camp, where the prevailing drug was dope, so, being an unregenerate alcoholic, I went down the pub that evening to get my fix. I ended up arguing with everyone in there about the road. I was burning with tension and a strange, exhilarating kind of anxiety. After the pub closed, I tottered off to my own little bed. There was a scrap of paper attached to my window, pinned there by the wind. It was a ripped page from a child's colouring book. There was a picture of a tree and, in the corner, in capital letters, was written 'OAK TREE'.

It was a magic moment.

I felt that the tree was calling me. I drove back up to the campsite and fell asleep among its curling roots.

The following day I was awake early. No one else was stirring, so I went over to collect Fen and take a look along the length of the road. As we passed the woods near where the camp was located, we saw three or four meat wagons full of police. They were evicting the site. We carried on driving. We got to the top of the road and Athie was there, in a phone box. She called over to us. She was speaking to a solicitor on the phone. I started talking to him, to find out what we could do. He was detailing all the possible tactics, while Athie was outside the box getting frantic. She kept telling me we *had* to be at the site *right now*. I was trying to talk to the solicitor, while Athie was gesticulating at me impatiently. She was constantly brow-beating me and it was getting on my nerves. I ignored her. When I'd finished the phone call I drove back to the pathway to the site; the camp was a good three-quarters of a mile along this path. I walked down there and was on site before Athie.

Later I went to see the farmer.

'I thought you said it was OK to stay on your land,' I said.

'I've been getting ear'oled,' he said, and he made the hand-sign for someone yakking away at his ear. 'The police. The neighbours. The magistrates. The council. Local businessmen, some of whom are villains. I'm fed up with it, and I don't want some little oiks coming round here and threatening my wife and children.'

I took that to mean that someone *had* been round there threatening his wife and children.

I went back to the site to inform them of what I'd heard. I gave Sunflower a tenner so he could buy some cider. Then I went driving round trying to sort out a new site and a van to remove all of the equipment.

Several of the local youths had become fully fledged road protesters by now, contributing their skills to the cause, lured by the excitement, the freedom and the large number of attractive young women that had descended upon our town. One skill in particular, nurtured by my council estate, had proved invaluable. When the police came to visit squat number two, they were impressed by the seamless entry. 'How on earth did you get in?' they asked. The building had seemed impregnable, sealed up and shuttered like the sarcophagus at Chernobyl. This had to be the first time in history that house-breaking as a skill had served the community at large.

So squat number two became the new base-camp. It was a luxury bungalow surrounded by about an acre of ground. It had central heating and an electric cooker, a bath, showers and several very large rooms. It was called 'The Oaks', which we took as a mystical sign. Mystical signs were the order of the day, though they never seemed to do us much good.

That evening, there was a meeting at the Oaks. Everyone was very frazzled. The talking stick didn't work. No one was paying any attention to it. They were just shouting at each other across the room.

There were rumours flying about like crazy. The farmer's children had been threatened by a bunch of gangsters with baseball bats. Everyone knew the names of all the people supposedly committing the threats. I realised that I was the source of this rumour and tried to scotch it. The farmer hadn't necessarily been threatened, I told them. He'd implied that he might have been threatened, or that he was worried about the possibility of threats. He'd never said from whom.

The pressure was intense in there. You had to watch what you said. Every little thing was picked up on, then repeated over and over again till it bore no resemblance to the original statement.

Sunflower blew up at me. He'd been drinking cheap cider all day. He said that he hated bullies and that when I'd informed him that the farmer had been threatened, he'd wanted to go round and sort out the perpetrators straight away. He'd spent the whole day brooding over it, getting drunk and falling out with all his friends.

I went to the pub that night with Fen and got roaring drunk. All week I'd been leaving messages on my answerphone, giving updates on the campaign. After the thirteenth arrest I'd said, 'Thirteen arrests. Thirteen is the number of lunar months in the year. It's the number of Christ and his disciples, the number of King Arthur and his Knights of the Round Table. It's a magical number.' A friend, who was at the pub, made some disparaging remark about the message. I blew up at him. I started ranting. I was burning with righteous indignation, attacking him and the whole world for their indifference and stupidity, railing against hypocrisy and deceit, and the quiet collusion of an indifferent population in all the injustices of the world. Then I was crying, there in the pub, in front of everyone.

My friend said, 'I was only being affectionate, Chris. It was a little harmless ribbing, that's all.'

I was losing it. I was losing my hold on reality. I was losing my perspective. Now I'd lost my sense of humour, too. That was too great a loss to bear.

Fen said, 'You need a rest.'

He was right. I went home to bed.

10 Beanfield

It felt like we were under psychic attack.

That sounds mad now, from this safe distance, and yet that is
precisely how it felt: a dark blitz; a war zone in the country of
the mind.

I pride myself in maintaining a certain rationalism, but when
you open yourself up to another person's rhetoric you tend to
absorb some of the content. I'd been spending a lot of time around
Fen. We were comrades in this enterprise and some of Fen's grand
historical/magical conspiracy talk was beginning to rub off.

Fen had said that bodies would be unearthed. And bodies
were unearthed. First, at the archaeological dig, where an Iron
Age cremation pot was found. Then later, a couple of the
protesters found a human skull in the woods while they were
cutting hazel for their benders. It was the remains of a suicide
some seven years previously.

Fen met an old woman on one of the footpaths that crossed the line of the road. She talked of ancient curses, historical massacres and weird conspiracies. She spoke of a hidden treasure soon to be unearthed, and future deaths, and a whole range of strange, unnerving stuff. Of course, Fen bought the whole lot.

I wasn't sure what to believe. I knew that I was suffering from deep levels of anxiety and that some odd things seemed to be happening around me. Those phone calls, for instance. They continued on a daily basis. I was being interviewed by a local reporter and was telling him about this when the phone rang. Silence. I handed the phone to him so that he could be a witness.

I'd been living in this town for nearly ten years, and had been writing my *Guardian* column for the last two of these, and hardly anyone had noticed. A few friends, that's all. I'd been fairly discreet about it. Now, all of a sudden, I was scared. I decided that the best form of defence is attack. I would go on the offensive, become so prominent that no one would dare touch me. I did an interview with a sympathetic local reporter, naming me as a key figure in the road protest and revealing my profession as a journalist. It went out as a double-page centre spread, along with photographs.

At the same time I was talking to all the local papers and the rest of the media. My name was being trumpeted throughout the town. You couldn't pick up a paper without me being in it. People were approaching me constantly to talk about the issue. The phone never stopped ringing. I was talking to people from all parts of the country, who were offering help, or asking for information or directions to the site. I began to suspect that my phone was bugged. The whole thing was getting out of hand.

I'd said to Fen a long time ago, 'The best we can do is to stop the road. The worst is that we can get up their noses and bring the issue to public attention. Either way, we can't lose.'

That had been my approach initially. I was going to do my best, that's all. But I was drawn into it as a life-and-death struggle. Every minor set-back seemed like a catastrophe. Every victory was a historic victory. I was losing my perspective.

At the same time, people were descending upon us from all parts of the country. A bunch of people turned up from the Pollock estate in Glasgow. Full circle. People were coming from London and Brighton and Northern Ireland. At one point there were about twenty vehicles parked up in the drive at the squat, and a huge bus parked up on the verge outside. I recognised some of them from my work with road-protest groups in the past. Then I'd met them with a certain front, with the dignity of a national paper behind me. Now I was just one of them. The images of me as a local bloke who likes a pint or two with his friends, and me as a journalist, were becoming confused. The line between my work and my life, which I had valued, was fast becoming blurred. I wasn't even sure who I was any more.

People were squabbling constantly. The meetings were a shambles: everyone shouting at each other, no one letting any one else talk, no decisions being made, no resolution of problems. Bad vibes and argument. Miriam hated Sunflower, who hated Athie, who hated Andy, who moped around glumly when he couldn't get his own way. Simon simply seemed like a braggart. He was always full of grand promises, none of which he ever fulfilled. He was going to climb the tower of the cathedral and abseil down naked, painted blue. It sounded spectacular. Instead of which he sat about drinking tea and sulking.

There was a meeting at the pub one evening. As usual, Athie was dominating the proceedings. Suddenly, Sunflower threw a tantrum. He was thrashing his arms and legs about like a five-year-old, swearing and banging on the table. He knocked my pint out of my hand.

I was getting it from every angle. People telling me what to do all the time. Too many chiefs and not enough indians. Everyone seemed to be turning into overblown petty dictators. I expect the same was true of me.

One day I was in the town. People were coming up to me to tell me that Rick was on the high street, pissed, and that he was collecting money for the road protest. When I found him he was staggering all over the place, waving a bottle of wine and a collection box at people, and picking arguments with the passers-by. When I tried to stop him, he blew up at me.

'I'm fucking pissed off with you always telling me what to do. Everything you say is negative,' he said, poking his bottle towards me.

Later, he turned up at the squat. There was no food in the house. We needed nails and rope and tools and wood and petrol for the cars. Rick handed over about 50p, then clambered in through the window. He took out a lump of hash and proceeded to make a spliff. That's what he'd spent the collection money on – a lump of hash.

In a way, Rick typifies everything I've hated about the counter-culture scene: shambolic, disorganised, drug-soaked, blurting out mindless slogans to a drunken audience, pleasure-seeking, middle class, thoughtless.

Now I have to make a confession. Rick is my nemesis. He's what I'd like to be. The truth is, I'm jealous. All of the descriptions in the previous paragraph are meaningless. They skate over the surface of things. Rick is popular, and I'm not. He's friendly, and I'm not. He's expansive, and I'm stuck in a shell. He's expressive, and I'm taciturn. He draws people to him, while I drive them away. He enjoys himself, and I don't. People feel indulgent towards him, while they feel defensive towards me. He is confident with women, while I just cry into my beer.

That scene from the Prologue, where Rick and I are rolling around drunkenly, lurching about, trying to get a New Year's kiss: typical Rick. Typical me, too.

Rick has a slogan. It consists of three words: 'Exuberance is holy.' I think he got it from William Blake. It sort of explains him, and it explains what is wrong with him, too: pure, undirected exuberance, like a flood. The best use of water is to irrigate the fields. For that you have to put it within bounds. Excess of exuberance is like a flash-flood. It washes the crops away.

This is the dark heart of the book.

Fen believes that everything in the universe is connected. As above, so below. Aches and pains in his own body represent conflicts on a cosmic scale. This is an extreme view, but there is some truth in it at least. As above, so below. On the social scale of things, this is certainly true. When the ruling elite employs violence and corruption as a matter of course, then the rest of us are infected. We are all corrupted to some degree, and these annoying little squabbles and niggling, egotistical little forms of behaviour are merely representations in microcosm of what is taking place in the wider world.

All of this was happening in late May and early June. Meanwhile, there was a handful of people causing headaches for the Wiltshire Establishment by holding a gathering at Stonehenge. Three people were arrested, under section 70 of the Criminal Justice Act, for 'trespassory assembly'. This was the first time this section of the act had been used: 1 June 1995.

The gathering was organised, ten years on, to commemorate an infamous date in British history: 1 June 1985. A date that signifies horror and disillusionment to anyone who knows of it. A date which reveals the poisonous worm at the heart of the British Establishment. The day that Wally Hope's dreams died. The day that the dreams of a whole generation died.

Evil. What we have to face is the presence of evil and what we have to know is that this evil is our master. It runs our lives. It lives in big houses and drives expensive cars. It makes our decisions for us. The law is its tool. The law wears jackboots. The law kicks in the faces of young mothers carrying babies. It destroys people's homes, destroys people's livelihoods. It destroys people's lives. It is the Enemy Within.

You see scenes of Fascist violence in faraway places and you say, 'Yes, but that's somewhere else. It's not here. That sort of thing doesn't happen here. This is Britain.'

But that sort of thing *does* happen here.

What I am about to describe is based on a TV film called *Operation Solstice*. It is a film which should be seen by everyone. It should be on the National Curriculum. Every child should be expected to see it, so that they know that evil exists. Evil is not an abstract principle. It has a name and it has an address.

For ten years the Stonehenge free festival had taken place, mostly peaceably. There'd been that biker riot, back when Crass had appeared. There'd been some trouble with heroin dealers. At one point, the old-style festival people had got together to drive the heroin dealers off the site. They were proving that the people's will was stronger than the strongest drug. And the festival was growing. Year by year, it was growing. It was becoming a beacon to the world. For one month every summer, the anarchist dream was being realised in this temporary autonomous zone. More and more people were taking to the road, buying large vehicles which they lovingly restored and fitted out, with pots and pans and working kitchens, with beds and settees and comfortable arm-chairs, which they would decorate with posters and ornamental knick-knacks, which they would paint in vibrant colours to represent the vibrancy of their own lives. This was life. For many people, this was the very act of being alive.

I spoke to someone at an anti-Criminal Justice Bill rally in 1994. His name was Bernard. He'd been on the road since the late seventies. I asked him what kept him on the road, what kept him travelling. 'It's the thought of the thousands of friends I haven't yet met,' he told me.

For four years, from 1981 to 1985, the numbers of people taking to the road had been doubling, year on year. And the Stonehenge free festival was the focal point for the whole movement. It was natural. It was right. Stonehenge was the symbol of freedom, built by early nomadic peoples to mark off the seasons, and as an indication of their intelligence and their ingenuity. Now a new breed of nomad, recognising its importance, was coming back to claim it as its heritage, as its birthright. The festival was as vibrant and alive as the people who went to it. It was a cultural masterpiece: a functioning economy that ran on light and love and mutual respect. Painted faces and naked children. Late-night revels and early-morning cups of tea. Celebration. Hope. Dreams of a better future.

The convoy that led the way to the festival was called the Peace Convoy. That says it all.

Nick Davies, journalist: 'I wasn't aware of it at the time it took place, but I later became aware that really the whole of the Wiltshire Establishment had sat down to decide what to do about the convoy, and this involved various landowners and the county council and the police and their solicitors. They didn't want these people occupying the land around Stonehenge, but there wasn't a law to enable them to keep the convoy out.'

They decided on a piece of legal subterfuge. English Heritage and the National Trust took out civil injunctions to prevent the festival taking place. It was these civil injunctions that provided the cloak for all that was then to take place.

So on 1 June 1985 the convoy set out, as it had almost every year since that long-gone summer in 1974 when Wally Hope and the prankster Wallies had organised the first festival. Some of them were no doubt aware of the injunctions. But what's an injunction, anyway? A piece of paper. They had right on their side. They had tradition.

They were proceeding down the A338 near Shipton Billinger, towards the A303 and Stonehenge. They were about eight miles away. They'd been staying in Savernake Forest, where many more potential festival-goers were still congregating. There were about 150 vehicles: buses, trucks, fire-engines, ambulances, London taxis, cars, in various states of repair. Most of them were brightly painted.

Police radio log, 1 June 1985, 2.04 p.m.: 'Vehicles 7 through to 15 appear to be the personnel carriers and the ones to concentrate on . . .'

'Personnel carriers'? This was the Peace Convoy. They were full of people going off to a festival.

Ahead of them, heavy lorries were disgorging tonnes of gravel across the road. The convoy was diverted down a narrow country lane (the B308, maybe?), then they found that this road was blocked too. They were trapped.

Suddenly a large number of police officers in riot gear, with truncheons and shields, rushed forward and started trying to arrest the drivers. They were hyped-up and violent. They started smashing windscreens with their truncheons.

Helen Reynolds, traveller: 'What's gonna happen now? No! Just tell me what you want me to do . . .'

The Earl of Cardigan, witness: 'One of the police reached through that broken window and grabbed a handful of hair . . . She was being pulled through a window which had been broken ten seconds earlier, which was framed with broken glass.'

The convoy reacted. There was a field near by. People attacked the fence with saws and axes, and the convoy broke through. This was the famous beanfield. And 1 June will be known as Beanfield Day for ever more.

Police radio log, 2.50 p.m.: 'It is stressed that we allow them to enter this field . . . We have a suitable breach of the peace situation.'

'Suitable'? Suitable for whom?

Detective Superintendent Burden, speaking on camera: 'We knew that there would be a confrontation. I am hoping that we can get through the day without too many people being injured, either policemen, or Peace Convoy, or the people in the field.'

By this time there were already people being carted off to hospital. Peace Convoy people, not policemen.

There was an uneasy stand-off, lasting about four hours. The festival-goers were trying to negotiate with the police, but the police were unmoved.

Reporter (off camera): 'Why don't you want to go to hospital?'

Husband, arm around his heavily pregnant wife: 'We don't want to be split up.'

Pregnant girl: 'I don't want to leave me puppies 'n' me 'usband 'n' me 'ome . . . '

Husband: 'If we leave here, we'll probably be arrested. We just want to get off this field as peacefully and quietly as we can, and this lot, all these coppers, are here for one reason, and that's to cause trouble.'

Man in CND helmet: 'They're trying to impose a police state. We're free-thinkers and we're gonna stay that way, no matter what.'

Man with long hair: 'What right have they got to tell us what to do?'

By 5 p.m. there were 1,363 officers from six constabularies available in the area.

Nick Davies, journalist: 'Eventually Lionel Grundy, who was then the Assistant Chief Constable, arrived on the scene and made it quite clear that there were to be no negotiations and that everybody in the field was to be, what he called, "arrested and processed".'

Assistant Chief Constable Lionel Grundy, Operational Commander: 'Those of you who come out under those circumstances will be interviewed and dealt with. If I suspect that you've been involved with any of the offences that have occurred today, then you will be arrested. I'm not here to bargain with you. I'm here to say something to you for you to consider.'

Reporter: 'What's your reaction to what that police officer has asked you to do?'

Phil Shakesby, traveller: 'Well, I'm well upset about it.' Voice rising to fever pitch, addressing the camera: 'We're genuine people, just like yourselves, and we need help. Help us, please.'

The police moved in at about 7 p.m. I challenge anyone to watch this film and not cry. If you don't cry, you're dead. Mass movement and strong-arm tactics. Shields, helmets, riot gear. Bludgeoning truncheons wielded with indiscriminate force. Roars, threats, screams, sickening violence. Here. In England. Where these sort of things don't happen.

Huddles of blue-clad bodies wielding sticks. 'Git out of it!' Pushing the cameraman aside.

'You stay there, boy!' Roar. Truncheon blows raining. A helicopter like a bloated insect hovering, roaring out encouragement to the frenzied police and warnings to the hippies, running scared: 'You have no escape.'

Lyn Lorien, traveller: 'They just started attacking the bus and they were hitting the window, the driver's window, with an iron spike about four-feet long. The windscreen finally broke and I went back, and this spike came through the window.'

A man with blood on his face being frog-marched by two policemen using restraining techniques: 'I didn't do anything, mate. They smashed me windows, they hit me over the head with truncheons, then they hit me when I was on the floor.'

A mass of policemen surrounding a bus. One of them tries to break a window and, when it doesn't give, proceeds to smash a window that is already half-broken. They're mad with frenzy, mad with hatred. Smashing everything indiscriminately. Shouting, 'Come out! Come out!' Kicking the bus. Climbing in through the smashed windows. A man appears at the door, looking frail and scared. He's shaking. They pull him down and, as one policeman tries to shield him from the camera's gaze, hit him over the head. The man falls. He is kicked. A policeman roars, snarling, 'On the deck! On the deck! Now! Stretch your arms out. Stretch 'em out, *now*!' You see a pair of boots standing over him, almost treading on his hair. Those boots, they remind you of something. Those boots. Those jackboots, those jackboots, those jackboots . . .

Is that what you fought the war for, Grandpa mine? Is that what your brothers-in-arms died for? To see the jackboots marching across Europe again, and here in Britain now, in this blessed isle? Is that why we suffered? Is that why we died? Is that why we withstood the dark nights of the blitz, huddled up in our shelters at night, keeping our spirits up with songs and laughter? To see the jackboots standing over our children again. Is that what Britain is about?

And seeing those jackboots there, positioned over a young man barely out of his teens – a young man who'd travelled there just to have a laugh with his mates, like young men like to do, to dance and to listen to music – seeing those jackboots, it makes you think about all the other pairs of jackboots around the globe, and throughout history; it makes you realise that it's the same people in control, everywhere. British jackboots, Chinese jackboots, Serbian jackboots, American jackboots, Russian jackboots. Capitalist jackboots, Communist jackboots. Just jackboots.

A woman is dragged away, screaming. Her top is coming off. She's struggling to stay upright, to pull up her top and to do what the police are forcing her to do, all at the same time.

Phil Shakesby, traveller: 'Just as we got to the brow of the hill there, these bobbies stopped me, span me round and said, "See that?" and I looked at me 'ome and there was smoke comin' out the side doors. They'd gone and set me 'ome on fire.'

Then, the worst scene: a brief glimpse of a bloodied, smashed face, so pulped that you cannot tell if it is a man or a woman. It's the voice that gives it away: 'Someone help me! Help me! Help me,' she screams, like the high-pitched squeal of a pig being slaughtered.

Another man, being marched along: 'See what they're doin' to us?! See what they're doin' to us?!'

Some anonymous testaments, not contained in the film: 'At one point I saw a youth inside a bus, surrounded by policemen, trying to give himself up. He climbed out of a broken window and found himself falling on a sea of policemen who, only a few feet in front of me, were leaning over each other to get a blow. I saw the young man's glasses swiped from his face and his front teeth break under the raining blows . . .' 'Above us a police helicopter, circling overhead, barked down encouragement from a loudhailer: "You're doing a great job. This is how they like it . . . "' 'The occupants pleaded to be allowed to leave. The windows were smashed by the police and occupants were dragged out through a storm of truncheons; broken heads, broken teeth, broken spectacles. Officers started to climb through the broken windows, lashing out on all sides with their sticks. Reporters screamed at the police to calm down.'

Kim Sabido, TV journalist, addressing the camera, with marching policemen at his rear: 'What we, the ITN camera crew, and myself as a reporter, have seen in the last thirty minutes here on this field has been some of the most brutal police treatment of people that I've witnessed in my entire career as a journalist. There must be an inquiry. I don't know what the results of it will be, but at this stage the number of people who've been arrested by policemen, who've been clubbed while holding babies in their arms, and in coaches around this field, is still to be counted . . .'

There was no inquiry.

You are probably wondering why you never saw any of this at the time. The film disappeared. From the offices of the BBC and ITN, the film went missing. Kim Sabido returned to the ITN offices the following day to look over the rushes. Most of it was gone. All of the really nasty scenes had disappeared. The only reason we have this much film is that a cameraman took his camera home with him with some film still in it.

Four hundred and twenty people were arrested and dispatched to holding cells across the South of England.

Social services were on hand to take children into care.

Two hundred and forty-one people were charged with unlawful public assembly, which carries a maximum penalty of life imprisonment. These were later dropped or reduced to lesser charges.

The estimated cost of the operation and subsequent court cases exceeded £5 million.

The irony of all this is that it hasn't destroyed the traveller's movement at all. Instead, it has created a politically motivated underclass who are the sworn enemies of the system. If the authorities had left the festivals alone, what would have happened? Nothing. The travellers would have gone on sitting in fields listening to music, and that's all. Instead of which, they're all up the trees stopping every road the Department of Transport want to build. At the heart of the road-protest movement are all those travellers that the government tried to stop travelling.

This was as true of our little road protest as anywhere else. Festival-goers no longer allowed to go to festivals. Travellers turned to protest.

I witnessed the eviction of one of the squats later in the summer. There'd been major defence-work going on. A tall tower had grown out of the roof and lock-on points placed strategically around the building. There were hundreds of police and dozens of media types. The police were trying to get on to the roof, where a lone girl stood defiantly, locked on to the flimsy tower. She was raising her arm in a clenched-fist salute. Eventually the police stood off.

Then it came, lumbering up from the main road: the huge

cherry-picker, like a prehistoric tank. It lumbered slowly, grinding along the road, surrounded by security guards. There were about a hundred and fifty security guards marching alongside it, like some cheerless army. Most of them were black, obviously desperate for jobs – any jobs – their faces set with the seriousness of the task. I looked at this lot: the poorly paid black security guards and the well paid white policemen, and the even better paid media types, two or three hundred of them, and all the equipment they had – the cutting tools, the vehicles, the huge, monstrous cherry-picker, the cameras and microphones. The whole operation must have cost a couple of hundred thousand pounds. Then I looked at the half a dozen scruffy hippies lounging on the other side of the road. All of this for a few hippies.

I had to laugh. What else can you do?

11   Mung Bean Stew

Her name is Mung. She said, 'Me and Stewart are getting married.'

They'd only known each other for a week.

'Are you in love?' I asked.

'Not really. I don't believe in marriage.'

'So why are you doing it?'

'I don't know.'

She's a protester. A squat lump of a girl, with long black hair, she called herself a white witch at first and wore a pentacle around her neck. Later, she changed her mind. 'I hate that expression, white witch,' she said, 'I'm a pagan.'

The ceremony took place under the Flat Oak. She described it as a 'handfast', which is pagan-speak for a wedding. Someone muttered some formulaic gobbledegook – 'Will you love each other till the thunder rumbles? When you look into the stars will you see his face?' – and did a variety of mysterious-looking gestures over them, while Mung wore flowers in her hair. Stew stripped to the waist to show his tattoos and wore a wreath on his head, while the press looked on, duly impressed. They made the front page.

Well, I'm a cynic about marriage at the best of times. I said, 'I'll give it two years.' I think I may have been over-optimistic.

The road protest was really getting me down by now. I didn't have a minute to myself and there was always someone asking a favour of me. 'Can I have a bath?' 'Can I wash my clothes?' 'Can you drive me to the shops?' The phone was ringing all day, my health was suffering and I'd hardly done a stroke of work for weeks. I'd been doing everything I could to get out of it, but there was always another impending action, some pressing need to be taken care of. Mostly, I didn't want to let my friends down. There were still people I loved and admired up there, though they were getting to be in the minority.

So I decided to take a holiday. I was busy preparing for this, warding off phone calls and trying to get my life into some sort of order when Mung rang me up.

'We want to ask a favour,' she said. 'Me and Stew are moving to Brittany, but before we go I want to collect some stuff from my dad's house in Newcastle. Trouble is, Stew has left his licence in Bristol. Can you hire a car for us?'

'I don't know. Maybe,' I said. 'Ask me again later.'

Then there was another phone call, the day before I was due to leave. 'About that car . . . ' Mung said. It was just another thing I had to clear out of the way before I could get on with the holiday. She assured me she would pay for it.

So we hired the car and I was vaguely wary. Something was niggling at the back of my mind as I signed the forms, but I shrugged it off. After all, nothing could go wrong, could it? I was just trying to help. The woman behind the counter said, 'It will be back by tomorrow, won't it?' and Stew said, 'Yes, definitely,' and Mung added, 'We've just got married.'

The following day my son and I set off on our holidays. Glastonbury first, then on to Wales.

Glastonbury is not a festival. It is a city without cars. It hums like a city. It breathes like a city. It has everything a city should have: cafés, bars, cinemas, clubs, shops, shopping precincts, emergency services, dustmen and women, road sweepers, street-lighting, TV crews and journalists, pop stars hidden away in their own little security compounds, winos, drug addicts, beggars. And the fact that it is all temporary only adds to its mystique. Tents huddle together in discrete sections, like suburbs. Every field has its particular feel. There's a West End and an East End, and maybe even a council estate or two, Housing Benefit Hill under canvas. It's like a huge sprawling shanty-town, an experiment in Third World living in First World Britain. Soweto on acid.

My son is fifteen years old. I thought he'd love it. I'd give him a handful of money and tell him to get on with it. 'You can stay up as long as you like,' I told him. 'You can eat what you like, when you like. You can do what you like. Just don't take any drugs.' Only he didn't like it. He didn't like the crowds. I said, 'It's only like Oxford Street.' And he said, 'I don't like Oxford Street, either.'

He spent the entire weekend in a friend's van reading *The Lord of the Rings*.

Well, I understood what he meant. In a crowd like that, nobody matters. You merge with the mayhem, like an amoeba drifting with the tide. I got lost. I went for a walk at 9.30, got drawn into the crowd, and didn't make it back till 2.30 a.m. Total disorientation. I'd find recognisable spots, but could never work out where to go next. Spinning round at a dusty crossroads, my head spinning, not knowing where to turn. This wasn't helped by the fact that whenever I saw a bar I'd have to stop for a drink. This is because I always feel at home in a bar, even if it is in a tent and you have to sit on bales of damp straw. Home is where the beer is.

Estimates vary as to how many people were there. Some say 100,000. Others as many as 200,000. It's just numbers. It was a sea of humanity. A vast cellular being, a giant with God-knows how many heads, stirring in the English countryside. This was because they had brought large portions of the fencing down. Glastonbury 1995 was a free festival, though there were a number of gangs who wanted it otherwise. There was a bunch of them, city kids fresh out of the ghettos, guarding a hole in the fence with baseball bats and wooden stakes, charging people £10 to get in. A hundred yards further on, there was no fence at all.

What struck me was how easy it would be to maintain it as a free festival, given that the majority of the ticket price goes to pay for security. The management need only sell the franchises to pay for the bands and the infrastructure, and the rest would see to itself. A weekend is not enough. It could go on throughout the summer. In fact, forget the bands. No one wants to see them, anyway. Tax the merchants and let the rest of us get on with it.

I love that Tory line about the Free Market. It's a total lie, of course. It's not a free market at all. It's a rigged market. It's their market. Glastonbury, on the other hand, is a real free market. Everyone has something to sell. Not just drugs. Melon slices. You'd see them crouched by the track, with a cut-up melon looking gaudy in the sunshine, and a piece of cardboard on which was scrawled 'Melon Only 50p.' One bunch of wags had found one of these discarded signs and had ripped off the bit that said '50p'. They were scattering among the crowd, holding up the sign and shouting 'Melon Only', like some surrealistic slogan. Melon only what? It made a strange kind of sense.

And hats. There were hats on sale everywhere. As I passed the millionth silly hat tottering by, staggering or laughing, on top of someone's carefully tended dreadlocks, I thought, 'Glastonbury is supposed to be so subversive, so sinister, and here we all are, lolling about in the sunshine being ridiculous.' And I remembered those kiss-me-quick hats you used to get at seaside resorts in the fifties and sixties. Wearing silly hats is not only a feature of Glastonbury, you see, it's a British Institution. We might as well have been in Margate.

Later on, I overheard an unaccompanied singer giving it his best shot:

'Environmental destruction through
human negativity,' he sang.
'If you don't watch out, if you don't watch out.
Environmental destruction causes
too much disruption.
If you don't watch out, if you don't watch out.'

Well, it didn't exactly scan. You could hear him stumbling over the complexities of the rhythm, like he was trying to hop, skip and throw pancakes all at the same time. 'Environmental destruction through human negativity' – you try it. But what made me crack up was when he started inviting the audience to join in: 'Environmental destruction – come on now! – through human negativity – sing along! – Environmental destruction causes too much disruption – yeah, join in now! – If you don't watch out – yeah! – if you don't watch out!' He meant well.

So I'm on my third or fourth pint of the afternoon and there's someone on stage addressing a small audience. 'Everybody wave,' he says. 'That's right. You over there: wave.' And they all wave. 'And you, the ones standing by the stall: wave.' And he waves at them, and they all wave back. 'Is there anybody here from the North?' he says. The audience roar. 'Is there anybody from the South?' Roar. 'I come from the Midlands, myself,' he adds, like some kind of a punchline. And now I have it. Now I see it. The hats, the singalong clichés, the audience participation. This isn't Glastonbury festival at all. It's a holiday camp with nose-rings. It's ordinary. It's British. Just a symptom of the summer.

I met a guy from the Midlands in a bar on the night before we left. He said, 'I made three New Year's resolutions this year. One, that I would get a Zippo lighter and keep it.' He showed me his Zippo lighter. 'Two, that I would get a tattoo.' He rolled up his sleeve to show me a tattoo of a pink pig shaped like a balloon. 'And three, that I would come to Glastonbury.' Which he must have done because he was there.

I got back to the van. Athie was outside selling brandy coffees. I sat down to talk to her, but found myself sitting on top of a huddled creature crouched in the darkness beside her. It was a tiny, insignificant bloke trying his hardest to blend into the earth.

Athie said, 'Watch out, you're sitting on my customer.'

The huddled creature said, 'What's happening, I don't know what's happening, I'm freaking out . . . '

Another bloke came and sat down beside her. He moved up really close. She made him a coffee and he didn't like it. 'What's this?' he said.

'It's brandy coffee.'

'I don't want brandy coffee, I want brandy. Give me a shot of brandy.'

She did.

'Is that all I get?' he said.

I was standing up in front of the fire. He looked at me aggressively and said, 'Let go of terra firma.'

'I like terra firma,' I said, tapping the ground with my foot. 'It makes me feel at home.'

He got up at that and stormed away in a raging mood, as if I'd just insulted him. Then he came back.

'And I *am* a Canadian,' he said.

I went to bed after that but woke up early, dying for a piss. There were people walking arm-in-arm in the dawn light, and in the background I could hear an acoustic band playing ragas. It was like being in another country. In the Dreamtime.

On our way out, clutching our oversized cheap sleeping bags, we passed one of the brew-crew trying to make it along the track. He was in rags, with a filthy mohican. He was staggering to the side, then back, one arm trailing the ground while his whole body leaned, putting all his weight on one leg, heaving and lurching, and making no headway at all. Like a beetle on the end of a thread, going round and round and round and round.

We had a wonderful time in mid-Wales. My son flew his new four-string kite which had taken six months to build. He could land it and take it off like a spacecraft. He spent five solid hours playing with it while the sun beat down on his face and I lounged around getting sunburnt. We also visited a waterfall. It was at the other end of a dank tunnel, and there was a rushing wind and the sound of the waterfall like a steam engine. From the cave we looked out upon a vista of dappled greens and shifting sunlight and the silver lines of the waterfall as it sent the air scurrying. There were huge beech trees like crooked giants and the smell of moss and damp in the woods. Later I took a dip in an ice-cold pool, and came out tingling and refreshed to my bones. In the evening we ate baked mackerel on the beach, and the smell of oil and lemon added relish to the smoke. Afterwards, we went to the pub and watched the sunset.

I returned home ready for work. Things were stirring in my head, urgent with life. But first of all I had to clear my answerphone messages. This was one of them: 'Hi Chris, this is Mung and Stew here. We're coming back with the car, but we don't know whether to take it to the police station or not. We didn't mean this to happen, it's a bit difficult to explain on an answering machine.'

Mung and Stew were still in Newcastle. Seven days after the car had been due back.

I spoke to them on the phone later.

'What happened?' I asked.

'I don't know.'

To this day, that's the only explanation I've had from them: they don't know.

'We can't apologise enough,' Mung said.

'I'm not interested in your apologies,' I said. 'Just get the fucking car back right now.'

The car eventually turned up two days later. Even then it was never returned to the hire company. It was repossessed from outside of one of the squats, still with Mung's stuff in it.

This is the other side of the road-protest movement: selfish little schemers who are out for what they can get. Not every road protester is like that. There are some genuine heroes among them, but a significant number are simply using the situation. They've crossed the line where righteous behaviour becomes merely self-righteousness. It's like a travelling road show scouring the country for the next cause to latch on to. They mutter grandly about saving the trees, only they're not really interested in trees. They're interested in making the front page. The talk is of anarchy and freedom. What they mean is a free ride, the freedom to rip people off.

Glastonbury had typified this. Everyone was blagging from each other. 'Got a fag? Got any mushrooms? Got any speed?' One morning someone had woken up in his sleeping bag outside the van. 'Cider!' he said. That was his greeting to the world. It was a demand. Everyone ignored him, so he changed his tack. 'Water!' he said. Then, when everyone ignored this too, he said, 'Fag!' In the end, he was pleading. 'Has anyone got a fag? Go on, give us a fag, will you? Go on, my leg hurts.'

I overheard someone else talking. 'I've got some mushrooms,' he said, 'and some speed. Someone gave me an indigestion tablet and it looked so much like an E, I swapped it. They thought they'd got a really good deal.'

It's partly the government's fault, of course. No one exists in a vacuum. When laws are designed that serve only the needs of the wealthy and the privileged – such as the Criminal Justice Act – then you invite people to break the law and a culture of lawlessness is created. There's a current slogan: 'When freedom is outlawed only the outlaws will be free.' Bob Dylan said, 'When you live outside the law you must be honest.' Unfortunately there are many who have not learned this lesson.

The road-protest site had become a squalid parody. Every so often people would throw a tantrum and smash up everything. The squats were filthy wrecks, scrawled with graffiti and not a window remaining. One night they had a fire which burned so high it singed the trees.

A friend of mine went to visit the squat. Mung was there, surrounded by filth and decay, with her voluminous breasts hanging out. My friend said, 'Don't you think you should do something about the washing up?'

'Back to nature, man,' said Mung, as if that explained everything.

Meanwhile, the police were ringing me up asking about the car. All I could say was I didn't know. I tried talking to the hire company. I said, 'I'm really sorry, I didn't mean this to happen.'

The manager said, 'What do you mean, you're sorry? I handed you the keys and you handed them straight over to a couple of scrungy hippies. You should have seen the state of the car when I got it back. It took me two days to clean it. There was puke all down the side. So don't come on with your fucking apologies, I'm not interested in your fucking apologies . . . ' and he slammed down the phone.

I drove up to the site to see if I could sort something out. It was clear that I might be prosecuted. Neither Mung nor Stew were there. I was nervous about seeing them in any case, but just as I was pulling out into the road Mung appeared, coming over the brow of the hill. When she saw me she started pointing at me and screaming: 'Where's my life, you fucking bastard? My whole life was in the back of that car.'

I was astounded. I'd tried to do the girl a favour, she'd messed it up, and now I was the guilty party. I jumped out of the car.

'You've got a nerve,' I said.

'Get a life, you paranoid git,' she said. 'This sort of thing happens all the time. It's normal. People are hiring cars and not taking them back all the time.'

I lost my temper.

'Have you got any brain cells in that skull of yours,' I asked, 'or are you really as thick as you make out? Don't you know what this has done to me?' I was screaming and pointing at her skull, emphasising every word with the appropriate gesture. I brought my arm around in a broad sweep, indicating the protest camp. 'You make a mockery of everything we stand for here. You're not into conservation, you're into destruction.'

'Don't talk to me about the road protest,' she said. 'You've done jack-all.'

The saddest aspect of the whole affair, for me, is that I'd've been quite willing to break the Criminal Justice Act myself. I'd got it all planned. I'd begin making a speech and when the magistrate interrupted, saying, 'This is a court of law, not a political platform,' I'd say, 'When you administer a political law it becomes a political platform.' Instead of which, I had to stand before a bored-looking police sergeant saying, 'I'm really sorry, I'll never do it again.' Kowtowing to a Freemason. It was humiliating. Fortunately, I was let off with a caution.

As for Mung and Stew's marriage, it exceeded expectations. They were divorced within weeks. Pity we couldn't get that on the front page.

I often wonder why I didn't get out of the whole thing earlier. It's difficult to say.

Maybe it was Fen. We'd been friends for a long time and I'd

promised I would help him with this protest. That land meant so much to him.

Maybe it was Miriam. Her fierce drumming was like the spirit of the protest, an insistent, compulsive beat.

Maybe it was Biff and Ernie, the two guys who'd found the skull in the woods. They were just ordinary blokes from the town who'd been drawn into this struggle.

Maybe it was Karl from my council estate who I'd seen blossom up there, finding a useful role outside the society which had rejected him.

Maybe it was Talia, the Belgian girl, who always greeted me with a growl and a hug.

Maybe it was Athie. I'd always loved Athie, even when she was nagging me.

Maybe it was Iggie, a guy I'd seen chain himself under a digger with a D-lock. He seemed like a genuine hero.

Maybe it was Brian, so cool and practical under pressure.

And there were all the other heroes and heroines I'd met, who'd placed themselves at risk for the sake of a patch of countryside and a few trees.

There's not enough heroism left in this world, I feel.

I wanted to believe. I wanted desperately to believe. That there was a better way. That we could get rid of all the greed and corruption and evil in the world, simply by opposing it. And I did believe for a while. I was a true believer. But I ended up hating the whole thing. I even fell out with Fen. It began because Mung and Stew were everywhere. When I rang Fen up, one of them was on the other end of the phone. When I went to the camp, or to the newly opened squat in the town, one of them was there, shouting threats and abuse at me. Fen didn't do anything to get rid of them.

After that, there was a squabble about money and another one about a woman, both on the same night.

Fen said, speaking to someone else, 'Me and Chris have fallen out. It's about money and women.'

When I heard that I laughed. I can never stay fallen out for long with a person who makes me laugh.

12   The Mother

If the law were rational, then perhaps we'd have more respect for it. If it treated everyone equally, then maybe we'd want to obey it. If it were intended to stop crime, then we'd all want to help. But the law isn't rational, it doesn't treat everyone equally and it isn't intended to stop crime.

We live in a state of economic apartheid. The laws are there to protect the haves from the have-nots. Thousands of square miles of beautiful countryside are set aside for the sporting and recreational pleasures of the economic elite, no-go areas for the vast majority who boil and fume in the city's burning ghettos.

Friday 7 July 1995, 6.30 a.m. Debby Staunton and Jim were flopped out, fully dressed, on a bed-settee in the front room of Debby's North London home. There was a loud crash and the sound of splintering glass. Jim sat bolt upright in bed, startled by the noise.

It was the police: ten officers, a mixture of uniformed and plain-clothed, from the Metropolitan and Hampshire police forces. One of them was wearing a red Fred Perry sports shirt and Bermuda shorts. (That's the sort of detail which burns itself into your consciousness when you're woken up at 6.30 a.m. by the sound of your front door being smashed in.) They were brandishing a search warrant under section 23 of the Misuse of Drugs Act. After a half-hour search they'd found a few dried twigs wrapped up in newspaper in the airing cupboard and a couple of stunted plants.

They were searching everywhere. They even searched the room of Debby's six-year-old son, Laurence. They woke him up and asked, 'Does your mother have any secret places where she puts things?' Laurence said no, then paused. 'But if she did have any, I wouldn't know where it is, anyway.'

During the search for drugs they'd also been rifling through paperwork, which struck Jim as odd. Later, they brought out a second warrant. 'Any documents relating to the free festival/demonstration known as "the Mother".'

Debby and Jim are both part of United Systems, an organisation set up to promote free parties and festivals. Talk of 'the Mother' had been doing the rounds for months. It was intended to be the largest free festival since the famous Castlemorton festival in 1992 and an act of defiance against the Criminal Justice Act. Debby runs an information line and she was certainly aware of it – everyone was – but she was taken aback at the ferocity of their entry that morning. She said, 'After all, this is a festival we're talking about, not an armed insurrection.'

Debby and Jim were arrested for 'conspiracy to cause a public nuisance', while Laurence was escorted to school by a uniformed WPC. Laurence was matter-of-fact about the event, though upset that the police had treated his Beaver suit with disrespect. The Beavers are a younger version of the Cubs and

Laurence is very proud of the suit. He said, 'They looked in my mum's draw and chucked everything out. It was my Beaver suit and it's not meant to be treated like that.' He also observed, wryly, that the police had left the room in a mess and not tidied up after themselves. 'And they should, shouldn't they?'

Debby said that afterwards, the house looked like an orgy at a bring-and-buy sale.

Debby is one of my favourite people. I first met her in 1994 on Victoria Station. I'd been given the contact by Nikki and Oz. We sat in a café and talked and talked for hours. She's the least likely criminal on the planet. In her mid-thirties, with a bright, effusive manner, she's very proper, very polite and middle class. She doesn't even swear. She's whippet-thin, with long fine fair hair and a pale complexion. I'm in love with her – but then again (as you've probably noticed by now), I'm in love with almost everyone. We became instant friends.

Debby is famous on the free-party scene. Her information line doubles as the Spiral Tribe number. Spiral Tribe are one of a number of sound systems throughout Europe who have helped turn the purely hedonistic rave scene into a political medium. They see free festivals as more than a weekend diversion; they are a way of life.

Debby first met them in September 1990. It was at a party in a squatted Victorian school. The party was called 'Detension'. The whole school was kitted out and painted. The gym, wreathed in camouflage-netting, was the chill-out area. The stairwell was painted matt black, with a continuous iron bar circling it in fluorescent yellow. All the classrooms were black and festooned with fluorescent stickers. There were three or four rooms playing different styles of music, but mainly heavy, full-on techno. Debby fell in love with the atmosphere. It was wonderful. Everyone was so friendly, just listening to the music and dancing. No poseurs. No pretensions. She really liked that. People were sharing with each other. People were communicating with each other. Yet what struck her most, what charged her with a fresh spark of life, was the fact that this whole, huge, wonderful aural and visual spectacle was being provided for nothing. Spiral Tribe became her family. That night changed her life. 'It was the first time I felt I belonged,' she said. It was more than a party. It was a recipe for the future. 'From that moment, I was hooked.'

During the winter of that year, there were a stream of parties. They were evicted from the school and threw an eviction party called 'Exspelled', which was broken up by the police. Then, the following spring and summer, there were more parties, this time in the open air. Debby says that part of the excitement was not knowing where you were going. 'It's like a magical mystery tour with a lesson in orienteering.' She remembers one party where the directions went something like: 'Along the lane to the cattle grid. Turn round. Back as far as the gate. Turn round. Take the track on your left.' She says that the directions had them fluctuating to the point of stillness in the middle. Even the directions seemed symbolic, somehow.

Then, in the summer of 1991, the rave scene hooked up with the travellers and festival scene, and a new philosophy was born.

Debby believes that Spiral Tribe were primarily responsible for this, though she admits that she's biased. The Spirals had captured people's imaginations over the previous year. There was something about them. Partly it was the style. They were very distinctive. They dressed the same: all in black with close-cropped hair. Everything about them proclaimed a unity. Their literature and graphics had a distinctive appearance (one of them was a trained graphic artist) and they played raw, hard-edged techno. It was like a corporate image with a point of sale. It was as if they'd learned all the lessons of corporate capitalism, but to a different end. They aped capitalism in order to subvert it: Thatcher's children in rebellion.

She remembers one festival in particular that year. It was

taking place near Cissbury Rings in Sussex. This was the same festival that Nikki, Oz and I had set out to find, but never got to. The police had encircled the Ring, enforcing the Criminal Justice Act before the bill had even been drafted! They'd driven all the way down there and were disappointed that they couldn't get to the site. They pulled into a petrol station to ask the attendant if he knew where it was. 'It's there,' he said, pointing to the local paper. 'It's on the front page.' So they bought the paper and, sure enough, there it was, with exact directions to the site.

Rival gangs of football supporters turned up and there was a stabbing. The police arrived with an ambulance. People were getting nervous. They didn't want the police on site. An MC known as Adrenaline Reggie took the microphone. He got the whole crowd to hold hands and raise them in the air. As the ambulance started nuzzling its way through the crowd, Reggie got them to part. Debby says that he was like a shaman performing a magical act. The crowd calmed to his words. 'The rest of the evening was absolutely great,' she added, in her usual effusive tone.

The next day was hot and uneventful. The police were about, wandering around in shirtsleeves and enjoying the event, like spectators. That was in early August.

Then there was the White Goddess festival in Cornwall. This was one of the turning points for the festival/rave scene. Lots of sound systems were there. It was on a full moon over the August bank holiday. The sun and the moon appeared in the sky at the same time. At dawn people turned to watch the sunrise. They were oohing and aahing as if they were watching the fireworks. Little pink fluffy clouds and a pink moon.

During the day, she remembers, everything was still, quiet. People flaked out sunbathing. But at dusk the music would pump up and Adrenaline Reggie would announce over the PA, 'Come on, all you dance warriors. Battle stations! Battle stations!' People would come pouring out from all corners of the site towards the Spiral stage, bodies pumping already to the relentless rhythm, waving their arms to the rhythmic flow. After that it was a full-on, kicking party till sunrise. The sound-system lights would bounce from the clouds, turning them kaleidoscopic.

In those days there was no segregation in the music. No deep house/fluffy house/techno rivalries. The DJs would blend the different styles – breakbeat, jungle, serious acid techno, dance, fluffy – into a huge harmonious whole. The festival lasted two glorious, sun-soaked, pumping, full-on, heavenly weeks. Heaven on earth. It's real.

As a footnote to the White Goddess festival: the following year it was cancelled. This was because the authorities had sprayed the whole area with liquid manure. When Debby saw the state of the site she thought, 'How could they do that? We don't leave a mess like that.'

Debby says that the joy of a free festival is spending your time with (by and large) like-minded people. She loves the initiative and the sense of can do, make do. For that period of time, life is reduced to the simple basics. It's a matter of community. You take along what you think you might need and all the rest you get on site. It's an *ad hoc* economy without too much importance being placed on profit. A circulatory process. People are making money, then spending it again, and the whole thing goes round and round.

People share what they've got. There's an openness, a sociability you tend not to find in other places. People talk. They get on.

Debby says she always liked to do a tour of the tea stalls. Tea-making takes time, especially on an open fire. So you'd sit on a blanket with a bunch of people and chat, while you waited for the kettle to boil. One day she met a man who'd just got back from America that week and another man who was philosophising about life. They were both interesting and she listened to them, fascinated, while they all sipped their tea and smoked a spliff or two.

Debby has two children. She's not some naïve young raver without a thought in her head. She's lived life and knows what it means to have to get on with the mundane things. But she's poor, and festivals, for her, were a cheap form of holiday.

I was reminded of my youth, how at holiday camps you'd always make friends with the people sitting next to you at the dinner table.

'That's right,' she laughed, 'holiday camps for hippies.'

She says she would take along what she could afford, and it didn't matter if she ran out, because there was always someone else who would help. She remembers one time, when she suddenly realised that the kids didn't have enough clothes with them. They'd been racing about all day in shorts and T-shirts and, as the sun set, she could feel a chill in the air. So she started asking round for extra clothes. Eventually she found a group of travellers who were selling off some items. So, for less than £10 she dressed herself and her kids in extra T-shirts, long trousers, jackets and jumpers. But the word had got round. Throughout the night people were coming up to her to offer her items of clothing and blankets to keep the kids warm. As late as 2 a.m. someone came up to her and said, 'I hear you're short of clothes. I've got some spare blankets if you need them.' She'd started looking some time in the early evening and at 2 a.m. people were still thinking about her. She was quite overwhelmed by the atmosphere of care and concern. People were thinking beyond the parameters of their personal being.

And, just like a holiday camp, she was able to get on with what she wanted while the kids could roam free, secure under the watchful eye of all the other parents. There was only one time when this went wrong, though even here there's a salutory ending.

They were on one site with a derelict building near by. The kids were told to go off where they wanted, but to report back occasionally, and that the building was strictly off-limits. So they went away and Debby got on with her tea-stall explorations. After a while she began to notice that it was getting late and the kids hadn't turned up to report back as they'd promised. She was a little bit concerned. She thought maybe they'd forgotten the time. When she found them she discovered the adventure they'd had. They'd been playing close to the derelict building and while they were there, one of the travellers' kids had climbed on to the roof and fallen through. He'd narrowly missed a large splinter of glass. So one of the kids (Phillip) had run off to find the child's parents, while Laurence had remained behind to comfort the hurt child. The parents ran a café. After the child had been taken away in an ambulance (he wasn't too badly hurt, just bruised and concussed) they invited Phillip and Laurence to eat with them. When Debby found them Laurence said, 'Come and have a cup of tea, Mummy.' He wanted her to go over to the caf and meet the parents. She got there to find that her children were the heroes of the day. Everyone knew them and all the travellers were talking about them, about their presence of mind and intelligence in sorting out this minor crisis. Word had got round the whole site, and everywhere the two of them went people were coming up to them and saying things like, 'Well done, you two. It's a good job you were there.'

The Avon free festival took place in May 1992. In 1991, avenues had been created between the free party and festival scenes; 1992 consolidated them. Everyone knew that the Avon festival would be big. Earlier there had been a large festival at Lechlade, with an attendance of 10,000, and the word was already going about there. It was the word on everyone's lips: 'Avon, Avon, Avon.'

In the end, the Avon free festival didn't take place in Avon at all, but in the Midlands, at a place called Castlemorton. It has since become remembered as just that: 'Castlemorton'. There's a resonance to that word. Castlemorton has gone down in the mythology as more than just a place. It's like an icon of remembrance, a mythical space where the world of spirit and the world of matter became temporarily united. A crossroads between the worlds, a place where, one day, gold ornaments will be hung from the trees.

The village itself is near Tewkesbury in Warwickshire, in the Malvern Hills. I used to go there as a child. There's a large common, with a half-made road running through. Debby had already started the phone line by this time and, after waiting to find if the event was on or not, she left a message on her answerphone. Consequently, she didn't get there until the Saturday. Her exhaust fell off on the way and they had to tie it on with a jump-lead cable and the cord from her anorak. When they arrived, they were directed to the site by the police. The exhaust finally fell off as they pulled on to the site. They pushed the car into a secure position, then left it.

The site was huge. It took half an hour to walk along the main drag from one end to the other. The road through the common was like a spine, with the festival taking place either side of it. At its far end, the road petered out into a track into the hills. It was beautiful. There was a large grassy area and, as you came to the end of the track, a woodland space. Beyond that there was a man-made lake, quarried out of solid rock, where everyone bathed, including the dogs. The scene from the surrounding hills was stupendous. It took Debby's breath away: 50,000 people gathered in the glorious English countryside to commune and dance with nature.

Castlemorton festival was a classic Temporary Autonomous Zone. It was the largest free gathering since the last Stonehenge in 1984 and a no-go area for the police. The police weren't needed. Debby gave me an example of this, of what she called 'site justice'. There was a posse of muggers going about. One of them was caught red-handed. He was surrounded by 250 angry people who he'd helped to rip off. Obviously, he was scared for his life. Just then, one of the sound systems grabbed him and hid him backstage. They 'chatted' to him. There's a certain amount of mythology surrounding what took place during this 'chat'. A legend has grown up around it. People say they fed him LSD and bent his mind. Who knows? Whatever the process, the result was that the ex-mugger went up on stage, admitted his faults through the microphone and appealed to the rest of his gang to return the stolen goods. And it worked! A substantial proportion of the property was returned.

Debby says that the statistical breakdown of crime figures for Castlemorton prove what a peaceable affair it was. In the week of 22 to 29 May 1992, there were 147 arrests. Of these, seventy-four were for minor drugs offences and were cautioned. Only eight drug arrests were considered sufficiently serious to require bringing charges. There were thirty-nine arrests for public nuisance, ten of which went to court (more of this later). There were two arrests for burglary, six for theft, and one for assault; six for the theft of motor vehicles, one for criminal damage, and another ten for miscellaneous offences which Debby's statistics fail to detail. There were 50,000 people at Castlemorton. Compare this with the crime figures for an inner-city borough of a similar size over a similar period of time and you have some idea of the 'public disorder' that free festivals actually represent.

But what made it for Debby, and for all the people who were fortunate enough to attend, was the atmosphere. It has become part of history. It was electric. She says she could see and feel every molecule as it hip-hopped and danced through the sizzling air. 'Joy, elation, that's what people felt.' Everyone was exuberant.

Debby would find herself hugging people, saying, 'Isn't it great?'

'Yes,' they'd reply.

No more words were needed.

A system of clearance arose spontaneously. People would undertake to clear the refuse from their own area. They'd hang carrier bags from their car aerials to use as rubbish bins. At the end of the festival, volunteers remained behind to clear up the site. Debby says that it is a myth that, when it was over, the place was a sea of rubbish and excrement.

This question was asked of her during the ensuing court case. She was a witness for the defence. The prosecuting barrister asked her, 'What did people do about going to the toilet?' He thought he would throw her with that one. She replied, 'I had a chemical toilet. The blue chemicals break down the excrement. Afterwards, we dug a hole and emptied the toilet into it, then filled it in again. No one would ever have known it was there.'

Those who didn't have access to chemical toilets used the divot method. You take a shovel and cut a small square of turf. You do the business in the resulting hole, then replace the turf. Again, you'd never know it was there. This is how people have been relieving their bowels throughout time. Those who'd brought shovels would leave them outside their vehicles for other people to use.

Talking of excrement (it's funny how these things relate: in one hole and out of the other), Debby began waxing lyrical about the food. It was something else, she told me. Mainly vegetarian: fresh fruit and vegetables, falafels, pancakes, tea, coffee, soups, rice, salad, curry, cakes, even freshly baked bread. And all at a reasonable price: 20p for a cup of tea, £1.50 for a good meal. All needs were catered for, she says. If anything was absent, the situation would be reassessed and someone would go and get it. There were also handicrafts for sale, clothing and jewellery, and artwork of all descriptions, all handmade and therefore unique.

'Humanity,' she says breathlessly, trying to find the right

word. 'Humanity with a strong spiritual element. Food for the soul.'

You don't miss things – things, that is, that are not essential to the art of living. The kids had no toys, no TVs or computer games. They'd go running about and playing, and, occasionally, people would arrange country rambles. And kids like dancing too. Laurence particularly likes the smoke machines. He refers to festivals as 'go camping, go dancing'.

All of the events are free, of course. The nightly parties, the kicking sounds and shuddering lights. There'd be a whip-round at a certain point. They'd pass the hat to get money for fuel for the generator. Some people would be generous – ten- and twenty-pound notes – while others would have nothing to offer. 'If you have nothing, you have nothing,' Debby said. But they'd offer gifts of food instead, or invitations to dinner.

The nature of a free festival is just that: freedom. You can do what you like, it doesn't matter how bizarre, as long as it doesn't impinge upon other people. No moralism. No prohibitions. Only the limits of common humanity, aware of our responsibility to each other and to the earth we all share.

I said, 'We have to talk about drugs, Debby. People will not believe what I'm writing unless we deal openly with the drugs issue.'

She said, 'We live in a drug-centred society and free festivals reflect that. If someone has an inclination to take drugs, they will take drugs. It doesn't matter where they are. It's not true that free festivals are places purely for drugs. That's not their *raison d'être*. They're about freedom. Freedom to do whatever you like. Certain things are frowned upon – for example, cocaine, heroin and excessive alcohol abuse. We don't stop people doing these things, but they know we disapprove. People go to festivals 'cos they don't have much money. They tend to bring a small quantity of drugs for their own use. Buying and selling does happen, but not to the degree that the media portrays.'

She compares the free-festival scene to the licensed rave scene. People who go to raves are well-off. If you can afford £25 for a ticket to a rave, then you can afford another £15 to £20 for your drugs. The legal raves charge that kind of money partly because they have so many palms to grease, but also because they know they can. If a dealer wants to sell drugs, he's much more likely to turn up at a licensed rave where everyone has money, rather than at a free festival where most people don't. He knows that people will be willing to pay whatever he wants to charge. They've forked out a small fortune to get in and they're bound to want to make sure that they enjoy it while they're there.

As for the possibilities of freak-outs, these are reduced at a free festival. For one, you are in the open air, in the countryside, where very little can go wrong. Your very surroundings are soothing. And you are supported by people who are experienced on the scene, who know how to help.

One or two abiding memories. Debby says that from the top of the hill it was not the sound of the music that was the most disturbing; it was the juddering, angry roar of the helicopters as they kept watch on the revellers. Also, someone had brought a crane with them – a huge crane – and they'd dangled a massive goal-sized net from the raised arm of the crane, which was filled with huge plastic fluorescent-orange balls. Debby says that it puzzled her. Of all the things you might think to bring to a festival – toilet paper, generators, marquees, sound equipment, food, a toothbrush – it had crossed someone's warped mind that a full-sized crane dangling fluorescent-orange balls was essential to the successful outcome of the festival.

She adds that the weather was gorgeous. So, in terms of the conspiracy, you'd have to charge God with it too.

The outcome of all of this (aside from the memories that everyone took home with them) was that thirty-nine people were arrested for conspiracy to cause a public nuisance: the very charge Debby is now facing for her supposed part in organising the Mother. There was a pre-trial hearing at the magistrates' court lasting three months, where the defendants were reduced to fourteen. Of these, three failed to attend and one pleaded guilty. The ten remaining sat through the ten-week jury trial. Each defendant had one solicitor and two barristers, at public expense. One defendant defended himself, thus saving the tax payer large sums of money. The irony of this is that because he was conducting his own defence he was denied access to many of the prosecution documents.

There were forty-four prosecution witnesses and four defence witnesses. All forty-four prosecution witnesses harked on about the same four points. Debby feels that they were coached. They all referred to the fact that they felt prisoners in their own homes, that they were disturbed by the incessant thump-thump of the bass beat, that they were, to quote, 'knee deep in excrement' and that the place was awash with drugs.

Debby was one of the witnesses for the defence. She talked about how lovely the site was, enthusing about the local flora. Debby has an encyclopaedic mind. She would certainly have impressed the jury with the extent of her knowledge and with her enthusiasm. She said that she had heard about the festival by seeing it on the news.

All of the defendants were acquitted, the three who failed to turn up had their warrants quashed, and the one who pleaded guilty was allowed to change her plea.

The cost of the court case was in excess of £4 million. Add to this the cost of the police operation and you begin to see to what expense the government are willing to go in order to stop free festivals. Debby rang me up with the statistics. Here they are: 632 police were deployed during the ten-day period. West Mercia Support Unit: nine police support units consisting of 198 officers and two traffic police support units consisting of forty-four officers. Plus: twenty dog-handlers, fifty CID officers, ten scenes-of-crime personnel, fifty traffic and operations personnel, fifteen command officers, ten charge-office staff, twenty (and this is sinister) tactical firearms personnel, thirty intelligence officers, twenty relief staff and twenty subdivisional staff. The financial cost of what they have called 'the Castlemorton invasion' is broken down into a number of items: police and civilian overtime, £502,600; National Insurance, £36,900; catering, £29,700; helicopter, a snip at £8,800; hire of vehicles, £10,500; transport running costs, £11,100; and lastly the cutely named 'miscellaneous expenses', £25,000. 'Miscellaneous expenses' probably refers to what they did in the pub in the evening. The grand total: £623,600.

As for the Mother festival in 1995, it took place in a number of locations. The original site, a piece of disused land near Corby in Northamptonshire known to be under receivership, was cleared by police at about 4 p.m. on 7 July. There were thirty to forty vehicles on site. Chief Superintendent Wilcox of the Northamptonshire police read out section 63 of the Criminal Justice Act, which relates to organising a rave, and told the assembled company that he would allow them a reasonable time to leave. However, he wouldn't elaborate on what 'a reasonable time' constituted. Helicopters and hundreds of riot vans were in evidence. Parties later took place in Cambridgeshire, in Sleaford in Lincolnshire, in Weston-Super-Mare, in Molesworth, at Grantham Water and near Hinckley Point in Avon. As someone put it, 'The Mother has had babies.'

Michelle Poole of the Advance Party went to Hinckley Point. She was one of a number of others arrested on the day of the raid on Debby's house. She said, 'There were a few police, but they weren't serious about keeping people out. There were two sound systems, it was really nice. Which just proves the point,' she added, 'what's it really all about? What's a "public nuisance" anyway? A few people sitting round a camp-fire listening to music and having a nice time?'

There was a party down in Kent, which I attended. Nikki and Oz were all prepared to attend the Mother but, hearing that it had splintered, decided to throw a party of their own. It took place in the woods. There was a mile-long track with a clearing at the end. All along the track you could hear the music thumping hypnotically in the night air. Beside the clearing was a trailer-load of logs, like a wall, and people were dancing on top of it. A couple of fires lit the site. I said, 'This is the Mother,' pointing at the earth. The police turned up in the morning. They read out section 63 of the Criminal Justice Act and were all prepared to make arrests. However, someone pointed out to them that, according to the act, a rave has to take place after dark and that it must consist of 100 people. There were about forty people there and it was light. The police went away disappointed and the party resumed somewhere else.

Nikki gave me an E, but, the truth is, I wasn't really in a party mood. I was sitting in a car which Nikki euphemistically referred to as 'the office'. There was a guy sat in the front spreading out lines of coke on a mirror. He had the disdainful air of a regular coke user. I made some vague comment and he turned round to look at me. He looked me up and down with a studied indifference. I was wearing sandals. I could almost read it in his face: 'I don't talk to people who wear sandals.' I suddenly realised that I simply didn't like him. What was I doing sitting in the same car as him? I got out and, without even thinking about it, found myself walking home.

I'm not a regular party-goer in any case and I'm famous in my circle as always being the first to leave. The truth is, maybe I'm getting a bit too old for it all, but that doesn't mean I want to stop other people from enjoying themselves.

There's a lot wrong with free festivals. There's a lot wrong with human beings. Rip-off merchants, drug dealers, people who won't give you a second glance when they're not E-ed out of their brains. Self-promoters and petty dictators concerned only with their own image and not with the needs of those around them. Liars and thieves. You find these people in all walks of life and considerably less of them in the free-party scene. I've had some of my worst moments at parties, but I've had some of my best moments too. That's life. It's a game. All any of us are asking is for the opportunity to play. Is this too much to ask?

13 1974

I was staying in mid-Wales, in a rambling, sturdy cottage infested with lanky spiders and a ghost. I'd come across the spiders lurking behind curtains or in washbasins or scuttling across the floor. And, on one occasion at least, I caught sight of some flitting shadow like a dark presence out of the corner of my eye and mistook it for the ghost. It wasn't. It was just one particularly nasty spider, the size of a child's hand. I caught it in a pint glass with a sheet of paper over the end and carried it across the road to invade someone's begonias. It seemed to like it there, once it had got over the trauma of being trapped in an invisible prison by an unshaven giant and transported across the road.

I'd gone there to attempt to pull the strands of this book together. The house was cool and dark, and in the mornings a single burst of light would shatter into prismatic colours through a crystal that was hanging in the living-room window, sending butterfly-wings of colour chasing around the room.

I don't know the ghost's name. She was an old woman, I was told. I would often feel her presence in the kitchen, like a half-forgotten dream, or the last silent ripple from a stone that had long-ago sunk to the bottom of the pool. I'd find myself talking to her, just explaining what I was up to. She didn't seem to mind me being there. Maybe she even liked the company.

The dialling code for the area is 01974. I took this to be significant.

One day someone came round to fix my computer and, over tea and cigarettes in the room with butterflies, he started telling me stories about his early life. He'd been to Glastonbury town one year, he told me, on the spur of the moment. And, hitching from London at midnight, he'd simply got one lift after another all the way there. He'd crashed out in the abbey and in the early dawn had woken up in a panic, only to feel a presence near by, like a guardian angel. 'Don't worry,' the angel had told him, 'go back to sleep. I'll look after you.' The time he spent in Glastonbury that year was like a dream. Everything seemed right.

I was in the kitchen.

'What year was this?' I called out.

'1974,' he said.

I already knew.

1974 was the year that Wally Hope started the Stonehenge free festival. It was the year that Windsor free festival had been clubbed into submission. James Callaghan was Home Secretary, later to become Prime Minister, and Ted Heath was the Leader of the Opposition. It was a kind of beginning and a kind of end. Two years later, punk hit the streets in a fury of jangling invective and breakneck chords. Anger had replaced the placid self-indulgence of the hippie era, but the institution of Stonehenge fitted in well with the DIY punk ethos. It was anarchy incarnate, a riot of self-expression and celebratory culture. A new breed of punk was born from contact with the festival scene: the so-called rainbow punks, hippies in all but name. They bought trucks and buses and took to the road. They became the core of what we now call New Age travellers. The fusion of hippie idealism with punk politics is at the root of the counter-cultural scene. The Stonehenge free festival of 1974 was – as it were – a seed dropped from the hippie plant, soon to burst into vigorous growth as it was fed from the mulch of post-hippie ideology.

On the way home from mid-Wales, I stopped off in Cardiff for the night. That's where I was in 1974: in Cardiff, south Wales. This had not been intentional. I'd not gone there to revive the era in my mind. I was passing through, that's all. But there was so much about the city that I recognised, many memories stalking the now-pedestrianised streets. I kept expecting to meet people I knew.

Then I bumped into Steven Andrews in a back street. I recognised him straight away. Same old lurching walk. Same old self-mocking grin. Only he wasn't hiding behind his hair any more. It was long, but braided and off his face. He was wearing shorts and a waistcoat, and he had on several bangles. He smelled of patchouli oil.

I said, 'All right, Steve? You're looking good.'

'Yeah, so are you,' he replied. 'What are you up to these days?'

'I'm writing a book about counter-culture.'

'I'm an expert on counter-culture. Ask me anything you like.'

I knew Steve in 1974 and he's never been away from Cardiff for more than a week or two in all that time. These days he's justifiably famous as the purveyor of whimsical pop ditties and a weird brand of New Age philosophical speculation that includes King Arthur and the Celtic myths, as well as UFOs and aliens from outer space. He thinks of himself as a pop star and dreams of a slot on *Top of the Pops*. I was a bit sceptical, but others I spoke to said, 'Yes he is, he really is a pop star.' He lives in a council house with his fifteen-year-old son, surrounded by plants, exotic insects and amphibians, and a vast archive of significant moments in his on-going quest to become an international superstar.

I have to admit, I hated the era. I was personally glad when it was all over. I was a student at the time, at Cardiff University. I smoked a lot of dope and took a lot of acid. I stayed up all night and slept all day. I got into drug-dealing for a while. It seemed a good way to keep me in free dope, but one day I got ripped off. I spent all of my money on a bag of dried leaves masquerading as Colombian grass. I didn't have any choice. I had to sell it. I went round to someone's house and, rolling endless spliffs that did no more than give you a headache, tried to talk up a ludicrous high. 'It's really good stuff, man. Far out.' Every so often I'd surreptitiously sprinkle in a little Moroccan to add credence to the rhetoric. I managed to blag my way out of a bag of privet-hedge and into a few quid, but after that I never felt the same about the trade. I gave it up.

I can't remember where I met Steve. Probably in the Pig and Whistle, which is where all us sexy young dope-fiends hung out. I had long black hair down to my nipples and a straight black beard. Steve had long curly hair that he used to hide behind like a curtain. He was characteristically hunched, being quite tall, so that his hair fell over his face. He would momentarily clear it with a sort of prissy vicar's two-handed flick, before it fell into place again. He wore tartan. Tartan everything. Tartan socks, shoes, shirt, jacket, trousers. I never saw his underpants, but I wouldn't be surprised to discover that they were tartan too. He took a lot of downers. Mandrax, Tuinal, Seconal, that sort of thing. I can't remember the names. I took Mandrax once and hated it. I hated feeling as if my head was crammed full of cotton wool.

I smoked so much dope I forgot who I was. I'd wake up to a spliff. I'd go to bed with a spliff. I'd smoke spliffs all day and chillums in the evening. It was deliberate. I was running away. Who from? From myself.

I remember one sunny day going to visit a friend. There was a willow tree on the way, by a stream, behind a green park fence. I leaned against the fence and watched the leaves shivering in the breeze. I felt the sun on my neck and (I don't know where the thought came from: from the breeze, maybe, from the trailing branches of the willow, from the sunlight, from the sky) I thought, 'I'm still here.' It seemed like a surprise that I should be.

Why do I hate the era so much?

Maybe it was because I was going along with something that simply didn't suit me. Peer pressure. A self-conscious attempt to alter the world by altering myself. This is normal. I was twenty-one years old. After you leave home, there's inevitably a period of rebellion, a breaking down of the old structures so you can remake your life by your own rules. Meanwhile, there's a lot of confusion, and a lot of bullshit. You can get sucked into all sorts of things.

Partly it was the drugs. I saw a lot of casualties. I remember someone coming to my door one sunny afternoon so out of his head that he'd forgotten to put on one of his shoes. He had on one shoe, but both socks. He was stumbling against the gatepost with streaks of urine down his trouser leg. He didn't care. He was so out of it, he didn't care that everyone turned round to look at him. He was in his early twenties but he looked about a hundred. That was junk.

Another bloke, Piss-Off Pete, thought he was an alien, half-man half-woman. He wore a dress and make-up. He flounced around, his muscular, hairy arms sticking out of the bulbous sleeves of his dress, and no amount of make-up could disguise the permanent five-o'clock shadow that darkened his chin. He ended up in a psychiatric hospital. That was acid.

I was in a pub one day when someone came out of the toilet with his prick hanging out – he'd forgotten to put it back in – and tried sitting on a chair, but missed it and went sprawling across the floor, then lay there giggling before he passed out. That was downers.

Someone I shared a room with for a while was so paranoid he thought he could hear voices constantly accusing him. He was in a permanently startled state, like a frightened rabbit. That was speed.

No matter what drugs you took, it seemed to have the same outcome. There was nothing heroic in it at all. It was all so squalid.

But most of all I hated the spirituality. Everyone was setting up as everyone else's guru. Everyone had something to sell you. Scientology. TM. Guru Maharaji. Acid gurus who'd met Christ and the Buddha on some trip or another, and who tried to assure you that the world was an illusion, but who'd rip you off all the same. Nothing matters. When the world is just an illusion, nothing matters at all. Even pain is an illusion. So people dying in agony because of imperialist wars in the Third World are only suffering an illusion.

Maybe there is a genuine spirituality. I don't know. I never came across it. I was always looking, but I never found what I was looking for.

The problem started in the sixties. Back then, people were spiritual and revolutionary. They wanted freedom and they recognised two blocks to it: the personal and the political. They saw that the two were interlinked. They wanted to change things. They protested against social abuse, poverty and war, while they tried to develop themselves by meditation. As long as these two activities were working together, they were truly revolutionary. Spiritual revolution: not such a weird concept at all. But at some point – somehow, by some means, by some force outside of the revolutionary spirit – the two were divided. One group went one way, marching the streets and chanting slogans, while the other stayed at home and contemplated its collective navel.

By the early seventies, this split was total. On the one hand you had the God-seekers, trying out all these experiments in personal-growth therapy, while the others turned to hard-line Communism (usually of the Trotskyite variety), took jobs in factories and tried to start the revolution.

That's what I did in the end. I got a job in a rope factory and read Karl Marx behind my machine. But that was much, much later. In 1974 I was a God-head, a seeker after the Truth. I read the I Ching and the *Baghavad Gita*. I read the works of Ramakrishna. I wanted to become an enlightened being. I listened to The Incredible String Band and tried to make sense of the convolutions of their blank-verse lyrics. It all seemed very profound to me.

Serendipity. It's my favourite word. It sounds like something magical. Which it is. It's a happy accident. A magical happy accident. Like life.

And now I'm taking you back again to that Welsh village on the coast. I'm rewinding the tape. You see, something happened there which was like serendipity. Another happy accident.

I'd sit in the room with the butterfly wings, drinking tea all day and letting my mind wander. It was as if my mind had butterfly wings scattering round it, idling, stirring, then chasing round again when a breeze caught the crystal.

In the evenings I'd go to the pub where I'd meet the man who was going to fix my computer for me but who never did and his wife, a social worker; both witches. Mid-Wales is full of witches. Witches and hippies. Witches and hippies and Welsh people. The

Welsh people would sit in the bar, where a pair of crotchless panties dangled above the till, listening to maudlin Welsh anthems on the jukebox, while the witches and hippies and computer buffs would sit in the back room discussing local politics and the tourist trade. Local politicians are corrupt, it seems, and the tourist trade is all but dead. No one was making any money any more.

Aside from witches and hippies and computer buffs there was also the ex-Lord Mayor and the ex-Lady Mayoress, ex-hippies too, no doubt, and certainly into computers. We talked about the Internet. Everyone talks about the Internet. Then my friend, the witchy computer buff, took me to the side and, in a conspiratorial whisper, told me that the ex-Lady Mayoress was also an ex-member of the Incredible String Band. And I couldn't help it. I kept glancing over at this glum-looking pixie, who seemed to come alive only when she had the ex-Lord Mayor for an audience, and found myself singing the words to an Incredible String Bang song silently in my head:

If I was a witch's hat
sitting on her head like a paraffin stove
I'd fly away and be a bat
through the air I would rove
stepping like a tightrope walker
putting one foot after another
wearing black cherries for rings

Hmmm.

I wondered if the lyrics might not have been prophetic in some way. The traditional Welsh hat does bear a remarkable resemblance to both a witch's hat and a paraffin stove. And here she is, all these years later, in an obscure Welsh village, drinking halves of lager in the same pub as me. I took this to be a significant moment. After all, it's not every day you meet an ex-Incredible String Band member turned ex-Lady Mayoress and find yourself picturing her with a paraffin stove perched on her head.

I was talking about spirituality. In fact The Incredible String Band were *the* spiritual band of the late sixties and early seventies. They played whimsical folk-rock tunes but became progressively more po-faced as they began to see themselves as spiritual gurus. One more coincidence. Steven – the old friend I was going to meet in Cardiff in a couple of weeks – is Robin Williamson's secretary. Robin Williamson is one of the founder members of The Incredible String Band. At this point I wasn't aware that I would be meeting Steve later, but it all adds up to something. Time is an ocean. It can't be measured with a ruler.

So I'm sitting in a pub in the nineties with a woman who was in a band in the sixties, which I listened to in the seventies, when I'd spent a lot of time with a guy who is now the secretary for one of the band, and whom I would soon meet, by accident, on a backstreet of a city I hadn't been in for nearly twenty years, in a couple of weeks' time. And who knows when you'll be reading this? Look at the clock and take note. It may be a Significant Moment.

Anyway.

I'd been sworn to silence by my witchy friend. 'She doesn't like to talk about it,' he told me, but I couldn't hold on to it. I had to talk to her.

I arranged a meeting.

Her name is Rose.

There's a photograph on the front cover of one of The Incredible String Band's LPs, *The Hangman's Beautiful Daughter*. That's the kind of title they went in for. The photograph shows a lot of people, wearing tapestry clothes with baggy sleeves, hanging round under an oak tree with a couple of Irish wolfhounds and a number of grubby-faced kids. It looks like a scene out of a Bruegel painting. It was the medieval-troubadour look. Very fashionable at the time, in a backward-looking sort of way.

So I asked Rose about it. Was it a deliberate attempt to construct an alternative lifestyle? I wanted her to give me the beef on what it was like to live like that.

'That was how we lived,' she said simply. 'A rural idyll. No one did anything they didn't want to do. We were the victims of various ideologies, as were others at the time. There were a lot of people trying to live an alternative lifestyle. It wasn't self-indulgent in any way.'

Hmmm.

I asked her about acid. It seemed to me that the String Band (as they were affectionately known) were the archetypal acid band. I had a picture of riotous acid parties where everyone took their clothes off and communed with nature under the stars.

'Acid was seen as a philosophical/experimental tool,' she told me. 'It was seen clearly in ideological terms. We took drugs as a psychedelic experience, not for fun. Of course, we enjoyed them, but we enjoyed them as a result of a better vision of the universe. Everyone's vision was regarded as limited by conditioning. Drugs were a way to throw off the constraints. We used other methods, too. It was about growth and development, rather than escape. Drug culture was one strand of a myriad strands – minor, as it happens.'

I was already beginning to realise that everything she said was wrapped up in philosophical terms. She used the word 'ideology' a lot. No matter what questions I asked, she merely philosophised the answers. There was no attempt to get through to the spirit of the age. It was as if she were covering up something. Not a scandal, nothing like that. Just an unpalatable truth. That she had been that person. That she and the band had taken themselves that seriously. Everything she said represented, everything I hated about the era. All that philosophical jargon.

All that po-faced, gelatinous, meaningful, life-enhancing gobble-degook.

She was insulted that I thought the lyrics were acid-inspired.

'I wouldn't see them as drug songs,' she said. 'I'd see them as part of the reality of the time. I'm sure Robin and Mike would not have wanted people to see the songs as drug songs.

'Between 1969 and 1970, other things were more significant. Scientology, for instance. It was a progression from Eastern religion to Maharishi to Scientology. That was the worst influence. It pandered to the worst elements, to people's weaknesses. It made people feel important, but it was facile. It aimed to be a philosophy, but it was on a nursery-rhyme level. It allowed you to think that you could buy your salvation.'

I was beginning to understand the reasons for the cover-up. There was a bitterness. Rose simply didn't like those times any more. She didn't even like to talk about them and, when she did, it was from a distance.

'Everyone wants salvation,' she said, 'life, health, etc., etc. Scientology appeared to give the answers . . . if you're weak enough or deluded enough. You don't have to work hard. It's very supportive. It makes simple people feel clever and weak people feel strong. It turned nice people into not very nice people.

'Cults are very dangerous,' she continued. 'More dangerous than drugs. Cults lift you out of known contacts so that you lose your sense of balance in the world. You need to make changes knowingly and thoughtfully. You can't be an influence if you're outside, if you lose contact with the majority of people. It's about changing the world. Most people want to change the world in a social way. Cults, on the other hand, become exclusive, and cultists have a superior attitude to the rest of us.'

I asked her why she joined. She was forced into it, she told me. It was either 'join the Church of Scientology, or leave the band'. There was no other choice.

I tried to get some sort of an understanding of what Scientology entails. It has something to do with the Immortal Soul, she told me. This is infinitely powerful in its pure form, but it is snarled up in our bodies. There are indelible blocks on the soul. If you remove these blocks, if you take the soul back through lifetimes, you can end up with a free spirit once more, eternally powerful. Something like that.

There's two electrodes, like a lie detector, that you hold in your hands. The aim is to make the needle float. Where there is pain or anguish, the needle will be stuck. When the block is cleared, the needle will float. Rose told me that it was the easiest thing in the world to make the needle float. She simply pretended to be going back through all those lifetimes of pain and anguish. Anything to get them off her back.

In the end, she left the band and took a job cleaning in Camden. Later, she worked for the DSS in Kentish Town.

'At least it's honest,' she said. 'I felt clean. We were only a bunch of twentysomething-year-olds who had set ourselves up as saviours.'

In this entire conversation I never detected one glimmer of affection for the period. She'd been in her twenties, remember. She should have been having a laugh, having fun, going out with people, dancing all night. They were well-off, a bunch of internationally renowned pop singers. They could have done what they liked and had a good time. Instead of which it was all po-faced worthiness and dreary philosophy. This went on. Maharishi Yogi, TM, Buddhism, Sufism, I Ching, Zen, Macrobiotics and Meditation. Reading, reading, reading: philosophy, philosophy, philosophy. And they didn't seem to have made any friends.

'They never knew what they were good at,' Rose said, referring to the rest of the band. 'They wanted to be what they weren't and they never knew what they were.'

The only faint moment of pleasure came when she told me

that she'd once played bass with Keith Moon of The Who.

'He was a good drummer,' she said, with a brief smile.

Hmmm.

Steve and I went for a drink. He'd been to all the festivals back in the late sixties and early seventies: both Isle of Wights, Bath, Knebworth and Phun City. Phun City was the first ever free festival. 'It was incredible,' Steve said, "cos it was all these people camped out in the woods there in benders and little tree houses and things. I've never seen anything like it, it just seemed so natural. I remember Kevin Ayers was there, who was somebody I was really into at the time. He was jamming with Edgar Broughton and he had purple hair which was, like, way ahead of its time. 'Cos the punks and things happened years later. That was a really good scene.

'I used to like festivals, I used to like the whole idea of all these people gathered together, even if the people weren't as wonderful as they made out they were, or you might think they were. But it was the whole idea that we were a different culture of people all meeting up and doing our own thing. You could feel it, you could feel a whole sea of people all around you, and you could see all these strange fashions and styles and people with all kinds of weird and wonderful stuff. There's nothing quite like it, the whole festival colour. I used to be into all that and the idea that we were all doing something, and we were all like minded people, even though a lot of them I suppose weren't. So I used to like festivals.'

Steve drinks cider and calls it Druid-fluid. Apparently it's what King Arthur drinks too. Steve is Quest Knight and Bard with the Loyal Arthurian Warband. King Arthur is an ex-biker turned Once and Future King, who realised that he *was* King Arthur when a bird's wing brushed his cheek at Stonehenge, and who owns the sword Excalibur that was made for the film of the same name. The man who'd made it had said he'd never sell it, but would give it to King Arthur when he returned. Then the current King Arthur turned up at his shop waving the deed-poll around with his name on it. King Arthur Uther Pendragon.

King Arthur hints that Steve might be Taliesin, the sixth-century Welsh bard, and Steve says that he has a picture of the bard on his wall at home and there certainly is a resemblance. 'If that's what you want to call me, Arthur, that's your business.' But he's happier just to be Steven Andrews.

One day, Arthur and Steve were at a party. Arthur had just found a source of really good meat pies to satisfy his lust for flesh. He kept away from Steve while he ate them, knowing Steve to be a vegetarian. Then he'd got completely pissed. He was drinking Druid-fluid and mixing it with someone's home-made wine. He'd not had any sleep for three days. So he was lying on the ground in Camelot (that's someone's back garden) with puke in his beard, snoring. A new convert saw him, hunched up there on the grass. 'I don't believe in him any more,' the convert said, kicking the comatose form. 'That's not King Arthur, lying there with puke in his beard, snoring. It can't be.' Steve was snorting with pleasure when he told me this story. 'How could that be King Arthur? King Arthur wouldn't get drunk like that. King Arthur wouldn't snore. Well, he wouldn't, would he? King Arthur wouldn't do any of those things. Or he wouldn't be King Arthur, would he?' But Steve says (and I agree with him) that this is exactly how a Dark Ages Celtic chieftain would act.

As it turned out, Steve was into Scientology too for a few years. That's how he met Robin Williamson of The Incredible String Band. In fact, he was the Scientology Executive Director for all Wales. He says it doesn't make any sense, but he still believes it was good for him at the time. Steve never regrets anything. He says it stopped him smoking. There were these tests, called drills. He had to sit perfectly still and stare into another person's eyes. If he so much as blinked, the other person would say, 'Flunk!' and he'd have to start all over again. He kept failing. Then he realised that the reason he kept failing was that he wanted a fag the whole time. So he packed up smoking and passed the test.

The worst crime in Scientology is to ask for your money back. There are a lot of crimes and a lot of punishments – and there's a lot of jargon – but the worst crime of all is to ask for your money back, any amount at all. If you ask for your money back you are condemned, not just for this lifetime, but for all lifetimes to come, to be excluded eternally from the Church of Scientology. So Steve asked for £10 back. The Letters Registrar for all Wales almost had a fit. She's in her eighties and Steve thought she might have a weak heart. She didn't want to see him condemned for an eternity to do without Scientology. So she offered to pay Steve £10 of her own money if he'd think again and cancel the request. Steve accepted the compromise in consideration of the old lady. However, when she's dead, Steve plans to ask for his money back anyway. It appeals to him to be condemned for an eternity. It appeals to his sense of humour.

Steve and I went to a party. We got rolling drunk together on Druid-fluid. This was at Pixie's house. Pixie is another of the Loyal Arthurian Warband. Pixie's back garden is Camelot. Steve showed me the exact spot where Arthur had been crashed out. Then he sang a few of his ditties: 'We all need a real love and communication! Yeah.' And Pixie sang some Irish folk ballads, and everybody joined in, while Pixie's face writhed and twisted with the strain of the melody. We're in a back garden in Cardiff at two in the morning, howling out these drunken hymns, with a fire skipping and leaping playfully into the night sky, and eddies of drunken chatter circulating about, and there's a security light which keeps going on and off whenever anyone crosses its path or moves about too much, and you can see the city lights twinkling all around and, just for a moment, I felt that I really was in Camelot – or somewhere mythical and distant and strange. For some reason, I felt like I'd come home.

What year is this again? I forget.

14   Back to the Garden

I was talking to a friend of mine, Toby. This was in the back
garden of that cottage in mid-Wales. He was lounged out in a
hammock in the dappled sunlight beneath the trees, reading
Heart of Darkness by Joseph Conrad. He said he was thinking
of using it as the theme for a dance/mime for a deaf dance troupe
he knew. His sister is deaf. The dancers use sign language as part
of the performance. The idea was to translate the journey of
discovery in the book into a journey of discovery into deaf
culture. I said I thought that the book was much too dark for
that. All the deaf people I've ever known always seemed to be
laughing.

It reminded me of the time I'd spent in Thailand. I'd run out
of money and was forced to stay and work in Bangkok. I was
teaching English as a foreign language. At the same time, I was
learning Thai. I'd thought, 'I already speak one of the most

useful languages in the world, I might as well learn one of the most useless.' The only people in the world who speak Thai are the Thais. I'd not been all that successful. Thai is a tonal language, like Chinese, which means that any word can have up to five different meanings, depending on how you say it. The Western voice is far too flat for it. I remember I was in a café one day. One of the waitresses asked me where I'd been. I replied, 'I've been to Koncaen.' It's a town in the north. At which point the waitress burst into hysterical laughter. She kept repeating it to all the Thais who were in the room. Soon the whole café was cracking up, screaming with laughter.

I got someone who could speak English to explain it to me.

'You said you'd been sitting in a vat of sweets,' he said.

There was a snooker hall near by. I went down there one evening. There was a beautiful blonde woman who I wanted to marry the instant I laid eyes on her. She was being chased round by what seemed like dozens of diminutive Thai people. The atmosphere in there was crazy. The Thais were running around, making these peculiar honking noises and waving their arms about. It was like a scene from Bedlam. Everyone was laughing and gesticulating.

It soon became apparent that the Thai people were deaf. The frantic waving of the arms was sign language. The honking noise was their attempt to make words. The blonde woman was translating for me.

'They're asking me if I'll marry one of them,' she said.

'Do you speak sign language?' I asked, unaware of the contradiction.

'No,' she said.

The blonde woman left. I wanted to run after her, but the deaf people were chasing round after me now, signing and laughing and honking in an absurd manner. One of them made a sign at me. He made out like he was holding a glass and tipping it to his lips. Then he indicated with his thumb, while putting on a questioning frown. He was saying, 'Do you want to go for a drink?'

We all trouped off to a street stall. These are one of the most pleasant features of Thai life: small-scale businesses that sell a variety of different things: food, cigarettes and drink. We sat out in the humid Bangkok night till three or four in the morning, drinking whisky and laughing.

I don't know how it happened. I'm in a country where the language is so alien to me that saying I've been to some place or another can sound like I've been sitting in a vat of sweets. And I'm getting drunk with a bunch of Thai people who don't even speak Thai, let alone English. They just make noises. All of a sudden they were making perfect sense. They were doing dumb-show mimes and mixing them with signs that seemed to indicate the grammar of the conversation. I can't say how it worked. I only know that I was caught up in one of the most entertaining conversations of my life, understanding everything and yet not saying a single word.

I've thought about the process since. People who know about sign language tell me that, although the languages differ greatly from country to country, there's enough understanding for any deaf person from one country to begin communicating with another deaf person from another country almost immediately. The sign I was given for 'Do you want to go for a drink?' makes that clear. The combination of the glass to the lips, the pointing and the questioning look was enough to tell me what was being said. I didn't have to speak Thai. They didn't have to speak English. The sign is universal. The sign for someone yakking in your ear is another. Make out your fingers and your thumb are like a mouth. Open and close them, while pointing the hand towards your ear. It's the sign for someone giving you earache. Add a pained expression and anyone in the world will understand you.

Deaf people might appear to have an almost unbridgeable barrier to communication. Yet those I met in Thailand were among the greatest communicators I've ever known.

The conversation with Toby about a journey of discovery into an alien culture also made me think about something else. It made me think about this book.

My friend Nikki, the sound-system guru, told me about an experience she'd had as a child. It was one of the most important moments of her life. She was brought up in Windsor. One year, she was in the car with her parents caught in a traffic jam. It was the end of the Windsor festival and people were pouring out of the park in hordes, all of these people with long unkempt hair, painted faces and bright patchwork clothes. Her parents were saying, 'Look at them. What do they think they look like? They're like animals. It's disgusting. It shouldn't be allowed.' But Nikki, who was about eight at the time, was transfixed by the scene. She was looking out of the back window entranced. They all seemed so happy. They were smiling and laughing. It was a riot of colour, like a carnival. It seemed to put a whole new perspective on life. Life for these people was not just a routine, as dreary as the relentless tick of the clock, and burdened with the inevitable pressures of duty. It was joyous. It was a cavalcade, a spectacle. It was fun. She'd never before seen adults who looked like they were having fun. It was more than all the adjectives you can attach to it. It was life itself.

My mother told me that when she'd first seen hippies she'd been frightened. She didn't understand what they were up to. Nowadays, she thinks that they were probably right.

The joke at Stonehenge was always that Hawkwind would appear. Hawkwind were the name band that had put their influence behind several of the festivals. Every year the rumour would fly around: 'Hawkwind are coming, Hawkwind are coming!' Mostly the bands were fairly mediocre: endless pedestrian replays of 'Smoke on the Water' and other dreary rock classics. Big-name bands wouldn't play because there was no intention of paying them. The story goes that Free turned up at a free festival one year, then left when they discovered that they weren't going to be paid. But Hawkwind were never like that, not in the early days. They were 'on the vibe', as the expression goes. They believed in the philosophy of the free festivals. So the rumour would go round year after year that this year they were going to appear. In fact they only ever played there about three times.

I went to see Nik Turner, who was in the band when they had their chart hit, and who turned up at Stonehenge almost every year, with or without Hawkwind. He lives in the Welsh countryside, in the hills near Cardigan, in a rambling pink cottage several miles down an isolated track. There were caravans parked all over the place and kids running round with space helmets shooting each other with electronic pistols. There was a cowed-looking dog and two pot-bellied pigs with deep frowns looking grumpy.

I asked, 'Are you intending to eat them, or are they just pets?' I was referring to the pigs, not the kids.

Nik Turner replied, 'We're not intending to eat them. They just wander around and we feed them occasionally.' He was probably referring to the pigs and the kids.

I took to him immediately. In a way he reminded me of Penny Rimbaud from Crass, only less serious. He's about the same age, in his fifties I'd guess. He was wearing only a pair of shorts, and his hair was cut short and dyed blond. He had on a copper anklet. We sat on the floor outside his workshop basking in the evening sunlight. He has a relaxed and easy manner, and sparkling blue eyes. You could tell immediately that he has enjoyed his life.

The first thing that he told me was that he didn't want to talk about drugs. He'd heard of a man in America recently who had taken some acid and then freaked out. He went to the police. They immediately charged him. He was banged up for about ten years. Such is the atmosphere of fear over there.

This was the day after he'd returned from an American tour. He talked a lot about America.

He was always into alternative culture, he told me. He was always involved, always found it attractive. Taking drugs (so he was talking about drugs straight away) was really groovy. Yet he never took heroin, though he was reputed to have been some sort of a dealer at the time and to have carried up to 15lbs of heroin around in his sax case. That was never true. It was just propaganda. He has some ex-junkie friends, some of whom are now in a bad way. He wouldn't recommend it to anyone. He only ever took drugs himself as a sort of experiment.

He was brought up in Margate, he told me. Margate is about fifteen miles from where I live. We chattered on a bit about places we knew.

He mentioned a lot of names: Richard Neville, Mick Farren, Michael Moorcock.

'You obviously knew all the characters,' I said.

'Yeah, I was involved in it for such a long time – counter-culture, or whatever you might call it – my first involvement in the whole thing, apart from being peripherally caught up in it, was going to UFO in Tottenham Court Road.' It had been his first experience of seeing bands and other people who were 'doing things', as he says. He saw Pink Floyd and a band called Suntrolley. This was in about 1966.

'I thought that was quite groovy,' he said. 'Groovy' is his favourite word. He says 'groovy' in a groovy sort of way. He's a groovy guy. 'Then I went to Berlin in 1969. There were these free jazz musicians and they convinced me that you didn't have to be technically competent in order to express yourself. So I started playing free jazz in a rock'n'roll band. That's how I became involved in Hawkwind.'

He spent some time in Holland in 1967. He worked in a rock'n'roll circus. 'The Psychedelic Circus it was called, Tent '67 it was known as at the time.' It was a huge tent taking up to 2,000 people. Nik was working as one of the crew and in the bar. They'd arrive on site in the afternoon, put up the tent, then do a show. They'd take the tent down at midnight and by 2 a.m. they were back on the road, heading for the next gig. They'd arrive there, kip out till about midday, and the whole process would start again. He laughed as he told me this.

'What was the nature of the performance?' I asked.

'The nature of the performance was we had this articulated lorry. It had flaps that would come out and make it about twice the size of the trailer, which was used as a stage, and we had a PA and a light show, and we had a bar and . . . basically it was a light show and bands and flowers we were giving away. You know, flower-power and all that sort of thing. There were a few shops in there as well – not exactly shops, but merchandising and things going on as well.'

I noticed the similarities to the current rave scene and mentioned this to him.

'Yes, it was similar,' he said, enthusing over the point, 'except it was legal and nobody even questioned it. Nobody hassled us. It was in Holland, which is pretty liberal, anyway. We did a different town every night and we travelled round for a couple of months.'

After that he became a roadie for a soul singer, a guy who did James Brown impersonations. The soul singer would fall to the ground as if overcome by emotion, and Nik used to have to rush up to him on the stage with a towel and try to mop his brow, saying, 'Davy, Davy, are you all right?' The guy would brush him aside, grab hold of the microphone and start up some heavy-duty song full of wrenched emotion: 'You know, "A Change Has Got to Come", something like that.' It was all part of the act.

As he was telling me this, the pot-bellied pigs were snuffling and grunting about, looking for food. It was as if they were snorting disparagingly at the whole notion of counter-culture, like a pair of grumpy aunties making an unfavourable commentary on our musical tastes.

While he was in Holland, he got to know these blokes from a band called Doctor Brock's Famous Cure. He kept in touch with them. Years later they asked him to join their band. This was before Hawkwind. It was a band which didn't even have a name, latterly called Group X. They did one gig. They barnstormed a place in Notting Hill Gate. They simply turned up there and asked if they could play for ten minutes.

'The people who ran the place said, "Oh, all right then." You know, reluctantly, "Oh, all right then".'

Everybody was impressed and John Peel, the DJ, advised a manager who was present at the gig to take them on board. So almost immediately they had a management deal and, soon after, a record deal, and they really didn't have much problem. They called themselves Hawkwind. It was a combination of Michael Moorcock's involvement – he was writing books about a character called Hawkmoon – and what was reputed to be Nik Turner's nickname.

'Rumour has it that it was a reference to my prodigious farting and spitting. You know, hawking and farting.'

Earlier in the conversation, when we'd been talking about Margate, Nik had told me that he'd run a stall there for a while. This intrigued me. I wanted to know more.

'Yeah, I spent about four years doing that, on and off. I had my own business there. A mate of mine's father was an importer of fancy goods and silly hats – kiss-me-quick, Italian hats, that sort of thing. We got them on credit, paid a minimal rent for a pitch on the seafront and ran it selling stuff to the tourists – you know, buckets and spades, and all that sort of thing.'

Kiss-me-quick hats on Margate seafront. The very thing I'd envisaged at Glastonbury.

This was in the mid-sixties, during the mods and rockers era.

He had been in the middle. 'I knew all the mods and all the rockers and they were all fighting. I was looking after the rockers' motorbikes and I was looking after the speed that had just come out of a chemist's shop – big boxes of Methedrine, etc. I knew all the local policemen as well. They'd stop and chat to me while I had all these drugs. They'd say, "How you doin'?" and I'd say, "Yeah fine, yeah, blah blah." "Everythin' all right? Quiet day, nice weather . . . " I was in the middle, really. I knew everybody. I suppose I was a bit of a mod. I had a scooter at the time.'

I couldn't help reflecting on the difference between Nik Turner and Rose from The Incredible String Band. Nik was telling me stories. He was laughing at all the things he'd got up to. He had obviously enjoyed his life. It was clear that he never regretted anything. I told him that this was my impression.

'Yeah, yeah. I don't regret anything I did. I don't see the point of regretting it. I've always been of the philosophy that, for better or worse, that was my life. That was what I did.'

I asked Nik about his involvement with Stonehenge. How many had he actually played?

'I think Hawkwind played at – was it the second or the third Stonehenge? Might have been the second one. They had the stage next to the stones. I think that might have been the first year that we actually played there. I sort of instigated it.'

'Had you had you had your chart hit by then?' I asked.

'No, we didn't have the chart hit, but by then we had an album out.'

'So you were a known album band?'

'Yeah, we had the first album out. You say the first festival was 1974? So I guess we played there in 1975 and 1976, and I believe Hawkwind did play there in 1977. I wasn't with them then. They erected their Atomhenge thing. It looked like a molecular structure, with pillars and pieces going across it, and great big crystalline shapes, star clusters of crystals. It was quite a large structure. In fact, we'd had it built for stage shows for part of the space-ritual thing, but that happened after I'd left the band. I was involved with having it built, but then I left.'

It was around this time, in 1978, that he moved to Wales. He also went on holiday that year and did some recording in the Great Pyramid, from which he made an album, and formed a band called Sphinx. He had a pyramid stage constructed for promoting the album and played at all the free festivals with the stage. The album was released in June, with a free concert at the Roundhouse, backed up by punk poets and New Wave bands. The next day they went down to Stonehenge. Nik was one of those responsible for the rainbow-punk phenomena: punks turned on by mysticism and the hippie ideal.

They toured with that stage, did lots of festivals. They were playing throughout the summer.

'We took it to Blackbush Airport, where Bob Dylan was playing, and set up outside the airport as a sort of protest gig – protesting against Bob Dylan and the price of his concert, and the fact that the only reason he was having a concert was to pay for his alimony. It wasn't really in the spirit of what I thought he was about, so we did this gig as a protest against him. He'd suddenly become very Establishment.'

I was interested in what makes people, who have once been counter-culture icons, turn to the Establishment. Nik had never taken that route, though I'm sure the temptations had been there.

'It's difficult to say. I mean, if somebody came along and said, "Here's a million pounds. Will you sign with Warner Brothers and make an album with . . . "'

'Pavarotti?'

'Well, I like Pavarotti, but I suppose it depends how you view it. I mean, I like Pavarotti, but then I like good music. I don't like bad music. A lot of alternative music is bad. One way of looking at it is that people are alternative because they're not talented enough to be anything else. I have my own principles. I suppose it's also the way you define "alternative". I live what you might call an alternative lifestyle. I eat only organic food. I don't like shopping at supermarkets because I think, on principle, they're a bunch of cunts. They offer you something cheap, they put everyone else out of business, then they put up the price. In the end, it's not cheap at all. On one level you can't go against progress; you can't go against what people want. Hypermarkets are in fact progressive, because they're a reaction to what's happening. In America you can go into one shop and buy everything on a credit card, and that's what they're trying to do in this country: they're trying to turn this country into America.'

'Do you think this is inevitable,' I asked, 'or do you think that there's a way of opposing it?'

'I think that materialism is a funny thing. People are brainwashed into it. I think people get brainwashed with television. I don't watch television myself. I haven't had one in twenty-five years.'

I was looking to Nik to guide me out of a dilemma I'd been caught up in. Counter-culture as a movement has been very strong in the nineties and it is very influenced by the sixties. It has some positive sides to it, but at the same time I want to remind people of the drawbacks. I was trying to draw upon Nik Turner's experience to help me get across my point.

I said, 'For instance, drugs aren't the answer because look who took drugs. Mick Jagger took drugs and he's the Establishment. Bob Dylan took drugs and now he's the Establishment . . .'

'Even the Grateful Dead,' said Nik. 'Although they're less Establishment, really. They're the exception that proves the rule, in a way, because they're probably the most popular band in America, I would say, although unfortunately Jerry Garcia has just died. He was in a drugs rehabilitation clinic where he'd gone to get himself off crack and he died . . . Well, they say he died from natural causes, but he probably had a heart attack or something like that. He was a figurehead; like a guru, in a way. He was like a father to a lot of people, because America is a soulless place and I think that he was someone with a bit of heart who people related to. Now there's a whole generation of parents who are from broken homes, and I think that Jerry Garcia represented a bit of stability and also something spiritual; something solid, something with a bit of foundation.'

The genesis of this book had been a dream featuring the now disbanded Grateful Dead.

'It's sad that it was crack,' I said. 'The story goes that Grateful Dead concerts were like the original raves. They carried on and on, like the original acid tests, and the drug was always acid.'

'Yes, that's right. But in the last few years it's come to pass that the Dead have stimulated a great following which is bigger than the band and also more spiritual. There used to be a great group of people that would simply follow the band around. They wouldn't even go to the concerts, they'd just park up in the car-park and that was where it was all happening – it was a social gathering. It's rather like Hawkwind gigs. Hawkwind were likened to the Dead in the early days for that reason: you knew at a Hawkwind gig that you would see loads of your friends, people that you hadn't seen for a long time. It's like Stonehenge. You'd see loads of people you hadn't seen since last Stonehenge.

'Festivals are gathering places. They're quite meaningful spiritual things. I've read books about megalithic culture. At Stonehenge there was a great gathering every year, and a great festival, and a great party, and everybody used to get totally wasted and it was like a real . . . a spiritual thing.'

'And you think that the latter-day Stonehenge, the more recent ones, were the successors to that?'

'People have a need for that sort of thing. They have a need for communion with each other and for communication.

Christianity sucks, and I think that the old religion is much more meaningful to people. That's what Stonehenge represents: the old religion, paganism, some sort of earth magic, to do with the seasons, the natural spirits and the fertility of the ground. That's what happened, initially. Some fairly wise people became aware of how the seasons worked, that there was a summer, a winter, a spring and an autumn, and the solstice and the equinox, the guiding points that they could take their calendar from . . . '

'So Stonehenge was basically a huge calendar?'

'Yeah, that's right.'

'So when do you think that people became aware – I'm talking about this generation – that Stonehenge was somehow significant?'

'A lot of people didn't realise it, but a few people did, and those are the ones who instigated and encouraged other people to become involved. A lot of people didn't know why they went to Stonehenge. They went there to see their friends, but their friends were probably there because they realised the importance of it.'

He went to his first Stonehenge in 1974, he told me, the year it was instigated. He was driving back from Wales and he saw some people there. He'd heard about the festival – it was being promoted by Radio Caroline – and so he stopped for a few hours. There were no bands, no PA, no stage. It was just a gathering of people to celebrate the solstice. He met a few people (he didn't have any recollection of any of them being called Wally and he never met Wally Hope), then he drove back to London. The next year he played there with Hawkwind.

They went to a few of the Windsor festivals, too. They did a gig there with Michael Moorcock in 1973, the year before it was trashed. They were happy to play free festivals, despite the fact that they were a name band. They were never materially motivated. They were happy simply to play and for people to enjoy it. He was aware of the free festivals as a spiritual thing.

Hawkwind were always a spiritually motivated band. Spiritual and social revolutionaries at the same time. That's why Michael Moorcock got involved with them.

We drew parallels between the rave scene and the festival scene. Same blend of the spiritual and the revolutionary. Same motivation, for political freedom and spiritual growth.

'You could say that the rave scene is the modern festival scene,' he said. 'Or it has been, although they've tried to suppress that as well.'

'Well, they have. They've suppressed it very successfully, in fact,' I said. 'Most of the rave organisations now live in Europe.'

'That's right, yeah. When I was in Germany, Spiral Tribe were living in Berlin. I met some of the guys. I think they call themselves SP 23 now.'

'Did they give any kind of a nod of recognition to you, as someone who had come before?'

'Oh yeah. They came to one of my gigs.'

He'd been in America recently, he told me, under the name of Nik Turner's Hawkwind. This had got up the nose of the current Hawkwind, who'd taken out injunctions against him, banning him from using the name.

'That's how Establishment they've become, that they'll appeal to a lawyer to take out injunctions against me, to prevent me using the name that I'd helped make successful.'

The tour was a great success. People were saying, 'We've been waiting twenty years to see you guys.'

'One guy came up to me, he looked deeply into my eyes and shook me by the hand, and he said, "I really want to thank you from the bottom of my heart," and I said, "Why's that?" He said, "In 1972 I was in Vietnam. When I came back from there I was a fucking killer. I was a complete psychopath. I didn't know what to do with myself. I found this album," and he produced *In Search of Space*, which is Hawkwind's second album. And he said, "This album really straightened me out, and I wanna thank you." I was flabbergasted. I thought, wow, it's really worth all the work I've ever done to have that one guy say that to me.'

After Nik returned from America he went on a tour of Europe. In Berlin he met the Mutoid Waste Company, who build weird sculptures out of disused cars, etc. Spiral Tribe were living with them, squatting a place in East Germany.

'They were all at the gig, and Spiral Tribe did have that attitude towards me – a sort of mutual respect. I know what they've been doing and they know what I've been doing. And' – putting on a parody biblical voice – 'It Was Good.'

We talked about the ethos of the free festivals, discussing the difference between the free festivals and free parties, and the licensed variety.

'Nothing's free,' he said. 'Somebody has to pay for it. A festival is as good as what you take there.'

'Yeah,' I said, 'but the difference in ethos boils down to: At a pay festival, where the point is to make money, for a start you have to pay for licences, which are vast, then you've got to pay for security fences because you've got to stop people getting in for free. Once you've paid for security, security fencing, policing and all the rest of it, the price is bumped up phenomenally. At a free festival you can cover the cost by taking a bucket round.'

'Yeah, but what I was saying about nothing being free: I had a stage constructed to promote my act, then I donated it to the people, because I didn't want to carry on going round to all the festivals putting it up all the time. Half the time I used to put it up single-handedly. I just used to take it to Stonehenge, where it was used as the main stage for the rest of the time, for as long as it was going. Nothing is free, but a free festival is what everybody brings to it. I'd take the stage, but I didn't want money for it. I saw it as my contribution. This is what free festivals were about: what people could contribute to them. It gives me a buzz to be involved and do something. I don't want thanks or anything, it's just a giving thing. This is what I've got.

I've helped as much as I can. I can work my bollocks off at these sorts of events in the hope that people will enjoy themselves.

'It's a spiritual thing – not in a religious way, but meaningful in other than a materialist way. A communion of people, communication; a bringing of people together in a nice, loving way. Brotherly love: what I've always been into. I suppose I'm a hippie, whatever that means – wanting to give, wanting to turn people on, not doing things for any other reason than for the joy of doing it.'

After Sphinx, he formed a band called Inner City Unit, a cult band of the eighties. It had a political/satirical edge. I asked him to define what he meant by that.

'It was a bit like Crass, except it was humorous. I always found Crass a bit too noisy, a bit self-indulgent, taking themselves a bit too seriously.'

'But you saw yourselves as kind of parallel to Crass?' I asked.

'We were on the same sort of level. We used to play in all kinds of squats, places like that, and we did loads of benefits, free concerts and parties. The difference between them and us is that they (although it's a bit of a contradiction in terms) tried to start the 'Anarchists' Centre', but they were doing quite a lot for young kids. I didn't do anything like that. I just did benefits. When people used to get a squat, I used to go and play there. I did a lot of parties at squats. I was involved. I was accessible to all those people living on the edge. We never really came together with Crass at all. I did do a gig at Stonehenge where they were playing. All these Hell's Angels were trying to smash up the stage and I was trying to stop them. I went up to a big gang of Hell's Angels and said, 'What's the problem?' They'd say, 'It's not me, it's him.' When it came down to it, it was in fact one really psychopathic guy who was out of his head on speed and booze, who was basically a troublemaker, and he was instigating all the others.'

'It was the idea of punks, wasn't it?'

'Yeah, yeah. "Fuckin' spiky-haired punks," he was saying. This was at the time when punks were becoming a bit of a cross-over, you know. They were becoming rainbow punks and were joining with the hippies, which had been something they'd reacted against. They suddenly found they had a lot in common with them.'

'Which is precisely what Crass were all about, what they were trying to do. They were trying to make the cross-over.'

'Yeah, because they were all what you might call ex-hippies.'

'There's an interesting parallel here. The first person I interviewed for this book was the drummer with Crass and he lives in a very similar setting to you.'

'Yeah, yeah. I always had a lot of respect for them, although I never went to one of their gigs. They were a very popular band and they were sort of a super-cult band. You'd see loads of punks around with the Crass symbol on the backs of their jackets. They had a really big following, which I thought was great, you know. I never knew them. I never got involved with them. One of my roadies eventually did. He became the guitarist with a band called Conflict, one of the Crass bands. He was called Kevin Webb. I think he played bass in the band.'

By now, it was getting dark and fairly cold. We were still sitting out in the garden as the peachy sky drifted into subdued splendour.

Before setting off for home I went to the toilet. I walked through their back door into the spacious, polished-wood-floored living room. There was a notice on the door: 'Please remove footwear before entering.' I was reminded of my dream and the rule at the Crass house.

All through the conversation there had been a peculiar honking noise. I'd looked round to discover that it was coming from a little girl. Later on, the girl (another of Nik's children) came over to talk to him. She was deaf. She pointed to his hair, then twirled her fingers in her own and made some signs.

Nik said, in a careful, laboured voice while signing, 'Yes. I had it done in America. I've cut my hair and dyed it blond. Do you like it?'

The look on her face was one of unrestrained affection, and the tone in his voice was gentle and filled with affection. The bond between them was palpable. Like love.

15 Drug Love

This is the final chapter. As I'm writing it, Kodan is downstairs in my poky little living room, lounged on the settee, reading *Fear and Loathing in Las Vegas* by Hunter S. Thompson. He's been staying with me for a couple of weeks now, on my living-room floor. He has a cut over his right eye, and the eyebrow is swollen and smudged purple-yellow. He's looking very drawn and pale.

We went out last Friday evening. We were in the Lazy Barman pub. I was talking to a friend of mine on the other side of the bar. To be honest, I was chatting her up, so I wasn't paying much attention to Kodan. Suddenly my friend said, 'I think you'd better go and sort Kodan out. He's just got hit.' I looked over and there he was, holding a bar-cloth over his eye, with blood pouring down his face, and the landlord and the barmaid both twittering over him. Someone had just given him a

Scotsman's kiss. A Scotsman's kiss is a headbutt.

Karma. A Scotsman's kiss for the kissing Scotsman.

While I was in Wales, I'd left Kodan and Marion in charge of my house. They were both homeless. Kodan had been kicked out of his house after a squabble about the washing up. Then again, he'd never paid any rent. He'd spent all his housing benefit on drugs. Marion had left her house after a squabble about Kodan. Marion's flatmate had decided he was a using bastard and had told Marion that she didn't want him to visit. There'd been a confrontation on the kitchen step. Marion's flatmate had screamed abuse at him, told him to fuck off and tried to kick him in the balls.

I met them on the beach. It looked like they'd been there all night. I was just packing up to go to Wales. It seemed like another of those magic moments. They needed a place to stay and I needed someone to look after my house. Perfect. They also agreed to look after my dog.

A week later I drove back from Wales. There were some things I needed to pick up. No one was in when I arrived, but the answerphone was flashing. It was a message from Kodan.

'Marion,' he was saying, in a little strangled voice, 'something terrible has happened. I've been done for shoplifting. I'm in Hackney police station right now, but they've copped me for jumping bail. They're taking me up to Scotland. Love you loads.' He sounded like an eight-year-old talking to his mum.

I went round the town looking for Marion. I wasn't sure if she'd got the message or not. When I told her, she simply sighed.

After that I went back to Wales and got on with my life. I wrote 'New Year', 'My First Rave', 'Everyone's Wally' and 'VE Day' in the space of four weeks.

I arrived home on the Sunday. The front door was open, but there was nobody at home. The toilet upstairs was flushing continuously and there was a circle of dog puke all over the sitting-room floor. I trod in it by accident. Later, I noticed a smell coming from my son's bedroom. There was an ancient dog turd festering in the middle of the room, on top of one of my son's comics.

The answerphone was flashing again. I pressed the replay button and it wound and wound and wound back. The messages were all from Kodan. He had that same whining tone in his voice. This time he was in hospital. He was saying things like, 'Can you bring me some clothes over?' and, 'Can you tell my pals that I'm in hospital? You know who my pals are,' and, 'Love you, Marion.' Things like that, punctuated with faint snuffles and woeful sighs. He was feeling sorry for himself.

I met Marion in the high street. She had my dog with her. The dog came bounding over, whining and wagging her tail, looking like an escapee from Belsen. She was literally a bag of bones. Her ribs were sticking out, her spine and hips were raised from her back like fins, and her face was drawn and haggard-looking. It looked like she hadn't been fed for a month. It was obvious she had worms.

I told Marion about the messages from Kodan.

'I know,' she said.

He'd got home one day with his hand all puffed up and infected, she told me. He'd claimed it was a bee sting, but then later admitted that he'd been shooting up in his hand.

'He was lying to me again. I've packed him up,' she said. 'I just can't be bothered any more.'

Kodan has 'Pretty Vacant' by the Sex Pistols playing at full volume now. He's bouncing around like a loon, waving his arms about and going manic. I want to tell him, 'Just because you've just come off junk, it doesn't mean you have to be enthusiastic about everything. And anyway, this is a writer's house, not a discotheque. Haven't you ever heard of silence?'

But no. I'll leave him. Whatever keeps the big man happy, I suppose.

I started getting phone calls. Kodan saying, 'I want to come up and see you, I need to talk to you.' I wasn't all that happy with him, but I'd agree, just for old times' sake. Also, there were things I wanted to tell him, but he'd never turn up.

Then one day he rang up to tell me how he was going to get his life together, and he was looking for a job, and he'd heard about this really good doctor who was going to help him by putting him on a methadone programme.

'What do you want to go on a methadone programme for?' I asked. 'You're not a junkie. Methadone is worse than heroin. What you need is counselling.'

He told me that he couldn't get the counselling without the methadone. That was the rule. It struck me that this was all part of the cycle. Methadone was just one more drug for him to play with.

'Methadone is the government's drug,' I told him. 'It's not really there to solve the drug problem. They don't want to solve the drug problem. It's there to make a nice fat profit for the pharmaceutical industry.'

He heard, but he didn't listen. He wanted his drug. Any drug.

I went to see him. He was staying on someone's floor. I knocked the door and he answered dressed only in his trousers. His eyes were glazed and when he talked, ribbons of saliva hung from his teeth. He was drawling. He went upstairs to collect some clothes so that we could go and sit out on the grass in the sunshine. It was market day and there were hundreds of people about. He carried his T-shirt and trainers across the road with him, not even bothering to put them on. I asked him what drug he was on this time. It was Valium, he told me. He was still waiting for his methadone. He was thinking of trying to buy some to keep him going.

I'd just about had done with him by now. If it wasn't the heroin, it was the speed. If it wasn't the speed, it was the alcohol. If it wasn't the alcohol, it was the Valium. If it wasn't the Valium, it was the methadone. It didn't matter what the drug was, just as long as he could put it into his system, just as long as he could absolve his life with chemicals.

I told him about all the ways that he'd pissed me off. How he'd borrowed money as a deposit for a flat, then used the housing benefit for drugs. 'So you took that money on false pretences, didn't you? You had no intention of keeping the flat. You wanted the money for drugs, that's all.' How I'd left my house in his care and he'd messed it up. 'Even my dog,' I said. 'If you hadn't have been so self-obsessed you'd've seen she was getting ill and got her sorted out. She only needed a few tapeworm tablets.' I was pulling no punches. Innocent creatures and personal loyalty: a potent mix. He started crying, but I wasn't all that impressed. They were Valium tears.

I got another phone call. It was Kodan again, trying to be chirpy. He invited me out for a drink. I went to meet him, but he didn't turn up. When he did turn up I bought him a pint, but he didn't drink it. He bought a lime and soda instead. That meant he was on smack.

There was enough residual affection in me to agree to see him one last time. We'd gone through so many things together. It was true that he'd as good as saved me when Gem and I had split up. Anyway, I felt sorry for him. He had nothing left. He was homeless and a junkie, he'd fallen out with just about everyone, and his girlfriend had left him. I was his last hope. I arranged to meet him in a café.

I bumped into a friend on the way.

'Kodan's in a terrible state,' she told me. 'I've just bought him a bottle of codeine linctus to help him with the withdrawals.'

When I saw him I asked what he'd taken that day.

'Nothing,' he told me.

The junk personality is like a parasite. It's like a tapeworm in the junkie's head. It is lying and devious and manipulative, and it feeds on the junkie's soul, sucking all the goodness out of it. You can't trust a junkie. He will wheedle and cajole, beg, lie, steal, make promises then break them, sell his best friends into oblivion for just half a gram of dreary forgetfulness. He has no friends. His only friend is junk.

But Kodan wasn't quite a junkie yet. I bought him a pint and he drank it. I bought him another pint and he drank that too. Junkies cannot drink. They have a physiological aversion to alcohol. So I agreed to let him stay at my house for a couple of weeks. Only there was to be no methadone, no Valium, no drugs at all in fact. I was putting him on my own personally tailored detox programme: three pints of Shepherd Neame's a night, to help him sleep.

We went shopping yesterday. Kodan had just got his Giro and he owed me £15, so he paid for it all. We bought fresh vegetables, rice, cereal, bread, butter and all the other basics. We also bought a frozen pizza and a packet of frozen chips. That's what we had for tea yesterday: real Italian pizza with oven chips. Kodan had also slipped a twenty-four-pack of Kronenbourg into the trolley. When I questioned him on it he said, 'But they're really cheap: 40p a bottle.' I wish you could have heard his voice as he was saying that. He sounded like a little boy. So we drank bottles of Kronenbourg after our pizza and chips. We finished them all off in one night, while Kodan recounted his life over the last six months. It was payment for my specially tailored drug-rehabilitation programme. I wonder how much a private clinic charges? Maybe I should go into business.

What puzzled me was how he'd turned so quickly from a decent human being with a minor drug habit into this manipulative, whining, wheedling monster I'd seen him become over the last few weeks. When we'd come back from Glasgow he was all right, wasn't he? He was still funny. He still considered other people. What had happened?

He'd discovered a source, he told me. In the beginning it was the fact that the heroin was available. It starts playing on your mind every time you have money. The first two times he'd taken it, it was free. The dealer had a source of cheap heroin, so he could afford to give it away. That was the explanation, anyway. He wasn't jacking it up. He was smoking it. Chasing the dragon. There's a wonderfully romantic sound to that phrase, isn't there? Chasing the dragon. It sounds mythological. The smack is heated up on a piece of silver foil. The user leans over and sucks the coiling plumes of smoke through a tube. Precious smoke. You can't afford to waste a single wisp.

After those first two times he had to pay for it. But he was being careful, he told me. He was avoiding getting a habit by taking time off, by shifting to other drugs for a week or so at a time. He thinks he kept this up till about June, though he can't be certain.

'When you're wrecked, time becomes confused,' he said. 'You become a Mister Man. Mr Forgetful.'

So he was chasing the dragon two or three times a week, with the occasional week off. He was also freebasing cocaine maybe once a fortnight. All these drug phrases – 'chasing the dragon', 'freebasing'. They mean the same thing. Freebasing is smoking cocaine in the same way that chasing the dragon is smoking heroin. He'd take a couple of ten-bags during the week, and a quarter-gram at the weekends. A ten-bag is ten-pounds' worth. A quarter-gram costs about £25. All this from his Giro.

I was puzzled. I mean, I like my drugs too, but for me it's a social thing. It's the excitement of a party atmosphere. It's the dancing, the beautiful women, the hypnotic sounds. Most of all, it's the fresh night air at an open-air party, the swirling lights, the early-morning glow. You take the drugs to help you stay awake and to socialise. I just couldn't see the appeal of sitting in a room with the same people night after night, muttering sweet inconsequential nothings to each other interminably. What was the appeal?

'At first it's a chummy thing,' he said. 'Heroin is the best drug on the planet for taking away hang-ups. You become Mr Intelligent, Mr Confident.'

'Always a Mister Man though,' I observed.

Junkies are the friendliest, chummiest people on earth, he told me. They're romantics, not only freeing themselves from their personal hang-ups, but being liberated from all the hang-ups in the world too. They just don't care about all the shit any more.

I started thinking about what he'd said. For some reason that word 'chumminess' haunted me. I could see him there, in a kind of glowing bubble, being 'chummy' with all his mates, and it scared me. I was trying to find the right word to describe my feeling to him.

'There's something not right about it,' I said, 'something not good.' I couldn't get any more precise than that. Then it struck me. That bubble of consciousness in which he coexisted with his mates was demonic. It was alluring, like some sort of a gilded insect which was attaching itself to his brain, promising to take away all his pain, but it was evil.

'Yes,' he said, and he put on a voice to describe it. It was a sort of lustful, throaty, baby voice: 'Chummy mummy scrummy, mmmmmm, yummy, snuggle-down duvet, yesss, soft blanket, warm-water bath, hmmm, yes.'

That voice made me shiver with repulsion, as if I'd just trodden on a snail and could feel the soft scrunch of its shell and the squelch of its jellified body under my bare foot.

I started thinking more about this idea, of a kind of demonic presence in the poppy plant itself. I'd heard stories that, often, when junkies are gouching out (as they call it), drifting into a waking-dream state, it is visions of the poppy, or of fields of waving poppies, that they have in their heads. Kodan told me that this was true. Sometimes when he was gouching out on poppies he would see himself picking poppies. Or, on another occasion, he'd seen himself at an ambient techno rave, where a huge billion-watt light burst across the sky. Someone had placed a handful of poppies into the light. He was standing before their shadow, watching their swaying movements, awe-filled, with his arms out, and that Plug-ugly look of gormless bliss on his face.

There were other common themes to the dream state. He said that often junkies would find themselves reading a book. They'd half-see the words before they melted away. They'd be reading the book, knowing that something very important was about to be said, but never quite reaching it. He said that when this had happened to him, at first he'd thought it was a reflection of the fact that he does, in fact, spend most of his time reading. But he'd spoken to other users and they'd told him that they'd all had the experience too, whether they were readers or not. It is the gouched-out reading dream. Another demonic hint: a minor deity pretending to a knowledge that it doesn't, in fact, have.

I said that the junk personality is like a parasite: it feeds off the real personality to provide justification for its needs. Getting off your head on smack as a pastime among friends is only the first level of the experience. Things are so apparently uncomplicated in that state that you begin to yearn for it all the time. The world out there is a complex, sometimes painful place. Why can't I be happy all the time? Why can't I talk to all of my friends in that straightforward, honest way? So Kodan started taking it by himself. Going out to meet his other friends in a smacked-out state. And maybe I'm never honest, never straightforward, never intelligent, never confident without it. The fact that all his other friends began to realise that something was up, that this was a false Kodan in front of them, and that they were starting to shy away, never occurred to him. He felt good, and that was good enough.

The unawareness is appealing, too. Junk draws you close to

death, but death doesn't matter any more. When there's nothing else going for you, turn blue a few times a week. Turning blue is the sign that you are nearing death. Junk is like a cosmic switch, and if you could simply switch off your life in times of trouble, wouldn't you be tempted to do it? No pain. Just a sweet, sleeplike death? Bravado. I can face death. Death isn't even important any more.

Some time in mid-June, another of the town's users met him on the street. 'Watch out Kodan,' he said. 'You're starting to look scagged-up all the time.' But Kodan didn't think he had a problem. He just lacked confidence, that's all. The heroin made it easy to face up to things. Anyway, he was on his Sid Vicious kick by now. Once more, I couldn't see the appeal. Sid Vicious is the least likely hero in my eyes. But then, I'm drawn to survivors, not losers.

'Sid's a classic young, beautiful, rebellious, mad, crazy romantic,' said Kodan. 'He never gave a fuck. He was the complete rock'n'roll animal, and at the same time a stupid big geek. Everyone who met him loved him. Everyone got pissed off with him too, in the end. So he ended up in the Chelsea Hotel with Nancy and . . . '

'OK, Kodan, we all know the end of that.'

Yet Kodan felt that there was a parallel there, to his own life. A stupid big geek. Johnny Rotten called Sid useless. That's how Kodan felt. He was attracted to the idea of being a philosophising bum, a nobody who knew more than most. He said he was reading William Burroughs at the same time and feeling that he was in good company.

It's back to that parasitic worm again. The self-justifications. The romantic imagery to disguise the self-seeking poisonous worm writhing in your head: 'Look, Sid did it, Burroughs did it, Dennis Hopper did it. They were all artists. They were heroes. You can do it too. You can be a hero too.'

Kodan had been doing this sort of thing since he was sixteen, getting out of his brain constantly. Taking drugs is putting off your life, putting off your life, putting off your life till the next day. In the place where he grew up it was all tied up with the fact that there were no jobs. I understood that. I'd seen Renfrew. It's a dull little town with nothing much going for it. In the schemes (as they call the council estates up there) you are surrounded by such a monotonous vista, rows upon rows of grim grey houses, all the same. That wouldn't matter too much if there was some money coming in, some dignity and pleasure in work, a nice holiday once a year, a degree of self-respect. Going out to work provides you with a purpose and it fills the time, but what do you do if there is no work, only hours following hours of the same dreary scene? Yes. You get out of your head. This is true of all the poorer council estates throughout the land. They're all awash with drugs.

The problem about Establishment propaganda is that it tells lies, and once you've seen through one lie, you disbelieve all the rest.

Fact: smoking hash does not lead to using heroin. The two drugs are as different as chalk and cheese. In fact, heroin users are psychologically incapable of touching hash.

Fact: heroin is not instantly addictive. At first you can take it or leave it. It is very hard to become addicted to junk. You have to really want to do it.

Fact: heroin is far less harmful to the body than cigarettes, say, or even alcohol. Junkies can live a full life span as addicts, as long as they have a regular and reliable maintenance supply, as long as they don't have to get involved with crime, as long as they don't have to engage in unhygienic practices to do it.

Fact: methadone, the so-called cure, is far more addictive, and far more dangerous, than heroin. It is manufactured in the laboratory – you don't even have to pay any poor Third

World farmers to produce it – and huge profits are being made.

Don't believe a word the Establishment says about drugs. It is all hypocrisy. It doesn't mind us taking drugs. It wants us to take drugs, but it wants us to take the drugs that serve it best. It wants us all on Valium and Temazepam and methadone. And cigarettes, of course: the most dangerous and addictive drug on the planet, and the most easily available.

This is a society based on drugs. The separation between legal and illegal drugs is purely arbitrary. Beer and cigarettes, coffee and tea – they're all drugs. As are aspirin and paracetamol. Not to speak of the legions of pharmaceuticals that are pushed on to us at every opportunity by the medical profession.

What we need is an intelligent approach to drug use. More of the truth, not more of the lies. Building up hysteria through misinformation merely encourages drug use. The user sees through one lie and immediately disbelieves all the rest.

Now here's the truth. Moderate use of clean, unadulterated drugs (preferably organic, such as mushrooms or hash or beer) as a social medium will do you little harm. The emphasis is on the word 'moderate'. Drugs are dangerous. They should be treated with respect. But, they are considerably less dangerous than driving a car.

In Scotland, Kodan was on a £6-a-day habit for years. DF 118s, di-hydrocodeine tablets, with maybe a Valium or two thrown in. Interesting that, isn't it? Valium and di-hydrocodeine are prescribed drugs, not illegal drugs, and they're freely available on the council estate where Kodan is growing up, just at the time when there were no jobs available.

Eventually, Kodan decided he needed to break from the cycle. First of all he became a Krishna monk. Then, when he couldn't cope with that, he moved to England. That's when I met him. When he first moved to England. He'd been two years without drugs in the Temple. He was a bright, shining being, bursting with intelligence and life. I'd had no idea that he'd once been so close to becoming a junkie.

That summer he got into the poppies. Free drugs available and they're growing in everyone's front garden. That was when he was seeing that girl we'd gone up to Scotland to visit. They were off their heads most of the time, but relatively civilised. I'd meet them in the pub. They'd be on lime juice and soda, while I'd drink my beer. We'd still hold interesting conversations and Kodan was always funny. So I saw no harm in it myself. It wasn't the same as junk. It didn't separate them from their peers.

Later, when the poppy season was over, they discovered another source: dried poppies from florist shops. So the season never ended. They were always on the poppies. There was always a pot of poppy tea on the boil.

The girl wanted to move away. She urged Kodan to take her up to Scotland. They moved back to Kodan's own turf, the place where he'd grown up. She got a job and Kodan got back into the DF 118s. Running round with all his old pals, doing the same things all over again. The girl packed him up and Kodan moved back to England. That was in the autumn of last year, about six months before our trip to Glasgow. I never knew any of this. I thought Kodan was an interesting, funny guy, with gallons of raw talent and a minor drug habit.

I bumped into him in the summer, during the dark period of the road protest. I wondered why he hadn't got involved. He was slumped in a chair in the corner of the pub, his hair limp and greasy, dark bags under his eyes. He was slurring and slouching and looking mean. He had a pint in front of him which he was drinking in greedy gulps.

I said, 'Kodan, why haven't you got involved? What happened to all our talk about the spiritual revolution? I thought we were on the same team, but it's like I'm always passing the baton on to you and you're always dropping it.'

237

'No, I'm not,' he slurred in a dark voice, with a resentful sneer on his face. 'I'm not dropping the baton. I'm selling it so I can buy more drugs. What you don't understand is that I'm a chemical being. You're an organic being, but I'm a chemical being. All that matters to me is that I have chemicals every day. Anyway, that road protest is all pish. They're all middle-class wankers. They're pish. They look down their noses at me 'cos they think I'm a junkie. Well, if that's what everybody thinks then I'll be a junkie. Fuck the lot of them. Fuck the lot of you.' And he stumbled out of the pub knocking into walls and chairs and people and everything that was in his way.

That was Temazepam and beer. Both legal drugs. He'd got the Temazepam on prescription, by claiming he was a junkie and that he wanted to come off. He'd been given two-weeks' worth, which he'd taken in the space of two days. In Scotland they call them 'government grapes', because they're provided by the government and they look like little grapes. They're also known as 'wobbly eggs', because they're shaped like an egg and they make you wobble. Take two of them – only two – with a pint of beer, and you're off into madness city, black-out city. And once you're in that place, you don't care any more. You just keep swallowing them. The name I like best is 'jellies'. People eat them like Jelly Tots and then turn into jelly. All these Michelin men wobbling about with rubbery knees and elbows.

You should see the road now, by the way: the razor wire, the miles and miles of fencing, the compounds, the security lights, the dogs. It's a gulag. They've employed 150 security guards to look after the site, on £3.50 an hour. If anyone asks me about it I say, 'We won.' It's cost them £5 million extra, by their own estimate. There's about half a dozen hippies left camped out in the woods. £5 million for half a dozen hippies.

The self-justification continues.

'A junkie is the only person who can lie in the gutter and look down his nose at the world,' he says. 'Us addicts have a genetic failure. It's a spiralling obsession. It's not my responsibility. It's my DNA.'

Admittedly this is Kodan remembering the way he used to feel, but there's still a degree of resignation in his tone, a form of self-justificatory myth-making. You see, what junkies are really up to isn't some heroic struggle against all that is base and low. What junkies really object to is the washing up. It's as simple as that. They make out all sorts of things – they talk about the avoidance of pain, the avoidance of shit, the lure of death – when all that it really amounts to is that they cannot cope with the mundaneness of life, they cannot bring themselves ever to do the washing up.

All junkies are still living at home with their mum, waiting for her to cook them a nice meal, then tuck them up in bed. Snuggle-down duvet. Mmmmm. Chummy mummy scrummy, yes, yummy.

It's the difference between the pleasure principle and the reality principle, to use the definitions first put forward by Freud. The pleasure principle wants immediate satisfaction. It's the level on which a baby operates. The reality principle is willing to sublimate the pleasure, to put off the pleasure, to wait until tomorrow, or until later in the day. The pleasure you get from doing the washing up is nothing to do with the act of washing up. It is the pleasure you get from knowing that the washing up is done and that now you can relax. Or it is the pleasure of doing the job so that someone else does not have to do it. The thing about the washing up is that it has to be done. Someone has to do it. If not you, then who? If not now, then when?

Old Zen saying. Before Enlightenment: chopping wood, collecting water; after Enlightenment: chopping wood, collecting water. Or, to give it a twentieth-century edge, before the revolution: washing up and going to the shops; after the revolution: washing up and going to the shops.

I'd been making the comparison between personal integrity and the washing up. It's something I'd been talking about to Kodan. Personal integrity is another thing that junkies are notoriously short on. That's because it bears no immediate yield. Mostly, personal integrity is something you know about only in yourself. No one is going to applaud you for it, but once you have undertaken the tasks that lead to the growth of personal integrity, once people begin to realise that you are absolutely trustworthy, absolutely honest, then they will begin to listen to what you say. Then they will begin to respect you.

Personal integrity is like the washing up: it gets easier as you get older.

In fact, I was talking to him about personal integrity only so that I could get him to do the washing up occasionally. Bugger personal integrity. I just want a tidy kitchen.

Things started to go bad as he began to suspect that he was losing Marion. Looking after my house while I was in Wales was his last chance to begin to make something of himself. He messed that up by getting caught shoplifting and then being shipped up to Scotland. That wouldn't have been too bad, only he got Marion to send him some money from her Giro, then used the money to buy drugs. He spent two weeks up there, getting off his crust as usual.

It was after he came back and she'd packed him up for good that he began shooting up in earnest. But even this was a ploy. He still wasn't really a junkie. It was all a little play-act to make her feel sorry for him, to make her want him back. Only by now, he'd gone too far. He'd played his last card. He was in hospital sending wheedling, lonely phone calls to an empty answerphone, and she was simply ignoring it. She couldn't cope with his childish tantrums any more.

Junk is the most childish game on the planet. It's all me, me, me. Look at me. Pay attention to me. I can't help it. Look, I'm standing near the cliff and if you don't give me what I want I'll jump, I swear. Me. I want. I want. I want. Me.

Me? What's happened to me? I seem to have disappeared.

Things started to get out of hand. While he was in hospital he stole a bottle of Valium from the nurse's trolley. Then one day he was in a car with someone else, they were both jellied-up, and they were trying to get over to the nearest town with some dodgy prescriptions he'd stolen from the health centre. (By now, he'd broken into the doctors' surgery about three times.) The car was swerving all over the place, scraping parked cars along the side of the road. Kodan was so out of it he didn't even know what was happening. Then it began to dawn on him. They'd been driving along like this for about fifteen minutes, going nowhere, with hot scripts in his pocket and hot drugs in the car. 'Uh-oh!' he thought. He told the driver to pull over. If they were caught she would lose her licence and he would go to prison. That's how close things were getting.

He woke up one morning with a terrible come-down. He reached into his pocket and found seven Temazepam, which he chewed for his breakfast. He sucked all the contents out of them, but he spat out the shells. They have gelatine in them. Bad Karma. He's a vegetarian.

Another day he was out in the high street, begging. He'd phoned an emergency doctor to say he was suffering from withdrawals. The doctor had given him twenty-one 10mg capsules of Valium. He'd taken about half of them in one go. He was trying to get money together for junk. He'd written a number of names and addresses down in a book, with '£2' written next to each name. He was going up to people, saying, 'Excuse me, I'm stranded. I'm trying to get to London and I'm £2 short of my train-fare. Can you help me?' The people would see the other names, with the figures written next to them, and they'd think it was legitimate. It was a technique he'd learned as a Krishna devotee. Except then, of course, he was begging for the Temple. Now he was begging for drugs. He was pouring on the charm; that famous Kodan charm. He made about £30 in two hours.

He left a trail of confusion behind him everywhere he went, as though his Valium state was being made manifest in the world. Liquid stupidity. Vile disordered dysfunction. But the scene that finally sealed it for him, that made him contact me that day and decide to get off the stuff for good, was when he saw Marion with another of his junkie friends chasing the dragon. It was the end. He thought, 'So Marion has packed up one hopeless junkie bum to go out with another hopeless junkie bum.' He thought, 'Fuckin' 'ell, man, this is the lowest of the low. Is this a joke? Is this real life, or did Monty Python write the script?' It was just too mad to believe.

My specially tailored detox programme seems to have worked. Kodan went through a few days of minor cramps and a certain amount of discomfort. He was deeply paranoid for a while, couldn't go out for fear that he might meet someone who knew him. Then again, he had good reason to be paranoid. He was looking like a startled rabbit for two or three days. Everything made him jumpy, but he took the pain with resignation. Every day from the first day he was looking better. More colour in his cheeks. More sparkle in his eye. Even the occasional joke. The dark rings around his eyes are fading and he wears his new scar with pride. It's a fashion statement. My son gets on with him really well. My son is a cool dude. They cook together and chat about inconsequential things while I'm up here writing.

I woke up one morning, it was about 7 a.m., and the sun was streaming in through my window as it had for most of the summer. But there was a faint smell in the air. I couldn't place it at first. Something fresh and clean. Something faintly melancholy. It was early September, a couple of weeks after Kodan had first moved in with me. Then it struck me. It's autumn. The smell is autumn. Just a hint of coolness in the breeze. The smell of ripe fruit and woodland damp. The smell of mists in the distant valleys.

I lay in bed luxuriating in the feeling. Soon the parties would be moving indoors. The party season was nearly finished and the club season was about to begin. The mushrooms would be out. Autumn is my favourite season. Kodan was supposed to be going apple-picking. I'd recommended it to him as perfect therapy – hard work and fresh air – but I decided to let him lie in this morning.

I got up at about 8.30. The smell was still there, drifting in through the back door. Kodan was asleep on the floor. I made him a cup of tea and he woke suddenly.

'I've been dreaming,' he said. 'I thought I was listening to "Stand!" by Sly and the Family Stone in full quadraphonic sound in my head.' He started singing: 'STAND, EVERYBODY, STAND, STAND, STAND!'

And did Kodan stand? Did he leap up, fresh, to take on the challenges of the day?

Well, not immediately.

He drank his tea first.